WINE with FOOD

for my parents and Poppy

First published in Great Britain in 1996 by
Mitchell Beazley, a division of Octopus Publishing Group Ltd

This edition published 2006 by Bounty Books,
a division of Octopus Publishing Group Ltd
2–4 Heron Quays, London E14 4JP
Reprinted 2008
Copyright © Octopus Publishing Group Ltd 1996
Text copyright © Joanna Simon 1996
Photography copyright © Octopus Publishing Group Ltd 1996

ISBN 978-0-753713-73-0

A CIP catalogue record for this book is available
from the British Library

Printed and bound in China

Senior Editor: Susan Keevil
Executive Art Editor: Fiona Knowles
Assistant Editor: Lucy Bridgers
Design: Fiona Knowles, Neil Wadsworth
Commissioning Editor: Sue Jamieson
Index: Angie Hipkin
Production: Juliette Butler, Christina Quigley
Photography: Jeremy Hopley assisted by Catherine Rowlands,
        Ray Moller assisted by Tim Kelly
Stylist: Wei Tang, Su Bentinck
Home Economist: Annie Nichols
Picture Research: Maria Gibbs

WINE *with* FOOD

Joanna Simon

Bounty Books

Contents

Introduction

The definitive book on the matching of wine and food is long overdue – but this is not it. The definitive book will, I suspect, remain unattainable. Every recipe, every cook's interpretation and execution of it, every set of ingredients and every kitchen's equipment varies. Each producer's wines differ from those of his neighbour and no two vintages produce wines with precisely the same character. It is hard to be definitive in such circumstances – even harder when one accepts that taste is elusive, taste is subjective.

This, then, is not a book of rules. It does not lay down the law. But it does aim to provide a set of guidelines and to explain points of principle, so that anyone who wants to drink wine with food can make informed judgements, or informed guesses, as to which wine (or, more likely, wines) might happily accompany a particular dish or a complete meal. By its very presence wine should enhance a meal, but where there is real compatibility between wine and food the experience is inevitably heightened.

I have taken time over specific ingredients that have a notable, and sometimes unexpected, impact on wine. I have also taken time over the question of cooking methods and preparation. These, as much as the ingredients, dictate the finished dish and yet they are apt to be overlooked, or at least underestimated. A sauce is often more important in terms of flavour and texture than the food it is gilding, supporting or surrounding.

Although this is not a book of dogma, it is meant to be practical. Throughout the various parts, I do not shy away from recommending specific types or styles of wine to partner specific dishes – and for those who want recommendation without the explanation there are quick reference sections, by wine and by food, at the back. Nor do I shy away from pointing out those combinations which it is safe to assume most people would wish to avoid. It doesn't mean that these combinations are somehow wrong, any more than in positively recommending something I am implying that it is right or more correct. There is no such thing as right and wrong with food and wine partnerships – just combinations that are more likely to please a crowd and those which are less likely to please it.

If this book achieves anything, I hope it will encourage people to experiment with different wines and alternative pairings of food and wine. I can see how irresistible the temptation to play safe is in today's wine world. The evolution and expansion of quality wine has been phenomenal in the last 30 years. Upward of 30 countries export their wines to the United Kingdom alone. No wonder people so often settle for the wine they always drink. At least they know they like its flavours – even if it does sometimes taste odd, or simply less interesting, with the dishes with which it finds itself sharing a palate.

If it was only wine that had undergone a revolution, it would be a lot to get to grips with. As it is, the changes to the world culinary map are no less far-reaching. There are still regional cuisines which stick fast to their traditional ingredients and ways, thank goodness, but, globally, cooking everywhere has been liberated from its home base (or mother country's apron strings). Like wine, only probably more so, food has travelled, mixed and merged: Asian spices have fused with Mediterranean vegetables, New World vegetables and Old World cuts of meat consort with Oriental dipping sauces. However valid they may have appeared in the past, the age-old food and wine rules based on colour codes fall very short when it comes to contemporary eating. This book, I hope, brings us up to date.

THE *Principles*

WHEN THE GASTRONOMIC MAP OF THE

WORLD WAS DIVIDED BY MUCH SHARPER

BOUNDARIES THAN IT IS TODAY AND THE

VITICULTURAL MAP WAS MUCH MORE

LIMITED, THERE WERE SOME VERY SIMPLE

RULES THAT COULD BE APPLIED MORE OR

LESS USEFULLY TO THE MATCHING OF WINE

TO FOOD. BUT CULINARY EXCHANGE AND

INTERPLAY AND A GREATLY EXPANDED AND

ALTERED WINE SCENE MEAN THAT THERE

ARE NEW – MORE EXCITING – WAYS OF

APPROACHING THE SUBJECT.

rules and how to break them
WEIGHT, INTENSITY,
ACIDITY, SALT,
SWEETNESS, TANNIN

tricky ingredients

cheese

Rules & HOW TO BREAK THEM

*I*f this book were about ethereal wine and food marriages, it would be very short indeed – just one paragraph. There are a few famous partnerships where food and wine seem magically to enhance each other (*see* list below), but, in general, matching wine and food is not about divining perfect and exclusive pairings. Most of the time it is about choosing food and wine that are happy together – each made more enjoyable, in part, simply by the presence of the other – and most of the time several different types of wine will cheerfully accompany any one dish.

In the past there were rules: white wine with fish and white meat, red wine with red meat and appropriate local wines with regional food. It is easy to denounce these today, for being sweeping, narrow-minded and limited in application, but in their context they made more sense. Cooking styles throughout the world were more strictly defined and self-contained. You didn't mix a little French *haute cuisine* with a little German, a touch of Thai with a tad of southern Italian, or a little Mexican with a hint of north Indian. Indeed, in English-speaking countries food was notable – even celebrated – for its plainness. And the wines people drank with it were either local or one of a handful of European classics; the New World didn't figure at all.

Against this background of greater simplicity, certain things stood out. It was very clear – and still is – that red wine quite often clashes with fish, the fish making the wine taste metallic or bitter (although cooking fish in red wine is a very useful way of ensuring that you can drink red wines – Pinot Noir-based wines are good to choose for this). And, because the tannin in the wine is the main cause of the clash, red wine with fish was presumably a more hazardous exercise in the past when red wines were generally more tannic than

they are today (*see* The Changing Face of Wine, page 51). As the one thing that successfully subdues the taste of tannin is the heavy, chewy texture of meat, especially beef steak, it was a short step to the red wine with red meat rule.

Equally, fish and white meats such as chicken are, overall, lighter in weight than red meats and game. And since they are lighter, they are more likely to be cooked by the sort of gentle method that reinforces their delicacy and is rarely appropriate to the heavier meats – poaching and steaming, for example. As there are more light white wines than light red wines and, conversely, more very full-bodied red wines than blockbuster whites, it was the same short step to generalize that white wine should be drunk with fish and white meat.

There is in fact no reason why you should not still use the colour of the protein on the plate as a starting point for choosing wine: when plainly cooked and served, lamb, beef and game are better with red wine than with white – but so, also, are the pale-fleshed pork and turkey; the majority of fish are easier to match with white wines – as are egg dishes; and lentils and dried beans are generally better with reds.

MARRIAGES MADE IN HEAVEN

OYSTERS with *blanc de blancs* champagne or *premier cru* Chablis

PLATEAU DE FRUITS DE MER with Muscadet *sur lie*

CHARCUTERIE with *cru* Beaujolais (or very good *villages*)

ROAST LAMB with Médoc, especially Pauillac and St-Julien

ROQUEFORT with Sauternes

STILTON with vintage port

GOAT'S CHEESE with Sancerre

White wines, meanwhile, are more successful than reds with the flavours of most vegetables. There are even some particular, but not exclusive, grape flavour affinities – lamb with Cabernet Sauvignon, game with Syrah and Pinot Noir, goat's cheese with Sauvignon Blanc.

But, if you use colour to set you off on the track, you must be prepared to override it when you start taking other elements into account.

The **WEIGHT** of the dish is the most important consideration – whether or not you have preconceptions based on colour – and this depends as much on the way the ingredients are cooked as on the flavours of the ingredients themselves: tuna is never lightweight, but it is certainly lighter when it is simply poached than when it is stewed Basque style with tomatoes, peppers, onions, garlic and potatoes; a steamed chicken breast with a hint of lemon grass is worlds away from a rich, dark *coq au vin*.

In most cases you should be aiming to balance the weight of the food with that of the wine, so that neither overwhelms the other – rich, robust food with rich, robust wine (game casserole with Barossa Shiraz, for example); medium-weight food with medium-bodied wine (roast chicken with a red Bergerac or a white St-Véran); light food with light-weight wine (poached shellfish with Pinot Bianco or Muscadet). As a guide, but not an infallible indication, full-bodied wines are usually high in alcohol (roughly speaking over 12.5%) and light-bodied wines are low in alcohol (below 11%).

INTENSITY of flavour provides the main exception to the matching of weight rule: fatty, rich foods can be partnered with light-bodied wines, the principle being to provide a sharp contrast – crisp, light wine cutting through the food. But it does not work with just any old light wine. It has to be a wine which, though light, is intensely flavoured – usually with fruit aromas and flavours coupled with brisk acidity and an element of sweetness.

The archetypal example is fine quality German *Spätlese* or *Auslese*, especially Riesling, with fatty meats such as roast goose, duck and wild boar (*see* Riesling, page 58, and Germany, page 106, for further details). Another is traditional Christmas plum pudding partnered by fresh, feather-light, frothing, sweet Asti.

If it is important to recognize the difference between the weight of a wine and the intensity of its aromas and flavours, it is no less important to distinguish between these two aspects in any food. A dish can be light, but powerfully flavoured. This may be the intrinsic flavour of one item, as in asparagus, or the result of combining ingredients and cooking them in a particular way: Thai food, for example, is often pungently flavoured, but it is very rarely heavy; the same goes for many Japanese dishes. These dishes and others are looked at in more detail under Tricky Ingredients (pages 16–21) and World Classic Combinations (pages 74–141). Suffice it to say here that an accompanying wine usually needs to be broadly similar in character – correspondingly assertive in flavour but not heavy – and it also usually needs to have a directness and freshness of flavour, rather than too much complexity. Young wines made from fairly aromatic grape varieties, such as Sauvignon Blanc and Riesling, fit the profile (*see* Grapes and Wines, pages 48–73).

Having gauged the weight and intensity of the dish, you need to look at the roles of some other other key components which can distort and influence flavour. These include acid and sweetness, in relation to both food and wine; salt, and to a lesser extent pepper, in food; the effect of tannin in wine; and the impact of the texture of some foods.

ACIDITY in a dish – in the form of citrus juice or fruits, other fruits, vinegar or the reduced white wine of a sauce – is very simple in its demands: it needs to be equalled, or echoed, by acid in the wine being drunk alongside it, otherwise the wine will taste flat and dull. This means that duck with orange will need a wine with discernible acidity, whereas duck with olives will not necessarily. A bonus of acidity in a white wine is that it can heighten the flavours of a subtle or simple dish, in the same way as a squeeze of lemon might do.

As a rule, acid levels are higher in white wines and in cooler climates. With white wines this steers you towards Europe's more northerly vineyards (rather than the hot Mediterranean ones) and to the New World's more limited number of cool climate regions (New Zealand, Casablanca, Constantia, Tasmania, Yarra Valley, Adelaide Hills and Long Island, for example). It steers you towards young wines (acid softens with age), to wines that have not been significantly oak-aged (oak maturation softens acidity) and towards such high acid varieties as Sauvignon Blanc, Riesling (whether dry, medium or very sweet), Silvaner, Aligoté, Muscadet, Gros Plant and Chenin Blanc (the spectrum from dry to very sweet). With the exception of Chablis, the new breed of unoaked Australian Chardonnays, some New Zealand Chardonnays and the relatively light north Italian Chardonnays, the search for acidity generally directs you away from Chardonnay, above all in its full-bodied, ripe, buttery, oaky New World styles.

The range of suitable red wines is much more restricted. Not only do red wines lack acidity, but acid in food is liable to clash with tannin in the wine. The reds that do have some appetising acidity tend to be young, low in tannin, light-bodied and, inevitably, from cool climates. They are also the kind of red wines that can be served cool or lightly chilled – Loire reds (whether made from Cabernet Franc, Pinot Noir or Gamay), Beaujolais, Barbera and its much rarer Piedmontese compatriot Grignolino, Bardolino, proper dry red Lambrusco (such as Lambrusco di Sorbara or Lambrusco Reggiano which bear no relation to the cheap, vapid versions produced for export), and the even more rarely exported astringent red Vinho Verde (lack of export here is not such a loss: red Vinho Verde is very much an acquired taste – acquired on holiday and rapidly lost back home).

Rosés, even when they taste fresh and lively, have a habit of being a touch too soft for very high-acid food, but Sancerre rosé has a notably refreshing bite.

Little attention is paid to the effect of SALT and pepper on wine – except to warn that eating salt makes you drink more. But salt, in particular, can have a great impact – and looking at the way salty foods are partnered with other foods is illuminating. The classic combination is salt and sweet, as in prosciutto with figs or melon, or even gammon with pineapple (that stalwart of dire, old-fashioned steak-and-chips restaurant chains in Britain). And the salt-sweet harmony has long been recognized in the famous matches of salty blue cheese with sweet wines (Roquefort and Stilton with Sauternes and vintage port, respectively). Similarly Gewürztraminer, which has a voluptuous spicy-sweet aroma and a flavour that can seem sweet until it finishes dry, is often partnered with smoked salmon. Personally, I prefer a slightly less overbearing wine with smoked salmon (*see* Tricky Ingredients, page 19), but I can appreciate the principle.

Another significant and often overlooked point about salt is its unhappy effect on tannin. Tannin is the dry, bitter, furrily mouth-coating substance that comes from grapeskins, pips and stems – and to a lesser extent oak barrels – and is found in young red wines which are intended to be aged (it is largely imperceptible in white wines – but all too perceptible in stewed, cold tea and the skins of unripe grapes, should you wish to experiment). Salt, which so capably enhances all sorts of flavours in food, does exactly the same, unfortunately, for the bitterness of tannin and it is noticeable that anyone who habitually takes a lot of salt with his or her food is likely to

favour white wines and low tannin reds, such as Beaujolais. And bearing in mind the salt-sweet affinity and the tannin clash, it is not surprising to find that wines with a generous, sweet fruit character – whether red or white – are the kind that go with salty (but not the most salty) foods. In white and rosé wines acidity is also an advantage, with the result that Germany's medium-dry and medium-sweet Rieslings and Scheurebes often come to the rescue. Red wines need to be low in tannin, or have the type of soft, ripe tannins that come from warm climates or benign summers in cool climates.

With typically salty foods served with apertifs, champagne and other dry sparkling wines in a similar mould go conveniently well, but so, also, do *fino* and *manzanilla* sherries. Not only do these pale dry sherries have a unique echoing salty flavour, but they are the only wines that go really well with the saltiness of olives and *tapenade*. (In cooked savoury dishes, the pungency of olives, like that of salted anchovies, should be sufficiently subdued by other ingredients to allow a fruity, not overly tannic wine to shine.)

Freshly ground pepper doesn't have salt's potential for bringing out the worst, but if you ever drink very old, fine, complex wine, you should exercise some restraint with the pepper grinder, as pepper is likely to obscure some of the wine's intriguing nuances and complexities. On the other hand, if you are drinking a rather simple, light, humdrum wine, you may find that a grinding of fresh pepper brings it alive and makes it seem bigger and more flavoursome – peps it up, in fact.

SWEETNESS in food, like acidity, needs to be matched in the wine. It sounds simple enough – and in the case of puddings and sweetmeats it is: the rule of thumb is that the wine must be at least as sweet as the food, and can be sweeter. If the food is sweeter, the wine will taste thin and tart. As with savoury food, balancing the weight of wine and food is critical, although it doesn't usually require quite such fine tuning because relative sweetness is the overriding consideration.

As a guide, the sweetest, heaviest wines are Australian liqueur Muscats and European fortified wines such as Malaga, PX sherry and various Moscatels, followed by Muscat de Beaumes-de-Venise and other Muscats from the south of France (Rivesaltes, for example). The liqueur Muscats and fortified wines are the kind of wines to try with the richest of chocolate, toffee or fudge elaborations, the heavyweight traditional Christmas pudding (if you decide against fizzy Moscato), and ice-cream. Botrytised and Late Harvest New World wines, especially Semillons, Rieslings and Chenin Blancs, tend to be heavier and sweeter than their European counterparts – Sauternes and Barsac, Austrian sweet wines, German *Beerenauslese*, *Trockenbeerenauslese* and *Eiswein* and the great sweet wines of the Loire (Coteaux du Layon, Quarts de Chaume, Vouvray etc). Sémillon-based wines such as Sauternes are fatter and more opulent than the Loire's Chenin Blanc wines and German sweet wines and are good with cream-dressed and cream-based puddings such as *crème brûlée*. Sweet Loire wines and German sweet wines have more marked acidity, which makes them particularly useful with fruit-based puddings. With the exception of Asti and other fizzy Moscatos, German sweet wines are the lightest-bodied; Austrian wines, though very broadly Germanic, are fuller-bodied.

Sweetness in savoury food is altogether more challenging, although a key point to have at the back of your mind is that, while dry wines are nasty with sweet food, there are sweet and medium wines that will go with savoury food. And it is not just with the famous marriages – Sauternes with foie gras, Sauternes with Roquefort – that it works. The more delicately flavoured types of shellfish, such as scallops, and white fish in creamy sauces can be served with German *Spätlese*, *demi-sec* Vouvray, Montlouis or Jurançon and *demi-sec* champagne, but the quality of these must be exemplary; cheap versions are not worth bothering with. Medium-sweet German Rieslings can also be set against the richness of goose and duck, pork and wild boar, above all when they are served with the sort of sweet fruit sauce or garnish which would desecrate a dry wine.

Sweet sauces, jellies and relishes are, as a whole, best matched by the combination of sweetness and acidity in good, estate-bottled German *Spätleses* and *Ausleses*. The snag is that these are not the sort of wines that go well with red meat and game, and even with many poultry and fish dishes, and anyway it is far more appropriate to match the wine to the main ingredients than the peripheral accompaniments. If the accompaniment can't or won't be sacrificed, if the sauce is an integral part of the dish, or if red wine is absolutely *de rigueur*, the answer is to choose a wine that has 'sweet' fruit flavours derived from very ripe grapes. Full-bodied, ripe, berry-flavoured red Zinfandel from California is the arch exponent, followed closely by Australian Shiraz and by New World reds in general. In the Old World, aim for warmly fruity Mediterranean wines, often blends including some Grenache (or Garnacha), Syrah or Tempranillo. If you stray in to the classic cooler areas, try to choose wines from the better (warmer, riper) vintages and make sure you avoid tannic wines.

With white wines (other than German), ripe fruit is again crucial, but marked acidity is just as essential as ripeness, if the sauce is, as they so often are, both sharp and sweet. The easiest way to ensure at least a modicum of fresh-tasting acidity is to choose young wine and to steer clear of the bottom rung, especially in blended whites and particularly those from the New World. It is also best to steer clear of heavily oaked wines, and wines, especially Chardonnays, with a rich, buttery flavour (this is acquired when the wine is allowed by the winemaker to undergo a secondary acid-softening fermentation called the malolactic). Neither oak not buttery flavours, particularly when they are in tandem, suit sweet, sharp fruit sauces and relishes. That a wine is oak-aged is very often mentioned on the label (often as '*élevé en fûts de chêne*'), although quite how oaky it will taste you don't know. Malolactic is rarely referred to: as a loose guide, it is favoured in Burgundy and therefore by aspiring producers in the New World (*see* Chardonnay, page 52).

So far, **TANNIN** has been cast largely as the villain of the piece. It turns nasty with fish and bitter with salt and equally nasty with eggs (*see* Tricky Ingredients, page 18) and with many cheeses (*see* Cheese, page 22). But, like acidity in white wines, tannin is essential to red wines, especially to those which are going to improve with age; it is

fundamental to their structure, giving a characteristic firmness, and contributes to their complexity. While winemakers can manipulate tannins to meet market demands and the trend is to make red wines less tannic nowadays, there are some grapes which are inherently more tannic than others – Syrah, Cabernet, Nebbiolo, Brunello and Tannat among them – while some, like Gamay, the grape of Beaujolais, and Dolcetto are naturally low in tannin.

It can't really be said that any foods positively need very tannic wines, but meat is tannin's major ally: rare steak and other red meats with a substantial, chewy texture partner tannic wines very well, because they moderate our perception of tannin. Equally, many top quality red wines, particularly from Bordeaux (ie clarets), which taste rather dry and austere on their own, only need food (especially meat) to render them supple, full of charm and tantalizingly complex in flavour.

As well as being a help – in the case of tannic wines – the texture of food occasionally presents itself as the unexpected banana skin. A few foods, principally eggs, chocolate and some cheeses, have a gluey, mouth-coating texture which blocks the tastebuds and generally interferes with the ability to taste wine. These foods are dealt with under Tricky Ingredients (page 16) and Cheese (page 22).

Tricky Ingredients

If weight and intensity yield the vital outlines and acid, sugar, salt, pepper and tannin provide the broad brushstrokes, filling in the details is a matter of looking at individual food flavours or textures, above all those which have the potential to modify, amplify and occasionally greatly to distort accompanying wines. Mercifully, clashes of entirely unpalatable proportions are rare. The foodstuffs and flavours listed here are simply those which you should be alert to when looking at recipes and menus – together with a few that ring false alarms. You will find many of them discussed in other sections of the book, but this is a checklist, with suggestions for the most suitable wines and, where possible, ways to mute offending flavours or textures. And one final word – remember that texture, though it is a less frequent problem, is not one to underestimate when it does arise: its impact can be very powerful and no less unpleasant.

VEGETABLES & FUNGHI

ARTICHOKES (GLOBE) Globe artichokes make most wines taste either metallic/bitter or strangely sweet. Squeezing lemon over the artichoke is good remedial treatment for this, as is serving the artichoke with vinaigrette, although the latter has its own potential for creating problems (see page 19). Young, moderately assertive white wines with highish acidity go well, for example Sauvignon Blancs from the crisper end of the New World spectrum (eg New Zealand), and young, crisp, medium-full Chardonnay works well with artichoke with a lemony hollandaise. But the best partner I have found is modern Greek white wine made from indigenous Greek or Cretan varieties which have a naturally sharp, lemon-and-pine character.

ASPARAGUS The powerful flavour of asparagus battles with many wines, but goes very well with a few, including those in which its distinctive flavour finds a companionable echo – namely Sauvignon Blanc wines (especially from New Zealand, Chile and the best from France's Bergerac and Côtes de Duras) and the cool climate Cabernet Francs of the Loire Valley (Chinon, Bourgueil, Saint-Nicolas de Bourgueil and Saumur-Champigny). Rounded but young Chardonnay (including burgundy and Chablis) is especially successful when the asparagus is served with melted butter.

FENNEL Fennel doesn't usually clash noisily with wine, but it doesn't positively go with many wines either. It is better with white wines (but if the rest of the plate demands red, go with that) and Sauvignon is its closest ally. The new wave, moderately aromatic, medium-full, dry white blends from the south of France work well and, when fennel is braised in butter, the herby, savoury and delicately buttery character of Chardonnay from Saint-Véran is good.

OLIVES See Fruit, page 21.

SPINACH Fortunately spinach is not often the centrepiece of a dish, as it can bring out a bitter or metallic taste in wine, particularly in reds. Modestly priced Italian reds and New Zealand Pinot Noir cope quite well, but the best policy with spinach is often to stir in cream, butter or parmesan to soften its flavour; or, if you are serving white wine, to squeeze lemon juice over it and then choose a fresh, young, not too aggressive white.

TOMATOES See Fruit, page 21.

TRUFFLES Finding the perfect match for truffles, both black and white, is difficult (and depends what they are shaved over), but youth and vivid fruit are certainly the wrong route. There is an affinity with the Nebbiolo grape, but Barolo is often too heavy; Barbaresco is a better match. There is also a musky affinity with Viognier, but you need a rich, creamy risotto, plenty of truffle and a top quality oak-fermented Viognier with a couple of years' age for the combination to work. Mature red burgundy, Saint-Emilion, top-notch Merlot and Rioja can be good; oddly, so can mature oak-fermented Chardonnay. And the Champenois drink mature vintage champagne.

SWEET

CHOCOLATE Death by chocolate is a common form of wine extermination. Chocolate is also one of the instances where an echoing flavour in a wine does not make an automatic marriage. Most of the wines which have a chocolatey flavour are dry, full-bodied reds, especially those made from Shiraz, Cabernet Sauvignon, Merlot and Nebbiolo. Very occasionally you can get away with a lush, ripe California Cabernet or Merlot with a chocolate pudding, but it's a risky business. These are all the kind of wines, however, which go with savoury stews and casseroles enriched with a little dark chocolate (a feature of some Mexican, Spanish and Italian dishes).

The difficulty with sweet chocolate dishes is two-fold: extreme sweetness and heavy, tastebud-smothering texture. Accompanying wines must be at least as sweet and they usually need to be full-bodied and high in alcohol, although the latter can vary according to the dish. There is a huge difference between the richest, densest dark chocolate truffle cakes and the lightest, frothiest mousses: Asti with a featherweight chocolate mousse is a triumph.

Muscat (the grape of Asti) is in fact the key with chocolate. While young, vigorous, top quality Sauternes will survive an encounter with many chocolate puddings (but not the heaviest) and ten-year-old tawny port will handle most of the heavier ones, there is a greater affinity with sweet Muscat. And, conveniently, there is a scale of sweetness/heaviness in Muscat wines which corresponds neatly to that of accompanying chocolate puddings, cakes and so on: Australian liqueur Muscats and Malaga are the heaviest and sweetest and so should be served with the very richest chocolate concoctions. Next down the scale are Muscat de Beaumes-de-Venise, Muscat de Rivesaltes, other Muscat *vins doux naturels* from Languedoc-Roussillon and many Moscatels de Valencia (the latter do vary in sweetness, though). Then come California Orange Muscat (especially good when there is orange in with the chocolate) and California Black Muscat; then other unfortified Muscats; and finally Asti. (Note that Moscato *spumante* and Clairette de Die are usually insufficiently sweet to be able to stand up to most forms of chocolate, and Portuguese Setúbal and Moscatel de Setúbal, though heavy, are not as sweet as other fortified Muscat-based wines and not usually sweet enough for chocolate either.)

ICE-CREAM The numbing effect of ice-cream is sufficient to wipe out the flavours of most sweet wines, but nothing wipes out Australian liqueur Muscat. It is best with chocolate, coffee, vanilla, rum and raisin, nut, praline, prune and ginger ice-creams and less good with fresh fruit based ones. Muscat de Beaumes-de-Venise and the ultra-sweet Spanish PX sherry are second choices.

RUM The powerful flavour of rum-flavoured puddings – babas, ice-cream, chocolate mousses – is best met by Muscat wines. Match the weight of the wine to the dish as usual (*see* Chocolate, above).

SWEET & SOUR SAUCE *See* China, page 136.

DAIRY & EGGS

CHEESE Matching cheese and wine is fraught with confrontations, but there are also many harmonious partnerships and a few heaven-made ones. *See* Cheese chapter, page 22.

EGGS Egg yolk coats the mouth in a very determined way. The crumbly dryness of completely hard-boiled yolk is difficult, but the texture of runny yolk is worse. Even so it is not an insuperable problem (although I wouldn't drink a precious bottle with eggs). What is needed is some kind of contrasting sauce or other main ingredient which the accompanying wine can latch on to, as in the classic Burgundian dish of Oeufs en Meurette (poached eggs in a red wine sauce), with which a Bourgogne Passe-Tout-Grains or other relatively modest red burgundy goes well. With most other egg dishes, particularly those involving cream, butter or cheese, white wines are better: in particular, not too oaky Chardonnays, Alsace Pinot Blancs and other medium- to full bodied Pinot Blancs (or Weissburgunders) that have a complementary echoing flavour. With the egg-based sauces hollandaise and mayonnaise, Chardonnay is usually the best bet, but Sauvignon Blanc is good with those which are markedly lemony. Soufflés and quiches should not be a problem either: again Chardonnay, including good burgundy, is usually a safe choice, although the ultimate decision will take account of other ingredients (cheese, onions, smoked salmon, bacon etc). Quail's eggs, with their finer texture, are delicious with *blanc de blancs* champagne.

MAYONNAISE *See* eggs.

YOGHURT Yoghurt is not a friend of wine, although cooked dishes with spicy yoghurty sauces are not impossible (*see* India, page 134). Dishes like Indian *raita* and Greek *tzatziki* are far more problematic, but, as they are seldom served alone, it is best to choose wines according to the other dishes and avoid sipping directly after a mouthful of the yoghurt dip or salad.

FISH

HERRING, KIPPERS, MACKEREL *See* Oily Fish, Smoked Fish and Vinegar.

OILY FISH Finding wines to serve with oily fish – sardines, to a slightly lesser extent herrings, and above all mackerel – is a question of making the best of a bad job. Unless you are drinking red Vinho Verde (in which case, commiserations) with sardines in Portugal, the wines have to be white, high in acid (to cut through the oil) and more neutral than fruity or flavoursome, because the fishy taste distorts the wine flavours. It is safer not even to consider New World wines. With mackerel the best bet is a Muscadet, or a Muscadet *sur lie*; Gros Plant provides an even sharper, more neutral (and cheaper) backdrop; and Gaillac (based on the acid Mauzac grape) and Mauzac *vins de pays* go with all three fish. Slightly softer options are Beaujolais Blanc, Soave Classico and other young Italian whites made from the ubiquitous Trebbiano (if there is no grape variety on the label the wine is likely to be Trebbiano-based). The rare Italian Timorasso grape, which is like a restrained and elegant Sauvignon, is particularly good with herrings. White Vinho Verde is good with oily fish, provided it is one of the bone dry, estate bottled wines and not one of the cheaper, sweetened ones. It is also worth bearing in mind that mustard helps counteract the oil in these fish, so, slashing a mackerel and filling the slashes with mustard, breadcrumbs and continental parsley before baking or barbecuing can expand the wine horizons.

SMOKED FISH The impact of smoked fish on wine varies enormously. Kippers really are best left for breakfast or a pungent Islay malt whisky, although *fino* and *manzanilla* sherries make acceptable partners. Smoked mackerel can be nearly as bad, although a light coating of cracked black peppercorns transforms it: fine quality Mosel and Saar *Kabinett*, dry Australian Riesling (Clare or Eden valley), bone dry Vinho Verde and aromatic Ribeiro from northeast Spain (but not the more aromatic Albariño) all go well. Smoked salmon is much more accommodating: champagne, especially vintage *blanc de blancs* is very good, as is Chablis (as expensive as you like), other white burgundies and high quality, lightly oaked New World Chardonnays; and some people swear by the more aromatic dry wines of Alsace. With the gentler flavour of smoked trout, stick with champagne or Chablis, or try a South African Sauvignon (they are usually less assertive than New Zealand's or the Loire's).

VINEGARS, PICKLES & SAUCES

CAPERS Even with top quality caper berries (larger and milder than capers), it is the vinegar, rather than the capers, which is the major force – and assassin – here, so *see* Vinegar.

SALSAS Whether red or green, Mexican-type hot chilli salsas are best with Sauvignon Blanc, but should you be matching the wine to the main ingredient instead? (*See also* Sauces, page 37.)

CHUTNEY Chutney is sweet, sharp and vicious. If you can't resist it, make sure you have palate-clearing bread, rice or other stodge, or cheese, pâté or plenty of water to insert between wine and chutney and then choose wine according to the main items, not the chutney. (For the record, late-bottled vintage port and high quality German *Kabinett* of various grape varieties survive better than most wines.)

CRANBERRY SAUCE Cranberry sauce is less punishing than chutney, but it still has a concentrated sweet-sharp character that does no favours to any wine and kills many, including fine, mature red Bordeaux. Top quality German Riesling *Kabinett* and *Spätlese* are best able to handle it, but if these don't go with the meat, fall back on the fruity character of a full-bodied Australian Shiraz or Mourvèdre (Mataro) or a California Zinfandel or Mourvèdre – and don't be too lavish with the sauce. (*See also* Riesling, page 35, and Sauces, page 36.)

MINT SAUCE *See* Herbs, Spices & Seasonings, page 20.

TARTARE SAUCE Sauvignon Blanc is best, but *see* Sauces, page 36.

VINEGAR, VINAIGRETTE & PICKLES Vinegar is a real danger zone for wine – even young white wine – and pickled anything is a problem. Acidity has to be matched to acidity and some sweetness is a help: German Riesling *Kabinett* is therefore usually more successful than bone dry Sauvignon Blanc, but, be warned, success is a relative word with pickled vegetables and fish (*see* Japan, page 140). With vinaigrette dressing you are on safer ground – or at least you can be if you make it with plenty of oil (perhaps five parts oil to one of vinegar). Using one of the more mellow vinegars – balsamic, sherry or Cabernet Sauvignon – also helps a great deal, as does substituting wine (but with less oil) and especially if you want to drink red wine; this is a trick employed in the kitchens of top red wine producers. If you are drinking Chardonnay, walnut oil will pick out and echo its nutty character.

HERBS, SPICES & SEASONINGS

CHILLI Surprisingly, chilli doesn't actually alter the taste of wine, but it numbs tastebuds and even burns them, with the result that it deprives you of some of your tasting capability: it is therefore daft to waste fine or venerable old wine on a chilli-laden dish. There isn't a specific type of wine that goes with chilli, but it needs to be fairly expressive to hold its own. Chilled, young white wines have the advantage of seeming to cool and refresh the palate. At the same time, it makes sense not to overload chilli-assaulted tastebuds with an obstacle course of heavily tannic red wines. *See also* India and Thai cuisines, pages 134 and 138.

CURRY *See* Chilli (above), Spices (opposite page), India, page 134, and Thai, page 138.

GARLIC When incorporated in cooked dishes, garlic is no problem at all, but a lot of raw garlic in a dish rather bullies the tastebuds. It's not a major hitch, but something to remember if you are thinking of serving a great wine; it is also worth bearing in mind that the dry, herby whites and rosés of the southern Rhône, Provence and Languedoc suit it well.

GINGER Ginger is not the saboteur that you might expect from its hot, insistent flavour, but it does need aromatic wines to stand up to it. Riesling, Gewürztraminer, Pinot Grigio, Muscat, Sauvignon and Viognier are all possibilities, depending on the dish: *see* India, Thai and Chinese cuisines (pages 134, 136 and 138 respectively). With ginger-flavoured sweet dishes, the most successful wines are sweet Muscats (choose the type according to the weight of the pudding – *see* Chocolate, page 17), botrytised Rieslings and botrytised New World Semillon.

HERBS Herbs are generally rather good news: they not only enhance food flavours but some enhance wine too. On their own the majority are more at home with white wines – rosemary and thyme are two important exceptions – but you should rarely let the herbs alone influence the choice of wine.

Note that sage can be rather domineering, so use it judiciously. *See also* Mint and Sorrel (below), and Thai food, page 138.

HORSERADISH Horseradish is hard on wine, sapping it of fruit and flavour. Unfortunately, the wine that stands up to it best, full-bodied Condrieu or California Viognier, does not go with beef (whether hot or cold) and is too powerful for smoked fish. If you cannot go without horseradish sauce, be generous with the cream and mean with the vinegar or lemon and try serving a Dolcetto or a Beaujolais *cru* with beef and a Chablis *premier*, or even *grand*, *cru* with smoked trout. Wasabi, Japanese green horseradish, is even more pungent and nose-tingling. When served with the raw fish dishes sashimi and sushi, try assertive Sauvignon from, say, New Zealand (and cross your fingers). *See also* Japan, page 140.

MINT & MINT SAUCE Mint is very happy with wine, including the Cabernet Sauvignons (especially Australian) in which there is a minty echo. But mint sauce and mint jelly, with their sugar and vinegar, ruin wine, especially red, and it is hard to temper them in any way.

MUSTARD Very hot, very vinegary and any rather sweet mustards should be treated with extreme caution, but Dijon mustard goes surprisingly well with both white and red wines and copes admirably with tannin. Whites need to be either round and full in the Chardonnay mould or have the concentrated acid-sweet balance of a good German Riesling (especially Mosel *Kabinett*). Reds should be medium- to full-bodied, and tannic if you wish, but spare very old and fragile wine. If you want to drink red wine with cold roast meat, where white might be better (*see* page 35), add mustard. It will cut through the cold fat and subdue tannin.

SORREL The sharp lemony flavour of sorrel has to be matched by a wine with high acidity. The punchy Sauvignons of the Loire, New Zealand and Chile are ideal, as is Savennières, a bone dry Loire white made from Chenin.

SOY SAUCE The saltiness of soy sauce demands white wine with marked acidity and, optionally, some sweetness. Fortunately, that is also the profile for wines that suit the broad range of Chinese and Japanese dishes (*see* China, page 136, and Japan, page 140). Where something such as a steak is dressed with soy sauce, remember the possibility of a tannin-salt clash and choose a full-bodied, fruity red wine (*see* Salt, page 13).

SPICES Chilli is dealt with opposite and the blend of spices in Indian cooking is discussed on page 134. Generally, spices are not a problem for wines, whether in sweet or savoury dishes. Most have a preference for whites, and you find echoes of their flavours in grapes such as Gewürztraminer, Pinot Grigio, Muscat, Viognier, Grüner Veltliner and Furmint, but you should concentrate on matching wine to the main ingredients and to the final effect of the dish.

FRUIT

GRAPEFRUIT Try the tartest white wine you can find (Gros Plant, Pouilly-Fumé, bone dry Vinho Verde). Or abandon the grapefruit.

LEMON/LIME Australian Verdelho and Hungarian Furmint have affinities with lime and Riesling has an affinity with both lemon and lime, but in savoury dishes the priority is to match the acidity of the citrus fruits with that of the wine (*see* Acidity, page 12). With lemon and lime puddings, botrytised New World Rieslings work well, as do Semillons, including Sauternes, especially when cream is served or incorporated.

OLIVES The saltiness of neat olives, whether green, black or purple, is best met by *fino* and *manzanilla* sherries. In cooked dishes, such as rich daubes, simply go with the main ingredients, or, if the olive taste is pronounced, choose a full-bodied, fruity and preferably herby red (from Provence, for example). In salads, crisp, dry whites and rosés, suit olives well, but you have to take account of other ingredients.

ORANGE Orange, like other citrus fruits, needs its acidity matched, whether the dish is savoury or sweet. Quite a wide range of sweet wines suit orange puddings and cakes, but it is well worth seeking out the complementary flavour of an aptly named sweet orange Muscat from California or Australia. Failing that, other Muscat wines are good. Match the weight of the wine to that of the food as usual (*see also* Chocolate): for example, drink sparkling Asti with an orange jelly or orange fruit salad and a liqueur Muscat with a very rich, dark orange-flavoured chocolate mousse. With a dense but not too sweet orange and almond cake, the marmaladey flavour of Setúbal Moscatel from Portugal is good. Botrytised Sémillons, including the wines of Sauternes, Chenin Blancs from the Loire Valley and Bouviers from Austria all work well, too.

The sweetness and acidity of an orange sauce with savoury food doesn't do wine any favours. If you are in charge of the cooking and want to drink dry wine, whether red or white, you will need to exercise restraint with the orange (juice and zest) and go easy on the sugar. Alternatively, with the classic duck dish, you can serve a German *Spätlese* or *Auslese* (Riesling, Scheurebe or Rieslaner), depending on the sweetness and the region from which the wine comes (Pfalz wines taste bigger and sweeter than those from the Mosel). You can even serve more opulent sweet wines, such as those from Sauternes and Austria, but for some people that is overkill.

TOMATO Beware the acidity of tomato. Sauvignon Blanc is by far the best all-rounder and there is a usefully large field to choose from. Vin de Pays des Côtes de Gascogne is a cheaper alternative. If you want a red wine, try an Italian Barbera or other young Italian reds (because of their tendency to astringency). The smoky intensity of sun-dried tomatoes in olive oil needs to be matched by equally intense white wines: the sweetness of a *Spätlese* Riesling from the Pfalz or the ripeness coupled with acidity of a New Zealand Chardonnay.

Cheese

The idea that wine and cheese are perfect companions is, I'm afraid, one of the great myths, perpetuated perhaps by the two most fêted and triumphant partnerships – port and Stilton and Roquefort and Sauternes. Generally speaking, cheese is one of the trickiest foods to choose wine for. But is it any wonder? Cheese is frequently strong and pungently flavoured; it is often high in fat; it may be high in acid; it is often very salty; and it can have a gluey, mouth-coating texture. Some cheeses even manage to combine all these wine- and tastebud-challenging features – and the whole subject is made more complicated by the fact that cheeses vary as much from producer to producer and according to maturity as do wines.

Contrary to convention, dry red wines tend to suffer more from cheese than dry whites (bang goes another myth) and sweet wines are often more successful than dry wines. Almost without exception, they need to be very sweet and at least moderately full-bodied (the lightness and elegant sweetness of German *Auslese* is rarely appropriate). The power of sweet fortified wines, especially port, and Recioto della Valpolicella (both dry and sweet) often come into their own with strong and blue cheeses. As well as port – both vintage (or vintage type) and aged tawny – bear in mind Bual Madeira and Banyuls.

If those are the broad generalizations, the points that follow are more specific nuggets to keep in mind.

• As it is the tannin in red wine with which cheese often clashes (spoiling the taste of the wine more than the cheese), reasonably mature red wines are often more successful than very young ones.

• Moreover, the complex flavours of reds with some maturity are more harmonious with the complex flavours of many cheeses than are the vivid, pure fruit flavours of young wines.

• Be wary, though, of subjecting a very mature, fine wine to cheese. If you do want to serve such a wine with cheese, choose Mimolette, or mature Gouda, as they do in Bordeaux.

• Red wines with some tannin meet their best match in hard cheeses, provided they are not too strong or salty (salt emphasizes tannin's bitterness). Indeed, hard cheeses (waxy or crumbly) are the most accommodating with wines across the board.

• Soft French cheeses of the Camembert and Pont l'Evêque types, particularly when they are mature, are some of the hardest on wine. For the sake of any wine, try to catch them before they have become too runny (and usually also pungent).

• Soft, creamy, high-fat cheeses (like Chaource) generally need wine with acidity, making white wines the easier choice.

• The more acid the cheese the more acid the wine needs to be – goat's cheese with Sauvignon Blanc, for example.

• Don't be lulled into a false sense of security by mild cheeses: Emmental, Jarlsberg, Edam and Caerphilly are not as easy as you might expect; and goat's cheese is pernickety even when mild.

• Trying to choose one wine to go with the sort of cheese-board that has a piece of blue, a ripe Camembert, a goat's cheese and a hard cheese is unlikely to meet with resounding success. Having one splendid cheese, instead, is as near to ensuring success as you can get.

• If at a loss, choose, where possible, a wine from the same region (or wine of similar type) as the cheese – strong, pongy Munster with Alsace Gewurztraminer, Maroilles with non-vintage champagne, Vacherin with mature Pinot Noir. (This doesn't help, of course, in a non wine producing area, like Normandy.)

• Cheese in cooked dishes doesn't usually pose a problem – and cheese soufflés are a rather good way of showing off fine red wines (and whites). *See also* Switzerland.

HARD CHEESES

The cheeses that go with the widest range of wines, including dry red wines from medium- to very full-bodied, are hard cheeses, provided they are not too old and strong. They include Cantal of *entre deux* strength (between the youngest and two oldest categories), Parmesan and Grana Padano, Manchego and similar Spanish cheeses, many French Pur Brebis cheeses, mature Gouda (Mimolette), Gruyère and English farmhouse cheeses such as Cheddar, Red Leicester and, above all, Double Gloucester. But not all British hard cheeses are equal: young white Wensleydale, with its crumbly, coating texture and acidity is very difficult (it is best with a New World Sauvignon or concentrated Chardonnay); the pungency and dense texture of mature Lancashire is difficult (try a full, spicy southern French red); so, also, is Caerphilly from Wales (try a top-notch New World Chardonnay). A full, rich Chardonnay is also good with Cheddar, Cantal and Parmesan.

SOFT CHEESES

Whether bloomy rind (eg Brie and Camembert) or washed rind (eg Pont l'Evêque), soft cheeses are among the trickiest to match, especially when they are unpasteurised and as they mature. Try Côte d'Or white burgundy with a creamy Brie and mature red with Camembert – a St-Emilion or Pomerol from a ripe vintage, a red burgundy or Chianti Classico Riserva. Ripe Pont l'Evêque is even more difficult: try a robust Sicilian red or a 10-year-old tawny port. Semi-soft Chaumes is easier: St-Emilion is very good, as are other mature, mellow reds. In contrast, the mild taste but rich fat of Chaource is best off-set by good steely Chablis.

BLUE CHEESE

Blue cheese and wine runs the gamut from celestial partnership (Roquefort with Sauternes, Stilton with vintage or old tawny port) to horrendous clashes. Danish Blue is to be avoided with wine at all costs – as are other very piquant blues such as the strongest Gorgonzola and caustic salty French varieties (often pitched as a cheap alternative to Roquefort – beware!). With milder Gorgonzola, try Recioto di Soave. If you are not sure of your cheese, settle for an aged tawny port or Bual Madeira. With mild, creamy blue cheeses, Tokay Aszú (4 or 5 '*putts*') often works well and with Dolcelatte try mature Rioja or Ribera del Duero. The latter is also quite good with Stilton; so is Sauvignon Blanc – surprising until you think of acid matching acid.

GOAT'S CHEESE

Goat's cheese's affinity with Sauvigon Blanc makes Pouilly-Fumé and Sancerre perfect. New Zealand Sauvignon comes a close second and is especially good with warm goat's cheese on a dressed salad. New Zealand Chardonnays, and other New World Chardonnays with good concentration and acid, are alternatives, especially with a salad including walnuts; white Crozes-Hermitage and Pinot Blanc (Alsace etc) are also good. Among red wines, Loire Cabernet Francs (Bourgueil, Saint-Nicolas de Bourgueil, Saumur-Champigny and Chinon) are a reliable choice. With a mature cheese (but not too old, hard or pungent), mature Syrah is complementary, if rather powerful, and sparkling red Shiraz is the off-beat option with a medium mature cheese.

SMOKED CHEESE

Very difficult: try Alsace Gewurztraminer, Australian Shiraz or a sweet wine.

See also Matching Wine, Matching Food – pages 144–155.

THE EFFECT OF

Cooking

INGREDIENTS COUNT FOR A LOT, BUT IT IS

IMPOSSIBLE TO OVERESTIMATE THE IMPACT

OF THE TECHNIQUES AND METHODS USED

TO PREPARE AND COOK A DISH ON THE

CHOICE OF ANY ACCOMPANYING WINE.

NO COOK EVER ASSESSES THE OUTCOME

OF A RECIPE BY ITS INGREDIENTS ALONE;

LIKEWISE, NO ONE CHOOSING A WINE TO

GO WITH IT CAN DO SO ON THE BASIS OF

THE ASSEMBLED RAW MATERIALS.

poaching and steaming

frying

braising and stewing

grilling

roasting

sauces

cooking with wine

Poaching & Steaming

One of the odd things about the standard rules on matching food and wine, and even about much contemporary advice, is that they focus entirely, or almost entirely, on the flavours of the ingredients and the overall weight and balance of the dish, but pay very little attention to cooking methods. Yet (if it isn't too obvious to say it) the way food is cooked can have a profound influence on its flavour. A steamed salmon steak is more delicate in flavour than one that is char-grilled. Vegetables that have been roasted in the oven are more intensely flavoured than those which have been boiled. All this inevitably has a bearing on the wine you choose.

Poaching and steaming are the most gentle of cooking methods and, accordingly, are mainly used for delicate foods: delicate flavours or flavours where freshness needs to be retained; or fragile textures or those where moisture and natural juices need to be saved. The Chinese, for whom the texture, freshness and appearance of food is of supreme importance, probably use these methods, above all steaming, more than any other nation, but any country which eats fresh vegetables, fish, shellfish, chicken, sweetbreads, eggs or delicate quenelle-type dumplings – that is just about every country – is likely to employ some of these methods some of the time. And the health concerns and fads of the last two decades have brought these, among other fat-free methods, more into vogue.

At its simplest, poached and steamed food needs an accompanying wine that is light-bodied, or at least no more than medium-weight, which means that there is a far greater choice of appropriate white wines than there is of reds. Tannin (found principally in red wines) is an enemy of this kind of food, whereas the acid freshness of crisp, light dry whites or rosé wines can enhance delicate flavours. On the whole the less ebullient flavours and lighter weight of classic European whites makes them more suitable than most New World white wines, and the most suitable red wines come from Europe's cooler wine areas, such as the Loire and Alsace in France, those of Germany and Switzerland, and northeast Italian regions such as Bardolino.

In practice, outside the convalescent room, food is seldom poached or steamed completely plainly and then served without any kind of sauce or accompaniment – even asparagus is usually served with melted butter, if not a rich hollandaise – and once you start adding other ingredients you have to take them into account when choosing the wine. The pithy, herbaceous fruit and piquant acidity of a typical New Zealand Sauvignon Blanc are far too powerful for poached scallops, but when you poach the scallops in a Thai-style broth (with lemon grass, ginger, garlic, lime and chillies) you suddenly have a marriage – the pungency of the wine matched by the hot, sour flavourings. Similarly, plainly poached chicken is worlds away from the classic French *poule au pot*, in which a flavoursome, elderly fowl, which is too tough for roasting, is packed with a meaty pork or ham stuffing, and simmered in water or stock with vegetables and herbs. The result is a dish with enough substance and flavour to drink with medium-weight reds such as Minervois and quite full-bodied whites. A more extreme example is the Italian *vitello tonnato*, where the rich tuna mayonnaise sauce is much more significant for wine than the mild flavoured poached veal (*see* section on Sauces, page 36).

Even in seemingly quite plain dishes you need to be aware of the poaching liquid. Water, stock and *court bouillon* (wine and water mixed) are the most usual, but milk (as in the classic Italian dish of pork cooked in milk) is sometimes used. Milk gives particularly moist meat and a ready-made sauce; wine can impart a good deal of flavour, and, in the case of white wine, heightened acidity which will usually need to be matched by the wine being drunk. A strong stock will also add a lot of flavour and, if made using mushrooms, particularly ceps, will probably turn the tables towards red wine.

Fruit may be poached in either a sugar syrup or wine. Pears in red wine is a French classic: serving this dish is one of the few occasions when a red wine incorporated in the cooking can be accompanied by a white wine to drink. German Riesling *Beerenauslese* and other botrytised and late harvest Rieslings make good partners for this and are the safest bets with any poached fruit (*see also* Braising & Stewing, pages 30–31).

Boiling is an altogether more vigorous (and more old-fashioned) method of cooking, used not so much to produce more vigorous flavours but to tackle different textures. With green vegetables it is used to preserve colour, crunch and flavour by rapid cooking. With meat, lesser, coarser joints, which would otherwise be fatty or tough (or both), can be boiled slowly (or rather, brought to the boil and then reduced to a simmer) with vegetables and spices to make them tender and enhance their flavour. Brisket and silverside of beef are often cooked in this way. The resulting flavour is less intense than for, say, roast or grilled beef, and, depending on the accompanying vegetables and sauces, a wide range of medium-bodied, not too tannic, not too grand red wines make good partners. The classic Piedmont *bollito misto* (various cuts of beef and veal, including the gelatine-rich ones, all boiled together and served with a sharp green sauce) is a more Rabelaisian dish which is naturally suited to more robust reds: Nebbiolo-based wines are ideal; Syrah (or Shiraz) and the bigger Tuscan wines are an alternative.

In fact, most dishes described as 'boiled' are usually simmered for the bulk of their cooking time: most meat would be toughened by hard boiling and the skins of boiling sausages would burst. But one occasion where boiling is essential is the making of *bouillabaisse* and other similar fish soups and stews. The liquid has to be kept boiling so that the olive oil emulsifies and does not float in blobs at the surface; the fish, or some of them, may be added towards the end of the cooking time, so that they don't become overcooked. Dry, medium-bodied, herby rosés, without too much floral or fruity character are the right sort of wines to drink with these chunky soups (particularly rosés from Provence, Tuscany and Navarra); or dry whites of a similar herby style from the south of France and Italy.

Frying

Frying has become somewhat unfashionable in the last 20 years, because of its association with the dread word fat and supposedly unhealthy diets. But frying is maligned: there are other cooking methods which rely on fat and, equally, among the variations on the frying theme, there is one, dry frying, which does not use fat at all. More importantly, frying, even deep frying, can transform the most ordinary of foodstuffs: a good potato chip is delicious, as are sage leaf fritters and freshly fried onions.

The essence of all frying is the fast cooking on high heat of fairly small pieces of food. Every country does it in one way or another. The variations depend on several things: the depth, the heat and the type of fat used – whether it is flavourless oil such as groundnut, fruity or peppery olive oil, lard, dripping or clarified butter; on whether the food is coated first; and on what sort of pan is used – a large deep pan for deep frying, a standard frying pan for shallow frying, a ridged, cast iron griddle for fatless frying, or a wok for stir frying. The potential for so many permutations means that frying covers a wide range of foods and dishes with very different results, producing heavy food at one extreme and gossamer-light at the other.

Deep frying uses the most and the hottest fat. Not only that but, to stop it drying out, food being deep fried is often

coated with batter, breadcrumbs or flour. The health lobbyists take a very dim view of all this, but dishes such as *fritto misto* (whether meat and vegetables, or fish), *tempura* (fish or vegetables), breaded veal escalopes, chicken kiev and even, when carefully done, the batter-coated staples of British fish and chip shops prove deep frying has a purpose and a place.

Considering how often deep fried foods are served with a refreshing wedge of lemon, it is fair to assume that a streak of equally refreshing acidity is a useful attribute in an accompanying wine. Fortunately, much of the food that is suited to deep frying is also suited to white wine. You need to be aware of the weight of the ingredients: a seafood *fritto misto* and *tempura* may be quite light, but, more often, deep fried foods have a certain weight which the wine must stand up to. Chablis, New Zealand Chardonnay and other stylish New World Chardonnays, including the new wave unoaked ones, tend to work with fish, chicken and veal. Alternatively, Sauvignons, such as Sancerre, Pouilly-Fumé and those from Austria, New Zealand and Chile, have an intensity and sharpness of flavour which provide a vivid contrast, particularly with fish. Austria's Grüner Veltliner does the same. The lighter fish and vegetable dishes need lighter wines, such as north Italian whites, Vin de Pays des Côtes de Gascogne, Rueda, Vinho Verde, New World Colombard, Swiss Chasselas and Sauvignon-Sémillon blends such as Bergerac.

Some dishes may be deep or shallow fried. Meatballs are a case in point. As a rule, they need red wines, but there are so many variations (*polpette* from Italy, *frikadeller* from Denmark, *keftethes* from Greece – all of which sound so much more tempting than meatballs) that it is hard to be very specific. As a guide, delicately flavoured veal ones can take quite classy, medium-bodied red wines; herby Greek-style lamb ones go well with medium-bodied southern French reds; and the heavier American beef ones, with garlic, onion, oregano and tomato sauce, deserve robust, fruity reds such as Teroldego Rotaliano, Montepulciano d'Abruzzo and reds like Copertino and Primitivo from Apulia. Only when meatballs

become very spicy – Indian style – can you revert to white wine – a dry Muscat perhaps, or a Viognier for a change.

Shallow frying spans the spectrum from a point close to deep frying, using very hot fat and similar coatings, to the gentle frying of delicacies such as Dover sole which deserve grand, subtle wine (Chablis or Arneis, for example). In between there are any number of steaks, chops, cutlets, fillets and other pieces of meat, poultry and fish which may be shallow fried to rare, with a browned outside, or thoroughly cooked. When choosing wine, you must go with the main ingredient, taking into account, as usual, any added flavours. Then bear in mind that shallow frying, if anything, will make the food richer than if it had been plainly poached and that a browned outside will give an intensity of flavour as in grilling and roasting (*see* pages 32 and 34).

Dry frying is sometimes used for delicate foods like fish and chicken, to give a very light, unfussy result, but more often it applies to the vogue of searing and rapidly cooking meat steaks and chops and fish steaks (such as tuna, salmon and swordfish) on a griddle pan – almost like upside down grilling. The resulting steaks and chops, with their griddle-stripes of intense, smoky-burnt flavour on the outside and succulent interiors, are very like those of grilled food. The similarity may be even greater if the food has been marinated first (*see* page 32).

Stir frying in a wok, invented and perfected by the Chinese, is a way of cooking quickly and evenly with very little fat to preserve colour, texture and flavour. It is particularly useful for vegetables and seafood, but strips of chicken and lean meat can also be cooked in this way, as can noodles and eggs. It is a method that allows the ingredients to speak for themselves, rather than imposing cooking flavours on them, and the resulting dishes tend to be light with notably clean, clearly defined flavours. White wines of fairly light body, especially German Rieslings of *Kabinett* and *Spätlese Halbtrocken* sweetness and weight, make many of the best matches, but it depends, of course, on the precise ingredients (*see also* China, page 136).

Braising & Stewing

Casseroles and *carbonades*, pot roasts and hot pots, *civets* and *salmis*, daubes and ragouts, ratatouille, *caponata*, braised chicory, fennel and all the rest are witness to the fact that practically every species of meat, poultry, game, firm fish and edible vegetable can be braised or stewed – and have been for centuries. They are indispensable methods for rendering tough cuts of meat and old birds tender (*see boeuf bourguignonne* and *coq au vin* under Burgundy, page 84) and for dealing with the less prized fatty cuts of meat, such as breast of veal. But more than that, some of the most appetisingly rich and complex tastes of any food evolve during the leisurely cooking process.

Despite all the different names, implying different methods and cooking vessels, there are just two main versions and the principle is the same for both: meat, fish or vegetables are cooked slowly in liquid in a covered pot with additional ingredients and flavourings, either in the oven or on a hob or fire. The difference comes with the amount of liquid used and the size of the main item, or pieces, being cooked. With stewing (often referred to as casseroling), more liquid is used, often covering the ingredients initially, and meat is cut into small pieces. With braising and pot roasting, less liquid is used – sometimes very little – and it is applied to whole joints, birds or fish, or whole portions.

So far as meat-based stews and braised dishes are concerned, the best of these is usually rich, even unctuous, precisely because of the theoretically inferior meat used. Cuts such as shin (beef and veal) and pig's trotters contain the all-important gelatine, which enriches both flavour and texture, and marrow and fat both lend extra richness and smoothness. Not only that but the meat from older animals and the most used muscles is often particularly flavoursome - and made more so if it has been marinated in advance and more so again if it is browned before the liquid is added. Tender, lean cuts, in contrast, are usually left dry and tasteless by such long slow cooking.

Quite apart from marinades, the cooking liquid itself is critical. Wine and stock may leave a deep imprint on the dish; certainly they will yield a much more flavoursome dish than plain water. If red wine is used, the wine to be drunk will almost certainly be red, whether the central ingredient is red meat, white meat or fish. If white wine is used, the opposite usually applies, but not always. White wine increases the acidity of a sauce more than red, but the other ingredients – meat, stock, mushrooms, for example – might give the dish a weight that needs red wine. Cider as cooking liquid, however, nearly always demands white wine with plenty of acidity (and flavour) to accompany it, while stews cooked in beer and stout need red wine, but one that is low in tannin, such as a Chinon, Bourgueil or Saumur-Champigny from the Loire.

Clearly, for so huge a span of dishes based on an infinite variety of ingredients, there can be no one type or narrowly identified group of wines that is the ideal accompaniment. What you can say is that the richer, more complex the flavours in the dish, the more substantial the wine needs to be, and more often than not it will be red wine. The meatiest stews of beef and dark fleshed game will often be able to cope with quite tannic reds (including Nebbiolo and Rhône Syrah), but where there is a greater proportion of onions, carrots and other vegetables (which give a certain sweetness), or where the base is poultry or rabbit, you will need less tannin and softer, lusher fruit in the wine – McLaren Vale Shiraz, Vacqueyras, a Côtes du Roussillon, New World Pinot Noir or Rosso di Montalcino, for example.

But by no means all stews and braises are dark, strong and concentrated. *Blanquette de veau* is an archetypal example of the reverse: the meat is mild in flavour; the sauce is both creamy (egg yolk as well as cream) and slightly sweet from the onions, carrots and nutmeg; and the cloves and nutmeg provide a touch of spice. White wine makes the best match: it needs to have some character and concentration, but it should not be too oaky, fruity, buttery or sharp. Dry Vouvray (and even *demi-sec*) works well, as do Alsace Pinot Blanc, Lugana, Favorita, the best dry Soave and fine, mature white Graves. Chardonnay is fine if you get one that has the right echo of buttery, creamy complexity – but that is the hard part: a Mâcon from a conscientious grower in one of the best of the villages is a good bet.

If *blanquette de veau* is not the easiest dish to find a perfect partner for, at least a glance at the ingredients makes it almost certain that your starting point and finishing point is white wine. Some stews are not so straightforward. *Osso buco* is veal, a so-called white meat; part of its liquid is white wine; the vegetables with which it is cooked – ónions, carrots, celery and tomatoes – generally favour white wines; and it is served with a risotto Milanese (saffron flavoured). And yet when you sit down and try it with red and white wines it is some of the red wines – Dolcetto and modern, young, freshly fruity, supple Pinot Noir – which make the most satisfactory matches.

Ratatouille, the most famous of vegetable stews, is even more the chameleon. As most vegetables, however they are cooked, are happier with white wines, it makes sense that dry white wines with good acidity and a herby or gently citrussy character (rather than ripe tropical fruit flavours) should go with ratatouille; it follows that rosés of similar youthful crispness from the Mediterranean should be equally suitable. But many of the red wines from Languedoc-Roussillon and Provence also work well and this is entirely a reflection of the cooking method, which produces a dish that is rich in flavours and relatively substantial.

Stewed fruit has something of an image problem, at least in Britain where school dinners of the sixties and seventies probably have a lot to answer for. There is no such stigma attached to poached fruit, however, which uses more liquid and which may be reduced at the end to produce a more concentrated syrup. In terms of accompanying wines, it doesn't make a lot of difference whether the fruit has been poached or stewed, although poached fruit may have a sweeter syrup. With their sweetness and acidity, German Riesling *Beerenauslese* and botrytised and late harvest Rieslings from elsewhere are the best all-rounders; sweet Loires, such as Coteaux du Layon and Vouvray *moelleux* are the next best thing; and Sauternes and other botrytised Sémillons are especially good when cream is added.

Grilling

The difference between roasting and grilling is cavernous at one extreme and almost a question of semantics at the other. Grilling over an open fire only becomes roasting by virtue of the size of the object being cooked: a chump chop is grilled; a whole lamb is roasted; unless it is done outside, in which case it usually becomes barbecuing, whatever the size of the beast or piece. Roasting and grilling both use dry heat, but roasting is sometimes slow and gentle, whereas grilling is almost invariably fast, blasting the food with high heat to brown or sear the outside and leave the inside juicy. Thus the quintessential browning process, which changes the flavour of the food, is more intense – more smoky and caramelizing – and affects proportionately more of the food than with a roasted joint or bird. Grilling over charcoal gives an even more intense smoky character.

It is an attractively minimalist and uncomplicated method in theory and practice, but uncomplicated doesn't mean easy. It is tantalisingly difficult to get it spot on, whether you are using an electric grill, an open fire or charcoal embers in the great outdoors. Timing is critical and there is precious little scope for correcting errors. Grilling, therefore, can only really be done with prime cuts of meat, but it has a much wider application in terms of types of food than roasting. It is used not only for all kinds of meat, fowl, offal, sausages and hamburgers, but for many sorts of fish and shellfish, for vegetables and cheese and even for salad stuffs, such as radicchio, and fruit such as pineapple.

Because of the more pronounced 'browning' flavours, wines for drinking with grilled food can usually afford to be more forceful than for food that has been roasted (or indeed poached). Young wines with flavours of fruit, oak, tannin or acidity that would be too vigorous for a roast meet their match with grilled food; and wines with flavours that are vaguely smoky, far from being too much of a good thing, often provide a complementary echo – for instance, Syrah and Shiraz, Zinfandel, Sangiovese, Nebbiolo, Pinotage and Mourvèdre among reds, oaked Chardonnay, Marsanne and Pinot Gris among whites. It is worth noting, too, that, because of the toasty, smoky flavours that ageing in (or with) new oak gives to wine, grilled food can generally take oakier tasting reds and whites than most other foods. This is not to be sniffed at in a world overloaded with oaky wines that don't sit easily with food.

Another point to bear in mind is the effect of rare meat on tannin: a chunky rare steak can be a useful ally for a tannic red. But beware, then, of overdoing the salt: salt makes tannin taste more bitter. Pepper, on the other hand, can bring out flavours in rather ordinary, simple wine, making it taste stronger and more complex.

As with roasts, grilled, and especially barbecued, food seldom goes completely unadorned. Garlic and herbs (see Roasting, page 34) are often used in profusion and the squeeze of lemon, which in some countries goes with roast meat, is even more likely to be the final touch to a lamb kebab, a spatchcocked *poussin*, a veal chop, grilled sardines or king prawns. It would almost certainly prove to be the death of any fine old claret; equally, it would flatten any cheap California Chardonnay with low acidity and a touch of residual sugar and any bland, neutral, low acid white. Where the meat demands red wine, you will almost certainly need a young wine with a touch of astringency. Italian reds from Tuscany northwards (including Chianti, Dolcetto and Barbera) often have it, but you need to avoid the tannic ones such as Nebbiolo: lemon brings out the harshness and bitterness of tannin.

Barbecue sauce is another potential trip wire, because of its sweetness. Sweetness and crystalline acidity in German *Kabinett* (Riesling and some newer varieties, but not the Pinot/ Burgunder family) is an easy match, but the delicacy of German wines is not suited to powerful barbecued foods. Gewürztraminer can work, but, equally, can be a touch overbearing. Red wines need to be deeply fruity, supple and low in tannin. Those that fit the spec include Australian Shiraz (including red sparkling), Zinfandel, Chilean and California Merlot, new wave South African reds and, with more caution, California Pinot Noir.

Then there are the marinades. While these can be used purely to make meat more tender and stop food drying out, the object is more commonly to enhance flavours – both by

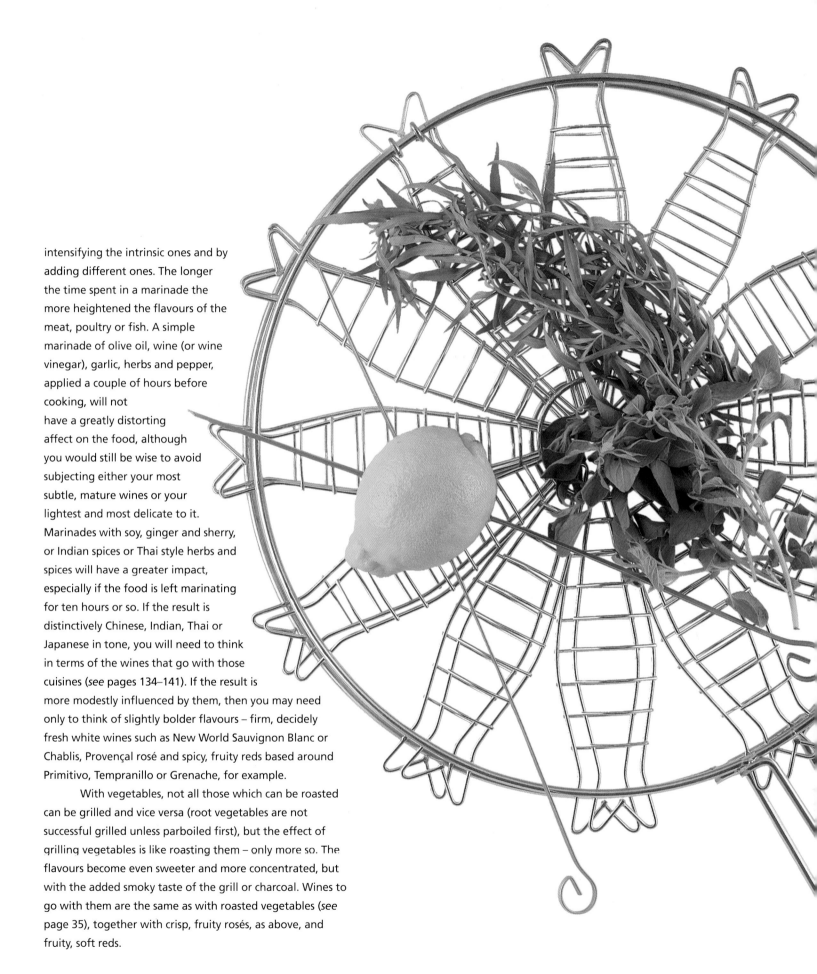

intensifying the intrinsic ones and by adding different ones. The longer the time spent in a marinade the more heightened the flavours of the meat, poultry or fish. A simple marinade of olive oil, wine (or wine vinegar), garlic, herbs and pepper, applied a couple of hours before cooking, will not have a greatly distorting affect on the food, although you would still be wise to avoid subjecting either your most subtle, mature wines or your lightest and most delicate to it. Marinades with soy, ginger and sherry, or Indian spices or Thai style herbs and spices will have a greater impact, especially if the food is left marinating for ten hours or so. If the result is distinctively Chinese, Indian, Thai or Japanese in tone, you will need to think in terms of the wines that go with those cuisines (*see* pages 134–141). If the result is more modestly influenced by them, then you may need only to think of slightly bolder flavours – firm, decidely fresh white wines such as New World Sauvignon Blanc or Chablis, Provençal rosé and spicy, fruity reds based around Primitivo, Tempranillo or Grenache, for example.

With vegetables, not all those which can be roasted can be grilled and vice versa (root vegetables are not successful grilled unless parboiled first), but the effect of grilling vegetables is like roasting them – only more so. The flavours become even sweeter and more concentrated, but with the added smoky taste of the grill or charcoal. Wines to go with them are the same as with roasted vegetables (*see* page 35), together with crisp, fruity rosés, as above, and fruity, soft reds.

Roasting

For the keen cook, a plainly roasted joint of meat is not the most exciting prospect, but if you are serving a red wine of great pedigree and perfect maturity, you could hardly be kinder to it than to serve roast red meat or pork dressed with no more than a scattering of herbs and garlic and served with the meat juices: it is hard to beat a leg of lamb for showing off the star quality of a fine Médoc or Graves. Simply roasted game birds, goose and duck can be equally flattering with fine Pinot Noir and Syrah-based reds.

As a method, roasting is the complete opposite of steaming, poaching and boiling. Where they use moisture or a mass of liquid to preserve the inherent flavours and texture of the food, roasting, as with grilling, depends on dry heat to intensify the taste and to add a specific 'roasted' flavour. This comes from the browning of the meat, which concentrates the flavours of the outside layers, where juices have evaporated, and gives a slightly caramelized taste to the crusty surface where juices have actually dried. Roasting fast at a high heat gives more of this character and is better suited to the naturally tender, superior cuts of meat which can be served rare so that they retain moisture within. (Rare meat, especially beef, has the useful attribute of making tannic red wines taste less tannic.)

More gentle, long, slow roasting produces a less intense roasted flavour, but is especially useful for making tougher cuts tender and for poultry and meat such as pork which must be thoroughly cooked. In practice, many people combine the two, starting with high heat to achieve the browning (it does not, incidentally, seal in the juices) and then lowering it for the remainder of the cooking. There is also the original method – spit roasting over an open fire – where the meat, being turned regularly, bastes itself with its own fat as it melts on the outside. Domestic ovens equipped with spits do the same job, but somehow the effect never seems quite so delicious.

If simply roasted meat is the ideal complement to fine red wine, the truth is that a great deal of roasts are not that simple. The meat may be served with lemon squeezed over it (the Greeks and Italians are partial to this) which might tip the scales towards white or rosé wines, or reds with some astringency such as Barbera and Chianti (*see also* Grilling). The juices may be deglazed with something quite powerfully flavoured, like Madeira or balsamic vinegar, which would suggest drinking a more powerful, deeply fruity red wine.

The addition of a herb, mustard or honey crust is also likely to have an impact. Tasted on their own, the majority of common herbs go better with white wines than with reds (rosemary and thyme are very useful exceptions), but the meat may shout out for red wine (beef, lamb, kangaroo, venison and most game). If so, it is worth thinking in terms of red with a herby, tobacco leaf or slightly spicy character – for example, wines from Provence and Languedoc-Roussillon, Sangiovese-based reds, Apulian reds (when not too hefty), Zinfandel, Portuguese reds and briefly oak-aged Tempranillo. Mustard, provided it is not fearsomely hot, vinegary or sweet, is not a problem with red or white. Used sparingly, honey may do no more than give a richer, more caramelized flavour to the dish, but, when used generously to give a distinctly sweet accent, it may well demand a white wine with some sweetness – a Vouvray or Montlouis *demi-sec* or a German *Spätlese*. Or try the ripe, sweet, berry fruit of red Zinfandel which can act as a decoy.

And that is only the start of it. The minefield begins in earnest with all the stuffings, sauces, jellies and relishes for which each country has its own traditions, particularly on the great feast days. Think of the traditional Thanksgiving turkey with chestnut stuffing, cranberry sauce, sweet potatoes, squash and succotash (creamed sweetcorn, beans and onions); or the British Christmas Day version with cranberry sauce, chestnut stuffing, sausage-meat stuffing, bread sauce, bacon rolls and chipolatas. The one thing that eases the way to choosing a companionable wine for meals like these is that the majority of the trimmings, and even the stuffings, are independent of the meat and so it is possible to look at them individually and decide what their combined impact might be. The trick is to be prepared to compromise on one side or the other. You can forego your favoured mature classic wine (the subtleties and nuances of which will be lost under a welter of vivid flavours) in favour of a bolder, brighter, quite probably New World wine; or you can let the wine take priority and sacrifice those accompaniments which are going to bring the most grief to a subtle, complex wine (could you eat lamb without mint sauce or settle for Dijon mustard instead of horseradish with beef?). Alternatively, you can go ahead with your vinous treasure and multitudinous food flavours on the grounds that you are bound to enjoy them, even if the combinations are theoretically less than ideal.

VEGETABLES AND FISH

Although fish, even when it is described as roast, never acquires the distinctive 'roasted' taste, roasting acts on vegetables very much as it does on meat, intensifying flavours by evaporating moisture. As the kind of vegetables that can be roasted tend to be at least slightly sweet (parsnip, onion, carrot, courgette, garlic, sweet potato, kumara, red pepper and, though not strictly speaking a vegetable, tomato), roasting them makes them sweeter again. White wines are usually more successful partners than red, especially quite intensely flavoured, aromatic wines with good acidity, such as New Zealand Sauvignon or Riesling, young Australian Verdelho, Alsace whites and Hungarian whites made from indigenous varieties such as Hárslevelü or mainstream varieties such as Pinot Gris and Gewürztraminer. But matching the wine exclusively to the vegetables is only relevant when eating them alone (as in the fashionable starter of roasted vegetables). When they are being eaten with meat or poultry, or, less commonly, with fish, there are other priorities for the wine, but you still need to be aware of a possible clash with a dry, tannic red wine.

COLD ROAST MEAT

A wine that seems perfect with roast meat or poultry one day often mysteriously fails to go with the remains of the same joint or bird the next day. When roast meat is left to go cold, the texture invariably seems to become denser and initially the flavour seems to intensify (before fading after a couple of days). The solidifying of the fat probably has a lot to do with the changes and may explain why wines traditionally served cool or chilled – that is wines with acidity which can cut through the fat – often work well. Tannin, on the other hand, is not at all comfortable with solid cold fat. Beaujolais-Villages and the *crus* are particularly successful with cold beef, pork and venison (although rare beef is also happy with Saint-Emilion, Pomerol and red burgundy). Lamb, surprisingly, goes well with white wines, including good quality burgundies from the Côte Chalonnaise and Mâconnais, and, less surprisingly, with mellow Saint-Emilion (providing it is not tannic). Well-structured, not too exuberant or oaky New World Chardonnay goes well with poultry, pheasant, partridge and pork; but game birds can also be partnered by vintage champagne, including rosé. German Riesling, especially *Spätlese*, is a good match for cold pork, duck and goose; with the powerful flavours of goose and Barbary duck, top quality California and Australian Cabernets also go well. And Pinot Noir, with its relatively low tannin, seldom clashes with any cold roasts.

Sauces

gnore sauces at your peril – it is impossible to overestimate their importance when deciding which wine will best accompany a dish. Very little food is served without any semblance of sauce, cooking juices, gravy, dressing or relish – and the only accompaniments that do not have any impact on the taste of the food and on the wine you are drinking are those that remain on the side of the plate uneaten.

There are various systems for categorizing sauces – basic sauces and compound sauces, cold versus hot sauces, or stock-based reductions, roux-based sauces, egg-based and eggless emulsions – and it is useful to have a basic knowledge of the methods. But only by looking at individual ingredients can you glean an overall impression of how the sauce will taste. After all, bearnaise and tartare sauce both have a distinctly piquant character, but the egg emulsion sauces on which they are based, hollandaise and mayonnaise respectively, are rich, a little lemony but by no means sharp. To find a matching wine for any sauce, you need to have an idea whether it is creamy, buttery, eggy, garlicky, herby, cheesy, concentrated and meaty, piquant with vinegar, sharply lemony, sweet, sweet-and-sour, hot and sour, hot and spicy, sweet and spicy, or salty with anchovy and olives. Of course, it could just be bland, like post-war Britain's ubiquitous white sauce, but you need to know that, too.

There is one other crucial question, which is worth addressing before you even reach the ingredients or methods stages. To what extent is the sauce/dressing/relish an integral part of the dish and to what extent is it an addition? Are the meat, fish or vegetables already in the sauce before it hits the plate, is the sauce added when the principal items are served, or is it an optional extra added, or not, at the table?

It is fortunate, although it is perhaps not by chance, that many of the trickiest sauces are of the self selection, optional extra kind – among them, cranberry sauce, redcurrant jelly, other sweet and often sharp fruit sauces, mint sauce (or jelly), *béarnaise*, chutneys and horseradish sauce. Top notch German Riesling *Kabinett*, with its sweetness and acidity, is better able to stand up to these kinds of flavours than most fuller-bodied wines, but it is not everyone who wants to drink Riesling Kabinett with red meat or turkey.

Other sauces are mostly a walkover in comparison with the above, although that doesn't mean that they are without their pitfalls. One of them is sauces based on heavily-reduced, intensely-flavoured meat stocks or glazes. This was more of a hazard in the eighties, at the tail end of the nouvelle cuisine era, but I am still always wary of any small puddle of dark, glossy chestnut brown sauce sitting on a large white plate. It is likely to be fiercesomely concentrated in flavour – too much so for most red wine, although powerful California and Australian reds, northern Rhônes, Ribera del Duero, Brunello di Montalcino and Barbaresco should cope. These wines generally handle red wine and Madeira sauces well, too, although you do not have to have such weighty wines unless, once again, the sauce is heavily reduced. When it is dry white wine that is heavily reduced, as in a *beurre blanc*, the resulting high acidity needs to be matched in a white wine, but whether that means Chablis, Aligoté, Sauvignon, Muscadet, Vinho Verde or some other white depends on the rest of the dish (particularly its weight) and on any other influential components of the sauce. A creamy white wine sauce, for example, will still need some acidity but will be able to take richer wines, including probably a variety of Chardonnays and the light sweetness of *demi-sec* Jurançon and Vouvray. A similar sauce with mushrooms will invite whites, but those with a savoury richness – burgundy rather than ebullient Australian Chardonnay.

Although the Sauternais introduce Sauternes into their cooking so that they can drink their wine with it, a sweet wine in a sauce for a savoury dish will not necessarily require a fully sweet wine to drink with it, but it will almost certainly require a white wine and one with some body and an element of sweetness – perhaps a Vouvray *demi-sec*, an Alsace *vendange tardive* or a Pfalz Scheurebe or Rieslaner *Spätlese Halbtrocken*.

Sauces in which vinegar is prominent (vinaigrette and devilled sauce), follow the same principles as those made with dry white wine – acidity to match acidity (*see also* Tricky Ingredients, page 19). But in other sauces vinegar may be merely a hint to relieve richness or blandness – eg in mayonnaise or a butter sauce.

Tomato sauces also require acidity: the insistent flavour and sharpness of Sauvignon go well with tomato, but if it is a sauce which also incorporates meat (such as a Bolognese *ragu*) a full, fruity, not too tannic red is likely to be more suitable – Chilean, Australian or Italian (Rosso Conero, Rosso di Montalcino, Montepulciano di Abruzzo and Torgiano).

Mexican-type raw *salsas* – red and green – usually based on chillis, tomatoes, onions, garlic, coriander and perhaps lime juice,

are hot and sharp to varying degrees. Again, Sauvignon is often the best bet, but if the dish invites red wine, simply avoid anything special, because of the palate-numbing effect of the chilli.

Egg sauces such as hollandaise and mayonnaise do not pose the same problems as eggs (*see* Tricky Ingredients, page 18), but they could not be described as flattering to wine. They are infinitely better with white wines than with reds (tannin is the sticking point), which is helpful in the case of tartare sauce with fish – Sauvignon is the best match – but less so when you want to eat steak with bearnaise sauce. Dolcetto and Beaujolais *crus* will get you by. Alternatively, be brave and try a more expensive, concentrated New Zealand Chardonnay (or a New World one of similar structure, intensity and quality): setting powerful fruit, buttery complexity, oak and firm acidity against steak is a surprisingly acceptable contrast. I don't say they positively enhance each other, but there is certainly no friction. Hollandaise, with its rich buttery character, and other butter sauces are ideal candidates for medium and full-bodied Chardonnays which echo the butter flavour, but, again, be wary of low acid levels.

COOKING WITH WINE
Whether half a glass is added to perk up a piece of fish or meat towards the end of cooking, or a whole bottle is used to enrich a slowly simmering casserole from the beginning, wine can transform the humblest to the most luxurious of dishes. You don't, in my view, need to use the grandest of wines, but it is a mistake to use wines that are clearly 'off' or tainted – whether vinegary, corked or musty. These flavours will be concentrated by cooking. Acidity will also be concentrated, so avoid tart white wines and add all whites with care: as a rough guide, they often need an equal amount of stock or water, whereas a red may sometimes constitute all the cooking liquid. Sugar, too, is concentrated in cooking, so add sweet wines with a gentle hand. The tannin in young red wines is not, perhaps surprisingly, a problem, but heavy oak flavour is, in whites as well as red. Don't waste beautifully aromatic, flowery, fruity wines in cooking: these volatile aromas will quickly be driven off – but do use full-bodied wines, as these will give more or less everything they have to the food.

Planning

CHOOSING THE RIGHT WINE FOR THE RIGHT
FOOD IS ONE THING. CHOOSING THE RIGHT
WINE FOR THE RIGHT PLACE AND OCCASION
CAN BE SOMETHING ELSE ENTIRELY. THERE IS
A WORLD OF DIFFERENCE BETWEEN
CHOOSING A WINE TO DRINK WITH SEVERAL
COURSES AND SELECTING A BALANCED AND
COMPLEMENTARY SERIES OF WINES TO
MATCH A SUCCESSION OF DIFFERENT DISHES;
AND WINES FOR A BREEZY BARBECUE ARE
LIKELY TO BE QUITE DIFFERENT FROM THOSE
FOR A FORMAL DINNER PARTY.

serving: THE ORDER
OF WINE

special occasions

special bottles

serving suggestions

Serving: THE ORDER OF WINE

Knowing the principles of how to approach the matching of wines to particular dishes, ingredients or styles of cooking is essential. Knowing the particular affinities between food and wine which have stood the test of time can come in very useful, but, just as you need to plan a menu so that you end up with a balanced meal – whether it is made up of a series of courses or a collection of dishes all served at the same time – so you need to plan the succession of wines when more than one is to be served. If that makes it sound like an onerous military-style operation, be reassured that it is not, and nor should it be in an angst-ridden exercise. Personally, I love the planning stage.

Fortunately there are some traditional serving guidelines: serve dry white wine before red, light wine before heavy, young wine before old, dry wine before sweet, and simpler wine before fine, complex wines. This means, for example, serving South African Colombard or Alsace Sylvaner before Petite Sirah or Nemea; or Pinot Grigio or Australian Riesling before Meursault or California Chardonnay; 1993 Rioja Crianza before 1989 Rioja Gran Reserva or 1988 Brunello; or New Zealand Sauvignon Blanc before *Beerenauslese*; and *vin de pays* before *cru classé* and Mâcon Blanc before Puligny-Montrachet.

It is all eminently logical: progressing from lighter and simpler to fuller, more complex and/or sweeter wine ensures that no wine is overshadowed by the quality, weight or sweetness of its predecessor. But these are no more rules than are any of the other food and wine guidelines: they are pointers which often provide a useful starting point, but which are easily turned on their head by the menu.

In some cases, the conventional order needs modifying irrespective of the food. The subtle rather fragile flavours of very old, grand wines may be overwhelmed after a series of high quality younger wines, particularly if the latter are still showing their tannin. A Mosel *Kabinett*, despite its sweetness, will nearly always need to precede a full-bodied Chardonnay. And a *fino* sherry served with a starter of olives and other tapas-type items need not be followed by a wine of equal or

higher alcohol: indeed, there are few wines of equal strength – exported *fino* is around 15% alcohol, but it has an appetizing, freshness and dryness that can make it an ideal start to a meal.

More often it is the food that dictates a change to the standard wine order – and it usually involves those strangely perfect marriages or instances where rich food (savoury or sweet) is cut by fairly light-bodied, but sweet or sweetish wine. The most obvious case is foie gras (or a liver pâté of similar unctuousness) served at the beginning of a meal with a very sweet and opulent wine, such as Sauternes, Monbazillac, Alsace-Pinot Gris Vendange Tardive or the slightly less opulent, but nevertheless sweet, Recioto di Soave. The combination of rich, sweet wine and rich, dense, silky liver is a heavy start to a meal, but for most foie gras eaters it is an irresistible one. Assuming that the meal is not to be a Sauternes-only affair (foie gras followed, for instance, by duck with orange and honey, Roquefort, then a French apricot tart), this course is best followed by a pause and a sip of water, and then, preferably, a wine that is fairly full-bodied and well flavoured. It certainly doesn't have to be sweet, but a light, dry wine would not be able to push its way

through the preceding richness and would certainly taste thin and tart if tasted directly after the last sip of sweet wine.

Rich, fatty meats such as goose and duck, as we have seen, can be cut with the intensity of a fine German Riesling of *Spätlese* or *Auslese* sweetness. This is not a problem for a preceding wine, provided you avoid anything fat, heavy or oaky. A German QbA or *Kabinett* – but not necessarily Riesling – would be a straightforward choice; other aromatic white wines, traditional, steely young Chablis, unoaked Chardonnays and breezy Sauvignons are other options. Even a light-bodied, untannic red (German, Loire, Alsace or northeast Italian) is a possibility. Nor does a *Spätlese* or *Auslese* pose problems for succeeding wines, because they are not extremely sweet and they are helpfully light in body. Any weightier, sweeter white wine can follow (German, Austrian, French, Spanish, Hungarian, Australasian, American *et al*); and dry red wines, because of their greater weight, are not ruled out. You do need to be aware, though, that sweetness in a *Spätlese* or *Auslese* will emphasize tannic dryness and any lingering hardness in a classic medium-bodied Médoc (claret). The perfumed fruit and low tannin of Pinot Noir is a better choice (after a palate-clearing pause, some water or bread), as are wines made with the richer, riper fruit of warmer climates and grapes such as Syrah (ie Shiraz), Portugal's Periquita and Zinfandel (Primitivo in Italy). Sweet red wines naturally follow well, but they are a rare commodity – Recioto Amabile, port, Banyuls, aged Rivesaltes and not much else.

Goat's cheese with the steely freshness of Sauvignon Blanc – from the Loire (Sancerre, Pouilly-Fumé, Menetou-Salon and neighbours), New Zealand and the best from Chile and South Africa – is another example of a perfect marriage which may break the traditional order. The difficulty with this delicious combination is that Sauvignon does not follow red wines comfortably (except Loire Cabernet Francs such as Chinon and Bourgueil). And nor is it at ease after many whites: full-bodied, oaky, buttery whites, like Chardonnay, emphasize its sharpness and rather one-dimensional character. There are two solutions: precede the cheese with asparagus, salads, shellfish and other fairly plain fish that will happily accommodate Sauvignon Blanc; or serve the goat's cheese as a starter, lightly grilled with a green salad with walnuts.

And, for a final break with established order, you might finish not with the heaviest, fullest wine, but the lightest: a light, frothy Asti with a fresh fruit salad, fruit or chocolate mousse, or as a refreshing contrast to the notoriously heavy, traditional British Christmas pudding.

Special Occasions

You can look at a dish and make a reasonable judgement as to what sort of wine will go with it; you know the red light ingredients that can easily sabotage an otherwise sound match; and you know how to plan a sequence of wines through a meal. So far, so good – but that isn't all. The occasion itself counts for a lot: the seasons, the surroundings, the company. It would be perfectly possible to serve broadly similar food, or at least some of the same dishes, at a party, a wedding, a picnic, a barbecue, a lunch, a casual supper, a formal dinner, at home or in a restaurant, but the perfect wines for the occasion might differ radically. Choosing wines appropriate to the occasion is likely to be just as important for its success as choosing wines that complement the food.

FORMAL DINING: WHICH WINE FOR WHICH COURSE?

In many ways these are the easiest meals to deal with, because you are likely to be choosing a different wine for each course, instead of trying to find one that will accommodate several disparate ones, and your budget is likely to be encouragingly more relaxed than usual. Quite often, too, the style of the food is more classic than dangerously inventive, so the tried and tested partnerships and conventional sequence are unlikely to let you down or upset anyone.

But that doesn't mean you need to stick rigidly with them. You could substitute high quality New World versions of European classics – a Clare Valley Riesling instead of an Alsace, a Marlborough Sauvignon instead of a Pouilly-Fumé, an Oregon Pinot Noir instead of a red burgundy, a mature Argentine Malbec instead of St-Emilion, a Shiraz instead of a Rhône. (This can also be a useful way of tackling restaurant wine lists.) Alternatively, you could break a progression of classic wines with something novel – an Arneis instead of a white burgundy, a red Douro instead of a red Bordeaux, a Canadian Ice Wine instead of a German *Trockenbeerenauslese* or *Eiswein*.

The biggest problem with choosing wines for this kind of occasion is perhaps temporary optional paralysis engendered by seemingly limitless choice – but I can think of worse problems.

WINES FOR INFORMAL MEALS: ONE WINE, PERHAPS TWO?

Ironically, the occasions for which choosing wine can seem trickiest are often the most casual, everyday affairs – meals where you plan to have only one wine, but with more than one course or, in the case of Far Eastern meals, several dishes (this can happen in a restaurant just as frequently as at home). Since dry wines simply do not go with sweet food, and sweet wines need to be at least as sweet as any food they are partnering, it is best to abandon the idea of drinking wine with the pudding at the outset (unless you know you can successfully create and appreciate an *Auslese*- or Sauternes-only meal).

With one wine, you should concentrate on matching it to the weight and flavours of the main course. You can always choose a starter to fit in (refer to the Grapes and Wines section for ideas) and/or choose a complementary cheese (see page 22). A Pinot Noir, one from Oregon, for example, could accompany salmon then game. Gamay, the red grape of Beaujolais, is another easy companion for both fish and meat. Red Loire wines made from Cabernet Franc (such as Saumur-Champigny, Chinon, Bourgueil etc) can be drunk with asparagus, fish, charcuterie and not too heavy red meat dishes, including spring lamb, rabbit and beef braised in beer. Medium- to full-bodied Chardonnays can accommodate a range of fish, meat and vegetables and, as we have seen (Wine Order, previous page), Sancerre and other Sauvignon Blancs are good with asparagus, many fish and goat's cheese.

Where one wine is feasible, two wines will broaden your horizons enormously – allowing you, for instance, to indulge a passion for huge, heavy reds by finding something crisp and aromatic, such as a dry Muscat, or simple and fruity, such as a wine based on the Colombard grape, to start with. If pudding is important, then it is worth having a sweet wine (see Sweetness, page 14; Tricky Ingredients, page 17; and Sémillon, Chenin and Riesling in the Grapes and Wines section, pages 58–61). Sweet wine might also have the advantage of coming in useful with the cheese (*page* 22).

WINING AND DINING IN THE GREAT OUTDOORS

To those of us from the chillier climes there is something magical about eating outdoors – despite the flies, the wasps, the sand, the wind and the wilting heat – and yet brilliant sunshine is not the place for savouring the finest, most venerable or subtle wines. Hot sun and the merest hint of a breeze will waft away wine aromas before you have had a chance to get your nose near the glass, thus rendering the wine a shadow of its former self. The best wines for drinking outdoors are those which are reasonably forceful in flavour and aroma (with fruity, floral, spicy or herbaceous characteristics), but not necessarily heavyweight. Indeed, high alcohol is positively undesirable on a very hot day, as is the high tannin of some red wines. Low tannin reds that can be served cool often come into their own (look to the wine regions of the Loire, Alsace, Germany, northeast Italy and consider any inexpensive, young, modern style of red). The acidity of white wines, and of rosés, is also a boon (provided the wine remains well chilled: *see* page 47) and a vibrant, dry rosé somehow always goes down well on a picnic – even pink champagne if the occasion demands it.

Naturally, the food, not just the ambient temperature and the surroundings, has a bearing on the choice of wine. A wine for drinking in the open may simply be a younger, slightly more assertive New World version of the Old World Cabernet Sauvignon or Pinot Noir that you would drink with precisely the same food indoors. But, equally, the food may consist of cold dishes – vegetables, salads, fish and meat – designed expressly for an outdoor meal. Chardonnay, Sauvignon Blanc, Riesling, Gewürztraminer, Viognier, Favorita, Pinot Grigio and new wave Portuguese dry whites (made from grapes such as Fernão Pires) are a few of the many white possibilities. Dry rosés, again, are another option. With reds, the answer tends to be fruity, fairly low-tannin style wines such as Beaujolais and other Gamays, New World wines made from the Pinot Noir grape, Dolcetto, young Chianti, Loire Valley Cabernet Franc, Merlot (not the most expensive bottles) and inexpensive Tempranillo and Australian Shiraz (or Syrah). Cold roast meat (as opposed to *charcuterie*) has an idiosyncratic character with its own potential problems, so, if this is a principal dish, refer to Roasting in the Effects of Cooking section (page 34).

Barbecued food, equally distinctive in a different way, is dealt with under Grilling (page 32). All that I shall say here is that the typically robust tastes – smoky, carmelized, spicy, herby – require wines which have a similar degree of flavour and often quite a lot of body, too. And barbecues, especially those involving rare steaks, are one of the occasions when high tannin finds a natural home.

Special Bottles

Most people choose wine to go with food rather than vice versa, but, at some point, it is likely that anyone interested in wine will have a very special bottle, or several, for which they want to devise a flattering meal. If there is one axiom in matching food and wine, it might be this: the finer the wine, the simpler the food. (Inconveniently for those who would like this to have been a book of rules, the reverse is emphatically not true.) The keep-it-simple advice is particularly worth heeding if the wine you want to show off is really quite old; as with people and antiques, old wine is fragile (it may also need decanting – see page 46). And this is all to be borne in mind if you are splashing out on a special bottle in a restaurant.

For recommendations for specific types of wine, there are two main sections of the book to consult, together with a wine to food quick reference section at the back (Matching Wine and Matching Food, pages 142–155), but your first port of call should probably be the brief list of marriages made in heaven (see page 10), always remembering that these are not the only foods that suit these wines. The more detailed advice is in the Grapes & Wines and World Classic Combinations sections (pages 48–73 and 74–141 respectively). The former, for example, will point you towards oysters and shellfish for fine, relatively young Chablis, but sole and turbot for more mature bottles; to lobster and richly sauced fine fish for prized white Côte de Beaune; and to game – especially game birds, not too well hung – for red burgundy (bearing in mind that they will flatter mature, fine wine better if they are simply roasted). Among the World Classic Combinations, you will find the dishes that accompany these great bottles on their home territory – for a mature Barolo, a rich beef stew, Brasato al Barolo; for a top Médoc, a simply roasted leg of saltmarsh lamb; for a Chianti Classico Riserva, a char-grilled steak. But be aware that there is such a thing as local taste: what the locals eat and drink together may not necessarily seem best in London, New York, Frankfurt or Sydney (pace red Vinho Verde with sardines).

THEMES, PARTIES, WEDDINGS

If you are planning wine and food from scratch and can't even seem to get started, choosing food and wines from a particular region is an attractively simple idea (it can also be a useful approach in a restaurant). The food and wine of Provence or Tuscany may not be the most original of European themes, but they are certainly both evocative, and you can always go for something a little more unusual – the far south of Italy or Basque Spain. Or champagne.

I have never really got to grips with the Champenois idea of drinking mature vintage champagne with game and red meat – with the honourable and surprising exception of cold roast game birds with vintage champagne – but a celebratory meal can happily start with a *blanc de blancs* champagne with smoked salmon, or a non-vintage *brut* with oysters or Beluga caviar, and then progress to a rosé or mature vintage champagne with fish such as lobster in a cream or butter sauce or poached, sauced wild salmon.

The bonus of regional themes is that they are as suitable for formal, sit-down meals as they are for buffets and parties. The tapas party may be an overworked theme in Britain, but, when it is done properly with authentic tapas and the freshest of *fino* or *manzanilla*, it is a marvellous experience (*see* page 100).

If you are happy about the food, but want a theme for the wine, alighting on a particular vintage (the widely successful 1990, for example) and then choosing contrasting wines from that year always makes for an interesting occasion, as does picking a series of wines made from the same grape variety in different parts of the world – Chardonnay, for example (although the latter can be more limiting on the selection of food).

So far as choosing wines for parties is concerned, the point to consider is not so much what type of food it is, but how much of it there is. If there is very little, avoid high acid whites (*see* Acidity, page 12), tannic reds (*see* Tannin, page 15) and heavy, alcoholic wines. Without being a killjoy, can I also point out that sparkling wine, though undoubtedly festive, goes to

the head quicker and that champagne, though a generous gesture, may not be quite as kind to stomachs as sparkling wines made by the classic sparkling method elsewhere: the latter tend to be lower in acid than champagne. Sweet wines pall after a while, but good *demi-secs*, together with off-dry and medium-dry German wines (providing they are not too acid) are often popular, particularly when food is sparse; German *Kabinett* also benefits from being low in alcohol (often 8–9%). Fresh, fruity dry rosés (French, Spanish, Italian, Australian) are the obvious choice when you only want to offer one wine – and they look pretty, too.

The comment about champagne's acidity is worth bearing in mind for weddings. For many people *brut* champagne becomes too much of a good thing after several hours' sipping. A switch to still wines is one possibility, but then you have the toasts to cater for, and one prospect you want to avoid is the drinking of *brut* or *demi-sec* with wedding cake, whether traditional British or a tower of *crème patisserie*-filled profiteroles. (Asti is better with both of these, but I admit that I did not serve Asti at my own wedding.)

Serving suggestions

If you accept that it is possible to spoil a good meal by serving it badly – hot food allowed to become cold and congealed, chilled food served on a hot plate so that it sweats or melts, a mass of different foods jumbled up on too small a plate – you must accept that the same can happen to wine. Serving both red and white wine too warm can ruin them, serving them in unflattering glasses can prevent you from enjoying the full aromas and flavours, and a mouthful of gritty or sludgy sediment is never a pleasurable experience. That said, there is nothing more likely to reduce people's enjoyment of wine than to be subjected to someone pontificating pretentiously or laying down the law about what is right and wrong. And, as with food, putting theory into practice may well involve some adapting to the occasion and the surroundings. Bringing your handblown crystal glasses on a country picnic is probably going to stress your guests more than impress them – however well-intentioned the gesture.

GLASS

The idea of a wine glass is that it should allow you to see the wine, smell it and sip it to the wine's best advantage. You can buy different shapes of glass designed specifically to enhance different types of wine and grape variety, but a vast battalion is not essential. There is such a thing as a good all-rounder for still wines and, providing you are moving from white to red and dry to sweet, you can use the same glass for more than one wine. The most suitable glass for the role is made from fine, plain and colourless, as opposed to thick, coloured or cut, glass. It should have a stem to hold (so that you don't have to put a hot hand around the wine unless you are trying to warm it up) and the bowl should be rounded, to allow you to swirl the wine around to release the volatile aromas, and tapering at the top to prevent all the delicious aromas from immediately escaping. For the same reasons, glasses, whether for red, white or rosé, should be generous in size (thus ruling out the meagre Paris goblet); you should never need to fill a glass more than half-full, if that, to get a good measure. For champagne, the classic, slender flute is ideal for preserving both bubbles and delicate

bouquet, while the unwieldy coupe or saucer dispels both. A traditional copita is perfect for sherry and, though rather small, can be used for port.

Having suitable glasses is not the end of the story. Cleanliness is next to Godliness where wine glasses are concerned. Traces of detergent and rinsing agent, the taint of dirty tea towels and of musty cupboards and cardboard boxes will all pass into the wine. It may be a relief to hear that dishwashers are much approved of by leading glass manufacturers – provided that glasses are washed alone or with nothing too grimy, that minimal detergent, if any, is used, that no rinsing agents are used and that the door of the machine is opened at the end of the cycle so that the glasses don't sit in heavy humidity. If they need drying use a linen cloth (wrapped round a wooden spoon handle for reaching into flutes). Store glasses in cupboards so that they don't gather dust, but upright so that they don't trap stale air, and wash them if you haven't used them for a while.

DECANTING AND BREATHING

The purpose of decanting is to separate a wine from its sediment. Better quality red wines designed to be aged (and occasionally expensive whites) often throw a deposit after some years in bottle. This is a good sign, especially in grape varieties such as Cabernet Sauvignon and Syrah which can throw a heavy sediment, because it shows that the wine has not been subject to over-zealous filtering (and thereby flavour removal). While top Médoc invariably throws a sediment, the deposit from a top red burgundy (made from the Pinot Noir grape) is generally lighter. Cheap and mass market wines of any variety rarely throw a sediment, but there is a general trend away from filtering, so more wines in the mid-priced bracket, from countries like Chile and Australia, are beginning to be bottled unfiltered (look for 'unfiltered' and 'non filtré' on labels). If you think a wine may have a deposit, stand it up for at least 24 hours before decanting it. (With a light or candle behind and below the neck and shoulders of the bottle, pour it slowly and smoothly into a clean decanter or bottle, stopping when you see the sediment approaching the neck).

Letting wine 'breathe' – come into contact with air by decanting or merely pulling the cork – is an altogether more debatable exercise and one on which countless experiments (more or less scientific) have failed to be conclusive. What is clear is that removing the cork commits you to drinking the wine, but permits little air contact. It is thus perfectly safe (and often convenient) to open most wines an hour or two before serving, but I would leave the uncorking of very old wines to the last half hour and the decanting of them as late as possible. Decanting wine aerates it to a greater degree, but whether in a young wine this softens tannins and acidity (a speeded-up mini maturation process), or allows aromas to be lost, or makes no significant difference is a moot point. Trust your own experience.

TEMPERATURE

If all other wine advice passes you by, at least take heed of temperatures. Serving wine too warm or too cold is the surest way of spoiling an otherwise sound bottle. Everyone knows that whites and rosés need to be chilled, but not enough people (and certainly not enough restaurants) seem to know that red does not need to be served at the temperature of the average centrally-heated room. The upper limit for reds is 18˚C – and that for the fullest-bodied wines. The lighter or less tannic the red (and many inexpensive modern reds are notably untannic), the cooler it should be – distinctly cool for ordinary Beaujolais (about 12°C for those who are counting, but personally I don't use a thermometer). The same temperature is appropriate for the fullest dry whites, but cooler is better for medium- and light-bodied whites and rosés, aromatic, high acid, sweet and sparkling wines, reaching a low 5°C for the very cheapest.

Although it is a shame to numb a fine wine senseless, it is better to err on the side of cooling it too much, because wine warms up quickly in the glass and you can always cup your hands round it to help it on its way. The quickest way of chilling wine (without one of the specially invented frozen sleeves) is to put it in iced water. A fridge may take up to two hours to chill a white well. Red wine can be warmed in a bucket of tepid water, or, with great care, in a microwave.

GRAPES &

UNTIL QUITE RECENTLY, MATCHING WINE

AND FOOD MEANT PARTNERING THE FAMOUS

CLASSIC WINES OF EUROPE WITH

APPROPRIATE CLASSIC AND REGIONAL

CUISINES. THE TRADITIONAL WINES ARE STILL

IMPORTANT, BUT THEY HAVE BEEN JOINED BY

A BOLD, NEW GENERATION OF WINES — WINES

WHICH, THOUGH OFTEN MODELLED ON

ESTABLISHED CLASSICS, PUT MORE EMPHASIS

ON GRAPE VARIETY AND ASSOCIATED FRUIT

FLAVOURS AND WHICH NEED TO BE MATCHED

TO FOOD ACCORDINGLY.

*the changing face
of wine*

chardonnay

sauvignon blanc

riesling

other white grapes

cabernet sauvignon

pinot noir

syrah

other red grapes

THE *Changing Face* OF *Wine*

If I had been writing this book 25 years ago, the chapter devoted to the main types of wine would have borne very little resemblance – certainly superficially – to that which follows. Above all, no one would have entertained the idea of calling it grapes and wines. Everyone knew that wine was made from grapes (well, one hoped that it was) and those grapes were the varieties which had always been grown in the locality. Admittedly, sometimes there was a little judicious mixing in of more robust grapes from elsewhere (grapes from the south of France or North Africa to beef up red burgundy and Bordeaux, for example), but that, too, was traditional and merely served to reinforce the established character of any region's wines. The vast majority of European wines, at all quality levels, were named after the area in which they were produced – Beaujolais, Chablis, Champagne, Chianti, Rioja to name but a few – and their producer, or after the producer only in the case of the most basic level, *vin de table*. German wine labels often acknowledged the superiority of the Riesling grape by naming it on the label; Alsace wines, most unusually for France, were (and are) largely named after their grape varieties; and there were a few wines like Italy's Brunello di Montalcino, in which the grape variety (in this case Brunello) had come to form part of the wine's name; but that,

really, was the extent of grape variety exposure in Europe until the eighties arrived.

Make no mistake: the established European wine styles continue to be named primarily after their place of origin, but in Europe, as throughout the world, grape varieties have assumed a much higher profile – some of them, like Chardonnay, almost to the point of becoming brands. This is a direct result of wine developments in the New World.

When California began making wines in the image of the great French classics, producers took the relevant grape varieties - Cabernet Sauvignon, Chardonnay and so on – as their starting point. Australia and others soon followed and, although at first many of these wines borrowed the names of their French and to a lesser extent German models, increasingly the wines were named after the principal grape variety used. The term varietal wine was born. Within a couple of decades, the wine world, or at least the world of drinkable, exportable table wine (as opposed to fortified wines, such as Australian 'sherry', or unfit-to-travel local wine), had expanded enormously and a handful of grape varieties had established themselves right across the globe.

But there is much more to the changes of the last couple of decades than mere expansion and the rise of high-fashion grape varieties. A technological revolution has taken place which has changed many aspects of wine production and, more fundamentally, its taste. For that, the New World can take the credit – or the blame, if that is your perspective.

At the crudest level, there is much less wine that is badly made and unstable, which means that buying cheap wine is not the risk it once was: its worst offence today is more often vapidity than total unpalatability. More significantly, wines at almost every level taste fruitier and riper than they used to – from inexpensive red Bordeaux to Barolo to Muscadet. In the past, French, Italian, Spanish and Portuguese producers did not seek fruit flavour per se. Indeed the Portuguese and Spanish, in particular, seemed deliberately to wait for any hint of fruit to disappear before considering either bottling or drinking their wines. Even in these countries local taste has begun to alter.

In general, white wines tend to taste fresher and crisper (even when they are mature) than in the past and red wines – young and old – taste softer, rounder, less hard and tannic. Red wines, especially, are being made for earlier consumption (ie with less tannin) not just because people the world over lack suitable, cool, humid storage conditions but because, for many people, the pace and style of life are such that they prefer to buy wines to drink on a daily or weekly basis, in much the same way that they buy food. There are still wines for laying down, but even the grandest red wines of Bordeaux tend to be approachable earlier. The jury is necessarily still out on whether they will last as long.

The other far-reaching change in the taste of modern wines derives from the ascendancy of oak. Originally oak was used as a convenient winemaking and storage vessel, but it must soon have been realised that, used in the right proportions (with the right amount of flavoursome, new oak and in the ideal size of barrel), oak barrels could add complexity in terms of both subtle flavours and richer texture. Inert stainless steel tanks, which began to replace old concrete and delapidated wooden vats from the sixties onwards, were largely responsible for freshening up the flavour of wine – they allowed winemakers to control the temperature of the fermenting liquid so that it did not become too hot and the resulting wine acquire coarse, baked and jammy flavours – but stainless steel adds nothing of its own to wine. Its role, essentially, is as hygienist.

When winemakers in the New World began using new oak barrels, because they had seen them in use in Burgundy and in Bordeaux, they used them lavishly – and they discovered that the flavours of oak in its own right – variously vanilla, toast, spice, smoke and coconut – could be rather seductive. The era of wine with a prominent taste of oak was with us. It still is (not least because winemakers have now found cheaper ways of instilling it), but there is also a trend away from overtly oaky wines – which is no bad thing for the diner as very oaky wine is not easy to match to food. It is apt to be overbearing. Smoked foods and barbecued foods are its principal allies.

For more on oak and other winemaking tricks and trends, *see* page 55 for the techniques used to fashion Chardonnay, the world's most fashionable and malleable grape variety.

Chardonnay

Chardonnay is the darling of almost every region where wine is made and can produce everything from long-lived wine of great complexity to simple everyday white, according to how and where it is grown and vinified. It can be light and steely or fat and powerful, minerally and austere or pineappley and exotically tropical. The foods its various styles go with are correspondingly varied – from fish and poultry to cheeses, spicy foods and nut sauces – but at the same time it is harder to go wrong with Chardonnay than with many other varieties. Mismatches seldom turn out to be truly nasty clashes simply because the flavours of Chardonnay are not that confrontational. Oily fish like mackerel and sardines are to be avoided and mushrooms treated with caution, but other than those its chief disadvantages for food are its tendency, in the New World, to low acid and very powerful fruit and (added) oak flavours – but the fruitiness can at least be harnessed to Far Eastern spices and bold Mediterranean flavours.

The reason for the extraordinary versatility of the Chardonnay grape is that it has little personality of its own. Instead, like a ventriloquist's dummy, it expresses the will of the winemaker and the fashion of the day. Only Chablis, in the north of Burgundy, produces a style of Chardonnay that so far can be made nowhere else, and that may be attributable to the distinctive Kimmeridgian soil found there. In other places the climate seems to be a more important determining factor, with cool climates producing light, leaner, appley wines, unsuited to ageing in new oak barrels. The warmer the climate, the more the wine fills out, until in Australia's very warm Hunter Valley it becomes fat and packed with butterscotch flavours.

The weighty wines are ideally suited to new oak ageing, which imparts vanilla and toast flavours well matched to Chardonnay's buttery character. In fact if you want to taste Chardonnay without oak your choice is limited. Unoaked Chablis is one option; the Chardonnays of Italy's Alto Adige are another.

Chardonnay and Food

The following are the different styles of Chardonnay seen around the world – whether as the principal grape variety in a blend or the sole variety in a wine. Some are so similar that, blindfolded, you would be hard-pressed to distinguish between them, but others are poles apart and need to be partnered by quite different flavours and types of food.

ALTO ADIGE & FRIULI

Northern Italian Chardonnays are among the lightest and crispest and are generally too delicate to bear much new oak. With their appley, floral-tinged flavours they make ideal aperitifs, but they are also good with the sort of food that would be swamped by too much flavour in the glass: gently flavoured pasta dishes and risotto; simple white fish with a squeeze of lemon; light salad starters.

HUNGARY & MOLDOVA

There is a handful of new estate-produced Hungarian Chardonnays that have an acidity and intensity of flavour reminiscent of New Zealand, but the bulk of production comes via Australia-trained

Flying Winemakers who turn out fresh, crisply fruity, inexpensive light-to-medium bodied whites with good acidity. They can be drunk on their own, or with lightish everyday dishes of fish, poultry or pasta (spaghetti with pesto, for example). The wines of Moldova (again made by Flying Winemakers) are similar, but a little fuller and riper; partnering food can be correspondingly weightier – pork for example.

CHABLIS

Traditional Chablis is the epitome of concentrated steely, minerally, unoaked Chardonnay, of a style found nowhere else. Some is now being aged in new oak, which makes for rounder, less uncompromising wine, but the unoaked style is the classic type for fish and shellfish. Choose a young Chablis for lighter flavours like oysters, and for salmon, turbot and sole a more mature *premier* or *grand cru*. The latter will also have enough weight for quite richly sauced fish and fatty cheeses such as Chaource.

MACONNAIS & CHALONNAIS

A lot of wine simply labelled 'White Burgundy' comes from Mâcon and the Côte Chalonnaise – the southern part of Burgundy – where the wines never reach the heights of the Côte de Beaune but

nevertheless have something of their savoury character. Single village wines will have more character, with good examples from the Maconnais, such as Pouilly-Fuissé and St-Véran, being quite creamy and appley, and those from the Côte Chalonnaise, especially Montagny, being fuller-bodied, nuttier and closer in character to burgundy proper. These are good wines with pasta, poultry and fish in creamy sauces (but save the finest fish for grander burgundies). They also go with pork and, when young, with Parma, Serrano and Bayonne type hams (provided they are not too salty) on occasions when you don't want a red wine.

COTE DE BEAUNE

This, the southern half of the Côte d'Or, is the heart of white burgundy territory (Chablis excepted). It is the home of such legendary names as Meursault, Puligny-Montrachet and Corton-Charlemagne: all of them expensive, full-bodied, complex and nutty; usually buttery, sometimes honeyed, sometimes smoky. Each village produces its own subtle variation on the theme. These are special occasion wines, deserving the best fish (lobster, wild salmon, turbot, scallops) and they are full enough to match rich sauces.

VINS DE PAYS

Vins de Pays du Jardin de la France Chardonnays are similar in weight and style to northern Italy's, but are less intense. They can be drunk on their own or with light dishes such as plain shellfish, dim sum or avocado. Vins de Pays de l'Ardèche have, at best, some of the nutty, savoury, buttery character of Côte Chalonnaise burgundies and are good with buttery sauces. The Vin de Pays d'Oc style offers a taste of ripe fruit and oak in the New World mould and goes with herby, garlicky fish and chicken dishes.

CHILE

Chilean Chardonnays are improving in leaps and bounds. With vibrant, ripe fruit and some oak, most are slightly lighter than Australia's and California's and are for drinking relatively young. They often handle spices well, but nothing too hot.

SOUTH AFRICA

This is another style in rapid evolution, especially since better clones of Chardonnay only became available in South Africa in the late eighties. There is still a tendency to over use oak, but the general direction is to a point midway between European subtlety and the more ebullient fruit of California or Australia. So far, they are wines for drinking fairly young, rather than laying down, and with a good cross section of dishes from mild kormas to roast guinea fowl or even lobster.

NEW ZEALAND

New Zealand's cool climate, particularly around Gisborne, is proving excellent for Chardonnay, giving wines with clear, vivid fruit and great intensity, but

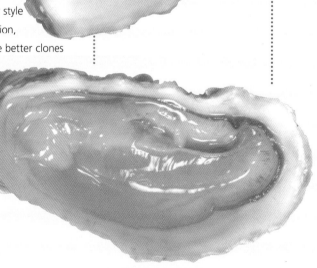

without the tropical fruit flavours associated with Australia. Good acidity and toasty oak add up to wines of balance and elegance comparable to good white burgundy. They are especially good with flavoursome fish, rich sauces and Mediterranean vegetables, but can also cope with grilled steak (beef).

CALIFORNIA

The original big, tropical, oaky style of California has become more subtle over the last decade – and hence a better match for food – but lovers of the powerful, upfront style need not despair: even the coolest parts of the state (Carneros, Russian River, parts of Santa Barbara, Monterey etc) produce riper, more exotic flavours than does Burgundy. Toasty oak, too, is still much in evidence, and acidity is relatively low. All but a few wines are made to be drunk within a few years of the vintage, and will not develop complexity with age. The least expensive lack individual

character, and have a touch of sweetness which can cloy. It is hard to generalize, but, with the exception of the wines which are most burgundian in style (of which there are not many) California Chardonnays are good with quite strongly flavoured food, such as smoked haddock with creamy saffron sauce, walnut sauce for pasta and the typical Mediterranean-influenced dishes of California itself, in which mustard, grilled bell peppers, cracked peppercorns, marinades and so on are lavished on main ingredients such as pork, duck and tuna.

AUSTRALIA

This, perhaps even more than California, is the traditional home of ripe, exotically fruity Chardonnay, but in fact that style is only part of the picture. Beyond the fat, oaky wines from the hottest areas like the Barossa and Hunter

valleys, which need to be drunk young with full flavoured food (eg, duck with orange), or no food at all, there are cooler regions, like the Yarra Valley, Margaret River, Adelaide Hills, Padthaway and Tasmania. These give wines of greater elegance and subtlety, which are easier to match to food, including spicy food. There is also a trend to fresh, unoaked Chardonnays – partly with Australia's marvellous native shellfish in mind.

CHAMPAGNE & SPARKLING WINE

Chardonnay is the least widely planted of the three champagne grapes. Pinot Noir comes first in terms of acreage, with Pinot Meunier just behind; but Chardonnay is nonetheless extremely important. It stands alone in *blanc de blancs* and, despite its reputation for elegance, is the longest-lived variety,

making it significant in vintage champagne. It is also much planted by makers of sparkling wine elsewhere. So far as food is concerned, champagne is the definitive apertif, but it is classically paired with oysters and smoked salmon and, inevitably, with other luxury foods – caviar and even black truffles and foie gras. It is also determinedly matched by the Champenois with every course on the menu. This is risky, but it is certainly worth trying dry champagne with shellfish of all kinds; fish when smoked or in a cream sauce; asparagus; Chinese, Thai food and sushi (*see* pages 136, 138 and 140); and with cold game birds. Typically, New World dry sparkling wine is fuller, fruitier and softer – less successful with oysters or game birds, but good with a gamut of lightly spiced dishes. Note that sweet champagne is seldom sweet enough for puddings.

TAILOR-MADE CHARDONNAY

Given basically hygienic conditions, crushed or pressed grapes will start to ferment and the result will be wine (without the hygiene, the outcome will be vinegar). With some grapes, that is all you need to do. They are the hands-off varieties, like Riesling and Sauvignon Blanc, which have forceful personalities which don't take kindly to being meddled with by winemakers. But other varieties are less inherently assertive and will do anything for anybody. Chardonnay, for all its flavour in the glass, is the ultimate submissive variety. Below are some of the techniques used and some of the other factors which influence the taste of the finished wine.

OAK: TRICKS & TREATS

Oak is more often used with red wine than white, but of all the white grape varieties it is Chardonnay which most often sees the inside of an oak barrel or a bag of oak chips. Chips? Oak chips, small pieces of oak suspended in huge tanks of wine, are the cheapest way of imparting oak flavour. Since their arrival on the scene a few years ago, especially in Australian wines, they have allowed cheap wines to be given a veneer of oak, where previously oak influence was the preserve of expensive wines. What chipped wine usually lacks is subtlety of flavour and complexity, although fermenting the wine with the chips, instead of adding them for a period afterwards, can give a more integrated result. The choice is not just between barrels and chips. There is the choice between expensive French oak, as used in the top French and California wines, and the cheaper American oak, with its stronger, spicy vanilla flavour, used especially in Spain and often in Australian reds. There is the choice of toast: high, medium or light, according to how strong you want the toasted character to be. With white wines there is the option of simply ageing the wine in barrels or also of fermenting it in them: the latter is much more expensive, but gives a deeper, richer-textured result. The amount of time – a couple of months or a couple of years – is critical, too, as is the age of the barrels: after three or four years use, there is little oak flavour left in them.

VINES: AGE, YOUTH AND YIELD

Old vines ('*Vieilles vignes*') are much valued because, as vines get older, they produce gradually fewer grapes but grapes of more intense and complex flavours. The very youngest vines (usually three years old) often produce very bright fruity flavours, but then lose that exuberance and go through a few rather dull years. Limiting productivity (which old vines do naturally) helps concentrate flavours.

YEAST & BUTTER

Wild yeasts (those present on the bloom of grape-skins and those which may accumulate in wineries) can produce excitingly profound wines, but they can also be unstable and therefore a risk. Moreover, many New World winemakers – above all those dubbed 'Flying Winemakers' who flit about the world making wine in several places each year – like the flavours given by specific cultivated yeasts. In the case of Chardonnay, these are yeasts which give extra peach, pineapple and tropical fruit flavours to wines that are intended to be drunk young.

Another characteristic that may be heightened is butter. Chardonnay inherently has a slightly buttery aspect, but this is often enhanced to a much richer, fatter butter flavour by a secondary fermentation, called the malolactic. Bringing out this flavour is not the only reason for the malolactic, however. Winemakers encourage it in most red wines (where the buttery effect is less evident) and in various whites, especially cool climate ones, because it lessens the acidity.

SOLO OR BLEND?

Until recently Chardonnay was not very often blended with other grapes – not like Sémillon with Sauvignon Blanc, or Cabernet Sauvignon with Merlot and friends. Champagne was the prime exception to this (together with wines made in the image of champagne elsewhere). But pressure on limited supplies and concommitant rising prices at the beginning of this decade concentrated minds wonderfully, especially in Australia where Chardonnay now frequently finds itself as part of a double-act with varieties such as Semillon, Colombard, Chenin Blanc and even the assertive Sauvignon Blanc. On the whole, it can't be said that these blends are better than the sum of the parts, or at least better than Chardonnay alone, but they are means to an end – the stretching of finite quantities of Chardonnay. Adding a small portion of Chardonnay grapes to hotchpotch southern French blends is rather different and has proved worthwhile. You often only need a small amount of Chardonnay to give a little extra body and fruit flavour – enough to make a more interesting wine.

Sauvignon Blanc

Sauvignon Blanc is one of the most instantly recognizable of grape varieties, for its grassy, flowering currant, gooseberry flavours and its bone-dry, pungent style. It has a far narrower range of flavours than does Chardonnay and adapts less well to climates that are cooler or warmer than the ideal. For example, in most of the wine regions of both California and Australia the heat typically produces rather clumsy wines with flavours that veer towards the tinned asparagus/green bean end of the spectrum and lack Sauvignon's quintessential vivid briskness.

At the other extreme, too little warmth produces thin, tart aggressively herbaceous flavours with no redeeming features. But Sauvignon is, without question, a cool climate grape, reaching its peak of classic aromatic intensity and crispness in France's Loire Valley and in New Zealand. It is to match this style, too, that the majority of Sauvignon Blancs, wherever they are made, are spared any contact with the vanilla roundness and creaminess of new oak. It is possible to make successful Sauvignon Blanc with new oak, but it requires a very delicate hand – and usually a fair amount of Sémillon blended in, as is the case in most of the white wines of Graves. Sauvignon, in marked contrast to Chardonnay, is not an adaptable grape in the winery either.

Even at their best, Sauvignon Blancs seldom repay cellaring. Indeed, most are best drunk within a year of purchase: left longer, the freshness usually fades without any accompanying increase in complexity. But the direct, rather one dimensional flavours and high acid are also the attraction, particularly with foods where acidity needs matching – tomato dishes, lemon garnished fish dishes, Thai food, goat's cheese – and, equally, with foods where the wine's acidity can act as a foil to richness. Go carefully, though, with green vegetables: broccoli, spinach and even courgettes are apt to accentuate the wine's herbaceous character.

Sauvignon Blanc and Food

The following are the different styles of Sauvignon Blanc seen around the world – whether as the principal grape variety in a blend or the sole variety in a wine. Some are so similar that, blindfolded, you would be hard-pressed to distinguish between them, but others are poles apart and need to be partnered by quite different flavours and types of food.

SANCERRE, POUILLY-FUME & OTHER LOIRE

This is France's prime Sauvignon Blanc region. There is a minerally, flinty character to Sancerre, Pouilly-Fumé and their neighbours, with a touch of smokiness in Pouilly-Fumé. Lesser Loire Sauvignons, from Touraine and Haut-Poitou, are simpler but have attractive grassiness. Goat's cheese is the classic match here, along with various fish dishes such as deep fried white bait, traditional British fish and chips, and any fish served with sorrel sauce. Also red peppers and/or tomato dishes, asparagus (but see Tricky Ingredients) and Thai food.

BORDEAUX, BERGERAC & COTES DU DURAS

Sauvignon Blanc in Bordeaux is traditionally rounded out with Sémillon for both dry and sweet wines (for the latter, see page 60), but even straight Sauvignon from here is less aromatic, less intense than in the Loire. It is a useful medium-bodied everyday wine with white fish and mussels and even with difficult oily fish like mackerel. The Bergerac and Cotes de Duras Sauvignons have a slightly fruitier character which makes them more wide ranging with food, but still at the lighter end of the food scale (try them with salads). Mature top notch Graves is a wine fit for grand, richly sauced fish dishes, including lobster.

AUSTRIA

Most of the best Austrian Sauvignon comes from cool Styria on the borders of Slovenia, where it is often called Muskat-

Sylvaner. It has a tautness and acidity that puts it on a par in terms of quality and food partners with fine Loire Sauvignon, but it tends to taste just a shade more fruity.

NEW ZEALAND

New Zealand Sauvignons are intense and vibrant with concentrated, crunchy gooseberry fruit. This vivid flavour, without any minerally flintiness, marks the difference from those of the Loire; the similarity is that they see no oak (or very little). Marlborough has the most pungently herbaceous; those of Hawkes Bay are slightly fatter. Although different from Loire Sauvignons, they go well with the same kind of food: shellfish, vegetables such as parsnip and kumara (both slightly sweet and often cooked with spices) and fennel.

USA

The oaked style of Fumé Blanc popular in California bears little resemblance to unoaked styles made elsewhere. Varietal character tends to disappear under oak and, sometimes, residual sugar, but this suits corn on the cob and other sweet vegetables such as leeks. For leaner, more classic Sauvignon, for fish and shellfish, Washington State is a better source. Texas, too, has some good results from high-altitude vineyards.

AUSTRALIA

A handful of winemakers, especially in cooler Adelaide Hills, has started making wines with true varietal character and finesse – ideal with shellfish.

CHILE & SOUTH AFRICA

The last couple of years have seen huge improvements in Chilean Sauvignon, with the cool Casablanca region in the lead and increasingly chasing New Zealand in style, quality and food matching ability. South Africa has yet to develop a very clear style, but its best Sauvignons, mostly from Constantia, have strong echoes of New Zealand fruit and intensity.

OTHERS

Hungary produces inexpensive, fairly light very zesty Sauvignons which go well with goat's cheese, asparagus, sushi and sashimi. The same sort of dishes also go well with the best of Italy's Sauvignons – those from Collio – while those from Alto Adige are lighter and best drunk on their own or with a light fish or vegetable *fritto misto*. Spain's medium-bodied, herby Rueda whites, which often owe something to Sauvignon, go well with white fish and seafood salads.

Sémillon

Sémillon reaches greatness in only two regions: Bordeaux and Australia's Hunter Valley. In Bordeaux it is almost always blended with Sauvignon, the latter adding bite to Sémillon's rich lanoliney character in either dry or sweet wines (*see page 60 for sweet*). Fermentation in new oak used to be reserved for great white Graves, but increasingly mid-priced wines are benefitting from a touch to give them more complexity and make them a match for slightly weightier food. Unoaked dry white Bordeaux should be drunk young with simple, light starters and plain, mild fish.

Much Australian Semillon is blended with Chardonnay for the lower end of the market, but varietal Hunter Valley wines, if unoaked, are lemony fresh in youth and age to toasty, honeyed complexity. Oaked versions, including Barossa's, are richer in youth, but age less well. Drink young, unoaked wines with spiced or barbecued fish, aged/oaked versions with eg honey-roast chicken.

Riesling

Currently a victim of fashion in the world at large, Riesling is none the less one of the world's few truly great grapes. Delicious in youth and yet capable of developing over a long period into a much more complex wine, it also has qualities, above all in Germany, which make it a match for a wide range of foods, including several of those which defeat other wines. Cold roast meat, particularly pork and duck, mustard, caper berries, green olives, Chinese food, beetroot, lobster, smoked mackerel and sundried tomatoes are just some of the range.

Most fine German wine is made from Riesling (the principal synonyms of which are Johannisberg, White, Rhine or Renano Riesling, but not Laski Rizling, Olasz Rizling, Riesling Italico or Welschriesling which are inferior varieties). Ironically, cheap German wine – Liebfraumilch, Bereich Nierstein et al – which has tarnished the reputation of fine German wine (and that of Rieslings from other countries) seldom contains a drop of Riesling itself.

Real Riesling is a complex patchwork of flavours – peaches, apricots, honey and apples, plus a whiff of smoke and minerals from parts of the Rhine and Mosel, a hint of spice from the Pfalz and a mouthwatering streak of lime from Australia. It makes bone dry wines, medium dry, medium sweet and beautifully sweet ones, and it can be drunk young or cellared until it attains a unique character that is both honeyed and petrolly.

In Germany it thrives in a cool climate, though in Australia, as though to refute generalization, it produces high quality in much warmer temperatures. These are fuller, toastier wines and are seldom as long-lived as those of Germany, where the classic medium-dry to quite sweet styles of *Kabinett*, *Spätlese* and *Auslese* have a tautness, a knife-edge balance between sweetness and acidity that is found in no other wine. The sweeter wines, the *Beerenauslesen*, *Trockenbeerenauslesen* and *Eiswein*, are immensely long-lived because of that same high acidity; and *Botrytis cinerea* or noble rot (*see* page 60 for more details), to which the grape is susceptible, gives *Auslesen*, *Beerenauslesen* and *Trockenbeerenauslesen* extra depth and complexity.

Riesling and Food

The following are the different styles of Riesling seen around the world – whether as the principal grape variety in a blend or the sole variety in a wine. Some are so similar that, blindfolded, you would be hard-pressed to distinguish between them, but others are poles apart and need to be partnered by quite different flavours and types of food.

GERMANY

The lightest Rieslings of all come from the Mosel, where the alcohol level may be as low as 6.5%. Nevertheless these wines, tasting in youth of green apples, smoke and flowers, have tremendous steely structure and can age for years. The Rhine makes weightier wines (relatively speaking), which in the river's southern reaches in the Pfalz and Baden can be quite spicy; they, too, age well. The sweet wines are sensational, honeyed and complex but never fat or cloying; sometimes, indeed, they are just too light to match food and are best drunk after a meal, when their elegance and finesse can show to best advantage. Good estate-bottled German wines make

lovely aperitifs, but they are also indispensable at the table. Try a fine Mosel *Kabinett* with Gravad Lax or sushi and a *Kabinett* or *Spätlese Halbtrocken* (literally half-dry) with Chinese food, or with scallops, trout or smoked fish. Try sweeter (*Spätlese* or *Auslese*) Pfalz or Rheingau wines with pork, duck and goose with fruit sauces. Or try *Auslese* with light, not too sweet fruit pies and tarts or raspberries. The sweeter styles can naturally take sweeter puddings – right up to pecan pie and treacle tart, although there is always a special affinity between sweet Riesling and apple puddings.

AUSTRALIA
The best Australian Rieslings come from the Clare and Eden valleys in South Australia, where the grapes ripen to full flavours of lime and passion fruit. They acquire a toasty, honeyed depth with age, but it is not the petrolly flavour of mature German Riesling. Match them with smoked fish pâtés, cold roast pork, mustard sauces, sun-dried tomatoes, red peppers and, providing they are not too hot, Asian spices. The botrytis-affected late harvest wines are heavier than their German (and New Zealand) counterparts and go with a wide range of puddings (cream, fruit, meringue and cake-based).

NEW ZEALAND
The cool climate produces Rieslings that are more Germanic in style than any others from the New World. Though they lack the steely, minerally pungency of the best Rhines and Mosels, they go with similar foods and slightly more spicy food. There are also some concentrated and very sweet botrytis-affected dessert wines that can be drunk much younger than their German equivalents, but which, like them, are relatively low in alcohol and never as fat as say, Sauternes. They are especially good with fruit-based puddings of all sorts.

USA
Riesling is seldom taken seriously in California, and most are off-dry, bland, inexpensive and not very interesting with food. There are, however, some excellent, concentrated sweet versions, which may be late-harvested, made in the manner of *Eiswein* and called Ice Wine or made from botrytised grapes. They should generally be drunk young with puddings, particularly those involving fruit, cinnamon or almonds. Washington State, Oregon, Ontario and New York State – particularly the last – produce more elegant, Germanic dry to off-dry styles which can partner Asian-influenced dishes. Ontario also produces very fine Ice Wine, for puddings.

ALSACE
Alsace produces both dry and sweet Rieslings in the only part of France where the grape is grown. They have a hint of spice typical of Alsace wines, are higher in alcohol and more substantial than their German equivalents and go with correspondingly fuller food – smoked fish of all kinds, fish in cream sauces and all sorts of pâtés. The sweeter *vendange tardive* wines can be matched to roast goose and apple sauce, while the very sweet *sélection des grains nobles* are better with puddings.

AUSTRIA
There are superb Austrian Rieslings. Drier and more alcoholic than German versions and less weighty but more fruity than Alsace ones, they age well, though they seldom get the chance. They partner a wide variety of fish, smoked or unsmoked, very well.

Other White Grapes

BOTRYTISED SEMILLON/SAUTERNES

Sauternes is one of the oddest of styles: wine made from rotten Sémillon grapes. But this is not just any old rot. *Botrytis cinerea* is a fungus which, under certain autumn conditions, attacks ripe grapes and feeds off the juice. The grapes first turn brown and mouldy and then shrivel, and this dramatically affects the flavour of the wine. It has an extraordinary concentration of sweetness and acidity, with a wonderfully opulent, fat texture and honeyed apricot and peach flavours – a taste that is hard to describe and yet instantly recognizable.

The main grapes of Sauternes are, as for dry white Bordeaux, Sémillon and Sauvignon Blanc, in that order and almost invariably blended: the acidity of Sauvignon balances the rich, luscious, lanoline-textured Sémillon. Great Sauternes is often delicious young, but it will also live and develop for years, even decades.

Because of its intensity and richness, it accompanies most puddings well and, when young and vigorous, can even deal with some chocolate puddings (a more mature, complex Sauternes is wasted). But it is also famous for its perfection with foie gras and Roquefort cheese, and in the Sauternes region it is often served with main courses – duck with peaches, honey-basted roast chicken, sweetbreads in a creamy Sauternes sauce, for example.

New World late harvest Semillon-Sauvignon blends (from Australia, New Zealand, the USA and Chile) have the classic flavours and concentration, but tend to be a little less subtle. This, though, makes them excellent with all sorts of very sweet, heavy or strongly-flavoured puddings – dense chocolate mousses and rich cheesecakes among them.

Lighter wines (for lighter puddings, or even as aperitifs) come from Sauternes' neighbouring regions, particularly Monbazillac, Cérons and Loupiac. In good years, there are some lovely wines (and bargains), but choose with care: standards overall are erratic and in mediocre years (of which there are many) most growers cannot afford to declassify their wine (ie, sell it off cheaply under another label or in bulk) as many do in Sauternes.

Some surprising looking grapes produce the most limpid of white wines. left to right: shrivelled, fungus-attacked Sémillon grapes of Sauternes and similar wines; Chenin Blanc, provider of wines from bone-dry to ultra-sweet; Colombard; and the distinctly pink Gewürztraminer.

CHENIN BLANC

Good Chenin Blanc is one of the world's most underrated wines, but poor Chenin, from too cool a year, has some of the sourest flavours of any wine. To transform the grape's flavours into apples and apricots, still with high acidity, but with a streak of nutty honey, it demands sunshine and a careful winemaker.

The wines can be dry, medium-dry, medium-sweet or lusciously sweet and botrytised. In the Loire, the European base of the grape, the very leanest, most acidic wines are at least ideal for turning into dry or medium-dry sparkling wines – Saumur, Vouvray and Montlouis; the dry still wines from Savennières have a steely intensity that allows them to live for years and develop considerable complexity; and the botrytis-affected sweet wines, from Coteaux du Layon, Quarts de Chaume, Bonnezeaux and Vouvray, have tremendous honeyed sweet fruit and an edge of almond marzipan. These are extremely long-lived, but are never as fat as Sauternes and should be spared the sweetest puddings. Fruit tarts and flans, especially apple, and cakes, pastries, biscuits or creams based on almond or hazelnut are ideal. The medium-dry wines make lovely aperitifs, but also go well with sweetbreads and fish in cream sauces.

Nowhere else in the world does Chenin reach these heights. The handful of New Zealand dry versions promise the most. South African Chenin (often called Steen) is crisp, fruity, not very concentrated, everyday wine.

COLOMBARD

There are times when you want a wine of no particular flavour – one that just gives a general impression of refreshing dry fruitiness to go with a light salad, a lunchtime snack, or a spur of the moment Thai takeaway. Vin de Pays des Côtes de Gascogne, made from the Colombard grape in Armagnac and foie gras country in southwest France, may well fit the bill. Aged in oak, it acquires a slightly fuller flavour and texture, more like a dry white Bordeaux, but it is never going to be a star. Californian, South African and Australian versions, predictably, have a more tropical fruit flavour and greater strength, but here, too, Colombard is a wine to enjoy but not to expect too much from.

GEWURZTRAMINER

There is no more distinctive, aromatic grape than Gewürztraminer. It is usually described as spicy – indeed, 'gewürz' means spice and there is often a touch of ginger and cinnamon to the taste – but the first impression is of a heavy, seemingly sweet, lychees, roses and Nivea Cream perfume. Even when dry it is opulent and one of

the perennial threats to quality is acid levels plummeting in hot years. With insufficient acidity, Gewürztraminer is flabby and oily.

It is at its most exotic (and renowned) in Alsace where it has three main styles: dry (sometimes actually off-dry), medium-sweet (*vendange tardive*) and lusciously sweet (*sélection des grains nobles*). Germany's Pfalz region runs a close second, followed by Baden and the lighter, slimmed-down, but still characteristic Gewürztraminers from Austria and Italy's Südtirol.

Outside Europe, Gewürztraminer is usually regarded as a source of easy, off-dry wines of no particular distinction, but growers who take it seriously in cooler climes (New Zealand, Washington State and Oregon) are often well rewarded. Chile and South Africa also show promise.

A wine of so strident character might sound a nightmare with food, and certainly can be, but there are similar food flavours that it complements. Spicy dishes are an obvious case, although beware the old idea that any Indian or Far Eastern dish will do: many are too subtle. The ones to try are highly spiced – but not ferociously hot – Indian curries and sweet-and-sour Chinese duck and pork. The sweetness of onions, leeks and red peppers is good with Gewürztraminer, as are some pungent cheeses, notably Alsace's very own pongy Munster. Then there is the marriage of foie gras and sweet Gewurz: *vendange tardive* is sweet enough, but *sélection des grains nobles* makes an extremely rich, irresistible combination. (Some people choose dry Alsace Gewurztraminer with smoked salmon: I prefer Pinot Gris.)

MARSANNE

With the more delicate Roussanne, Marsanne is one of the grapes of white Hermitage and Crozes-Hermitage. It is also found in the south of France and, as a varietal wine, in Australia. It is quite weighty, with a distinct savoury, herbiness and, in Australia, a tangy, spicy lime-marmalade flavour. Good acidity means it can take oak maturation and age well. Its weight, savoury character, freshness and subtle fruit make it well suited to food – a pity we don't see more of it. Australian examples can be notably good with spicy, even Indian, food.

MUSCADET

The grape of Muscadet is more properly known as Melon de Bourgogne, but now that it is grown virtually nowhere else it is often known by the wine's name. It is one of the most neutral of white grapes and its virtue on France's Atlantic coast is that it has enough acidity (and a whiff of the sea, if you're feeling imaginative) to wash down the local oysters, shrimps, clams *et al*. If you want to drink it with anything else, light *antipasti* or salads, for example, choose a nutty, yeasty *sur lie* wine.

MUSCAT

Very few wines actually taste of grapes: those made from the Muscat family are the exception, whether dry, sweet, still, sparkling or fortified. Other key notes are orange, rose, musky scents and, in the case of fortified wines, raisins.

Different strains of Muscat are grown in different places, but most wine growing countries have one or more. The main difference between them is one of finesse: Spanish Moscatels, for example, are usually very sweet and high in alcohol whether fortified or not, while Beaumes-de-Venise is very sweet, quite alcoholic, but usually more refined; Alsace Muscats are elegant, dry, rose-scented wines (usually drunk as aperitifs). Apart from in Alsace, dry Muscats can occasionally be found, but sweet versions are much more common.

The fortified Muscats of the south of France, from Frontignan, Saint-Jean de Minervois, Lunel and Rivesaltes, as well as Beaumes-de-Venise, are often drunk locally as aperitifs,

but they go well with puddings, especially very sweet ones. The much darker and sweeter liqueur Muscats of Australia (generally of very high quality) are too powerful for many puddings, but can be drunk with the richest, densest chocolate concoctions, ginger-flavoured puddings, Christmas pudding, mince pies and – otherwise impossible to match – ice cream.

At the other end of the scale are the freshly grapey, low alcohol, fizzy, sweet Italian Moscatos (Asti is the best known). Though often despised, these are versatile wines: drinkable with light fruit salads and jellies, feathery chocolate mousses and even as a palate refresher with plum pudding. Clairette de Die, from France, is similar, but less sweet and more alcoholic.

PINOT BLANC

It is easy to see why there has been confusion between Pinot Blanc and Chardonnay. Light, unoaked Chardonnay has the same sort of leafy, buttery fruit and appley acidity found in dry Pinot Blanc. The vines look similar, too, but they are not related, and Pinot Blanc, though pretty widespread in Europe, has never reached the heights of popularity – or quality – of its near-double.

It may not be as exciting a grape, but it has its uses when partnering food, because it seldom fights (like Muscadet, only more interesting). At its most flavoursome – which means Alsace, where it takes on a little of the region's aromatic characteristics, and Austria, where it is more nutty (and called Weissburgunder) – it can be good with dishes with just a touch of spice; not a complex blend of spices of the East, but an aromatic hint in a lightly creamy sauce with fish, for example. Fish pâtés, mousses and terrines are also a good bet, as are most plain fish dishes, many *salad composés* (but not with chicken livers), *crudités* and *prosciutto*.

Another source of characterful dry Pinot Blanc is southern Germany where, in the Pfalz and Baden, it is often aged in new oak and produces a wine for richer fish dishes. In Austria and in Burgenland it also yields wines up to *Trockenbeerenauslese* level – intensely sweet, long-lived and complex, and deserving of rich puddings. Northeast Italian Pinot Bianco is dry, light and leafy, eg from Alto Adige, but some Collio wines are very exciting.

PINOT GRIS

Pinot Gris makes everthing from bone dry to richly sweet wine. It is planted throughout central and eastern Europe, as far south as northern Italy (where, as Pinot Grigio, it is at its lightest and most neutral), but outside Europe only Oregon has shown much interest in it, with medium-weight, dry, lightly honeyed wines.

The finest Pinot Gris come from Alsace. They are somewhere between Pinot Blanc and Gewürztraminer in style, richer than the one, but less exotic than the other. Even when dry, they are full and honeyed with some spice; as they get sweeter they take on fatter, more honeyed, nougat flavours. In their sweetest incarnations they can partner foie gras, rich smooth liver pâtés and puddings. Drier ones are good with quiche – onion, bacon or smoked salmon – and with smoked salmon itself. It is also a good white wine with mushrooms.

Germany, Austria and Switzerland all make attractive wines in various styles – from dry to super-sweet, unoaked and oaked – and under various pseudonyms (Ruländer in Austria and Germany, Grauburgunder in Germany and Malvoisie in Switzerland). In Central Europe, Hungary is making some particularly successful, honeyed but dry wines.

UGNI BLANC/ TREBBIANO

Whatever name it goes under, this is not a grape to set the adrenalin going, but it is so widely grown it cannot be ignored. It is one of the grapes in Vin de Pays des Côtes de Gascogne and it crops up in Languedoc (it is also distilled into armagnac and cognac). In Italy it makes a host of light,

Three of the most characterful of white grape varieties – Pinot Grigio (second from left), *Viognier* (fourth from left) *and Muscat* (lower wine previous page)*; together with two of the most neutral – Ugni Blanc* (third from left) *and Muscadet* (top, previous page)*; and one which falls somewhere between the two – Pinot Blanc* (far left).

neutral whites – Soave, Frascati, Orvieto are only the best known. As it never manages to muster much character alone, it is often blended: good, nutty Orvieto, for example, depends on Grechetto and Malvasia; Frascati with any flavour contains Malvasia; and the delicious sweet Recioto di Soave (made from grapes dried to concentrate the sugar) generally features Garganega rather than Trebbiano. The dry wines need simple pasta and white fish (if any food); the Recioto is a wine for not too sweet puddings and French and Italian blue cheeses (even Gorgonzola).

VIOGNIER

Until recently the headily-perfumed wine of Condrieu, made from temperamental, low-yielding Viognier vines in the Northern Rhône, had little competition: California's handful of Viogniers were impressive but no less expensive. Cheaper versions are now emerging from the south of France, but, while they have the apricot-cum-peach character, the complete lime blossom, may blossom, apricots, peaches and musk experience still only comes from Condrieu, where the wine is also notably full-bodied, even fat – but still dry. Not everyone agrees, but I think it should be drunk young to enjoy its extraordinary scent.

It is quite a hard wine to match with food, but is good with the rich, sweet flavour of crab and lobster and with Cantal cheese (admittedly one of the easy cheeses). Surprisingly, it can also complement, rather than compete with, the flavour of black truffles and has an affinity with rosemary, so much so that it will partner roast pork if well flavoured with rosemary.

Cabernet Sauvignon

Cabernet Sauvignon is grown just about everywhere in the winemaking world and, with admirable consistency, yields the familiar aroma and flavour of blackcurrants, perhaps with a vanilla whiff of new oak. There might be a touch of cedar or lead pencils if it is Bordeaux, mint if it is New World, especially Australian, jam if it is a young Eastern European or tobacco and spice if it is more mature, but first and foremost it will taste of itself (far more so than the malleable Chardonnay).

Yet its popularity as a varietal is ironic, because the wine that sparked off all these imitations – claret, or red Bordeaux – is a blend of grapes in which Cabernet Sauvignon may not even be the senior partner. The truth is that the noble Cabernet is almost always better and more interesting if it is mixed with other grapes – the whole much more than the sum of its parts. California producers increasingly mix in a little Merlot and Cabernet Franc for complexity. In Australia Cabernet Sauvignon with Shiraz is highly successful. Chile adds Merlot; Tuscany sometimes blends it with Sangiovese grapes and in Spain it may be added to Tempranillo.

On its own, in a cool climate, it can be lean and angular, with the green pepper flavour too evident and the blackcurrants and chocolate not evident enough. In Bordeaux the softer, plummier Merlot rounds it out, aided by the raspberryish Cabernet Franc – and the result can be anything from a simple, everyday red, drinkable soon after the vintage, to a complex, concentrated wine of great depth and the tannic structure to last 20 years. New World versions are generally fuller bodied with riper fruit, more chocolatey richness and more obvious new oak.

So far as food, is concerned, Cabernet Sauvignon, blended or solo, is above all a wine for red meat, and to a much lesser extent game, with a particular affinity for lamb. Ideally, the higher quality the wine, the more simply the (necessarily high quality) meat should be prepared, but it is worth remembering that the fuller and riper the style (New World versions), the more it can handle richer flavourings and sauces.

Cabernet Sauvignon and Food

The following are the different styles of Cabernet Sauvignon seen around the world – whether as the principal grape variety in a blend or the sole variety in a wine. Some are so similar that, blindfolded, you would be hard-pressed to distinguish between them, but others are poles apart and need to be partnered by quite different flavours and types of food.

BORDEAUX, BERGERAC, COTES DE BUZET & DE DURAS

Bordeaux is the home of the classic lead pencil/cedar/cigar box flavours of claret and a quality spectrum that ranges from generic Bordeaux, with its often slightly stalky, blackcurrant fruit, and rises to some of the world's greatest, most subtle and long-lived wines, the *crus classés*. In the Médoc and Graves, Cabernet Sauvignon is the principal grape variety, but in St-Emilion and Pomerol (and the less elevated appellations such as Bourg, Blaye and Castillon) Merlot and Cabernet Franc are more important, and the wines are consequently softer and plummier. The outlying regions of Bordeaux use the same grapes and produce similar styles, with Bergerac and Côtes de Duras tending to be grassy and blackcurrant, and Côtes de Buzet firmer. Lamb is the classic match for Médoc, but beef is particularly good when the Merlot element is high. Fine Pomerol has the richness to match duck and goose and a mellow (ie not tannic), middle ranking claret can partner roast chicken.

PAYS D'OC & PROVENCE

France's fullest, ripest Cabernets come from Provence, where they are herby and well-structured and usually blended with other grapes, and from Vins de Pays d'Oc, where their full, supple, blackcurrant fruit, and sometimes oak, has shades of Australia. Drink with garlicky, herb-strewn red meat dishes and game.

USA

California's Cabernets are powerfully fruity, oaky and often tannic – upfront, but at their best on a par with the finest clarets (but drinkable sooner and less long-lived). The lesser wines have one-dimensional, though vibrant, blackcurrant flavour and sometimes a touch of eucalyptus. They can overpower food, so choose full flavoured dishes – meaty casseroles, marinaded grills and so on. The Cabernets and Merlots of Washington State are more akin to Bordeaux in weight, but more intensely blackcurranty and minty – good with turkey and traditional sweet accompaniments.

AUSTRALIA

The keynote of Australian Cabernet is ripeness and succulence, with the Coonawarra region being particularly noted for depth of flavour (often mint-tinged). Tannins are invariably ripe; oak is seductive and spicy; and the best wines age well, but can almost always be drunk young. These are adaptable wines, but typically need more rather than less flavour in food – liver, kidneys, kangaroo, as well as beef and lamb.

NEW ZEALAND

With a cool climate grassy-herbaceous Cabernet character, the most successful New Zealand Cabernets are

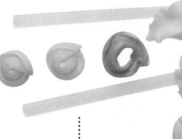

usually those plumped up with some Merlot. In good vintages they have a Bordeaux-like elegance but with slightly crisper fruit. Lamb and kid are natural partners.

CHILE & ARGENTINA

Chilean Cabernet is improving all the time, with the best wines now showing deeper more complex flavours beneath the vibrant cassis fruit. The cheapest wines have simple, supple, fresh charm. Argentine Cabernet is fuller, with a more solid-spicy chocolate character, well suited to full flavoured food, especially beef.

SOUTH AFRICA

South Africa has yet to develop a national style of Cabernet and there is a still a tendency to tarry, aggressively tannic flavours which need rather robust food – rustic stews and barbecued meats. But there are also growing numbers of claret-like blends with Cabernet and Merlot which can be drunk with food as if they were claret. Equally, the growing numbers of modern, fruity New World styles can partner meat with more herbs, spices and garlic.

EASTERN EUROPE

Bulgarian Cabernet Sauvignon, with its mellow, cedary, tobaccoey style, is a useful stand-in for lesser clarets; Moldovan Cabernets have more vivid fruit, the hallmark of Australian winemaking; and Romanian versions can be excellent value, with soft, fleshy fruit. Drink them with anything from sausages to lasagne, lamb casserole to turkey and the trimmings.

ITALY

Tuscany produces superb Cabernet and Cabernet-Sangiovese blends of intensity, spicy richness and the ability to develop extra complexity in bottle. These are wines for the best chargrilled meat, roasts and game such as wild boar. The typically light, grassy Cabernets (often Cabernet Franc) from the North east are better with pasta.

Pinot Noir

Pinot Noir is the most seductive of grapes. Its wine combines a clarity of fruit perfume and flavour – raspberries, strawberries, cherries, cranberries, roses – with an extraordinarily silkiness of texture and occasional hints of sandalwood, incense and exotic spices. It is less tannic than Cabernet Sauvignon and less long-lived, but the best wines from Burgundy's famed Côte d'Or, especially those of the more northerly Côte de Nuits stretch, do improve with age, developing extraordinary complexity in an endlessly fascinating range of rich, savoury, gamey, farmyard flavours. At least, they should.

They don't always, because Pinot Noir is the trickiest to grow and vinify of all the fine wine grapes. It likes a fairly cool climate, which is why it is at home in Burgundy, but the trouble with the Côte d'Or is that many years just aren't quite warm enough. The result is pallid, thin tasting wine.

The New World generally has the opposite problem. With too much warmth, Pinot Noir speedily develops jammy, baked flavours that banish elegance and silkiness. The best New World Pinot Noirs have glorious fruit (almost invariably slightly fuller and riper than in burgundy), but they never quite have the magically complex *goût de terroir* of great burgundy. Nor, indeed, do their producers always want them to. Instead, they often have a little more vanilla or spicy oak, which sits well with Pinot Noir's fruit and floral aromas, provided it is not overdone.

Although less forgiving of climate, soil and winemakers than Cabernet Sauvignon, Pinot Noir has a wider food span. It leaves lamb to Cabernet Sauvignon-based wines, but can partner most other meats and game, including those cooked in classic red wine sauces, and it is the most reliable red wine with fish, whether the fish is cooked in red wine or not. Try Pinot Noir, particularly New World, served cool, with salmon, red mullet or tuna.

The following are the different styles of Pinot Noir seen around the world – whether as the principal grape variety in a blend or the sole variety in a wine. Some are so similar that, blindfolded, you would be hard-pressed to distinguish between them, but others are poles apart and need to be partnered by quite different flavours and types of food.

COTE D'OR

Pinot Noirs from the Côte de Nuits – Gevrey-Chambertin, Chambolle-Musigny, Vosne-Romanée, Nuits-St-Georges et al – are more substantial and tannic than those such as Pommard, Volnay and Santenay from the Côte de Beaune to the south. Both go with game – furred, feathered, plainly roasted or casseroled – but avoid anything too well hung. Côte de Beaune is better with milder game: pheasant, wild boar and rabbit, for example, while Côte de Nuits can take bigger flavours – pigeon, mallard, venison, jugged hare. Equally, a light Beaune wine can be served with delicacies like sweetbreads and veal kidneys, while heavier Nuits wines are better with beef casseroles. More affordably, a skilful Côte d'Or grower will

be able to produce an appealing, regionally expressive Bourgogne Rouge for drinking early.

COTE CHALONNAISE & MACON

Wines from the Côte Chalonnaise echo the style of the Côte de Nuits to the north, but are less deep, complex and long-lived and there is a touch of earthiness rather than silkiness. They can be drunk with game (nothing too grand), but also with casseroles of chicken in red wine and with pork. Mâcon reds are largely made from Gamay (*see* page 71) and are altogether less interesting, suitable for pork or charcuterie, but nothing too challenging.

ALSACE & SANCERRE

With the occasional Alsace exception, the northern French regions produce wines that are light, strawberryish and far removed from the vegetal gaminess of the Côte d'Or. Alsace and Sancerre need warm summers to acquire depth of colour and flavour, but served cool they make lovely summer wines, especially with fish such as red mullet and salmon, and Sancerre is a hit with brandade.

CALIFORNIA & OREGON

California has made great strides with Pinot Noir, locating appropriately cool spots in Carneros, Santa Barbara and Russian River Valley to produce delicious and, at the top end, increasingly complex Pinot Noirs. Their lush raspberry and cherry fruit, underpinned by French oak, makes them a good match for a lot of dishes, including quail, duck, turkey, ham and 'meaty' fish. At their best, Pinot Noirs from Oregon (once hyped as the Côte d'Or of the New World) have California's clarity of fruit, but harnessed to a seam of the quintessential burgundian savouriness, which can make them better partners for game – but California is the more consistent producer.

AUSTRALIA, NZ, SOUTH AFRICA & CHILE

Many winemakers in Australia long to crack the Pinot Noir code, but their success so far is erratic. The Yarra Valley, Mornington Peninsula and Geelong, all in Victoria, are so far producing the most elegant, supple wines, though they can lack complexity. In terms of food, they have the same sort of versatility as California's Pinot Noirs.

In New Zealand's cool climate, and in the country's fast progressing, youthful wine industry, a handful of fine Pinot Noirs has already been made. With their penetrating dark fruit, the best can be drunk with game (particularly venison), and with quail and duck, while the slightly lighter ones can partner fish like John Dory.

There are only a couple of star Pinot Noirs in South Africa to date, but these are so good, with more than a hint of burgundian complexity to match to game birds, that this must be a country to watch. And in Chile Pinot Noir is just beginning to emerge in an attractive, soft, medium-bodied, fruity style that goes well with salmon, red mullet and hams and pork.

GERMANY, AUSTRIA & SWITZERLAND

In Germany Pinot Noir is called Spätburgunder and usually makes light, sweetish reds which can be drunk with charcuterie, fish and even some Chinese food (*see* China, page 136), but in Baden in the south there are some wines of exceptional standard made with oak-ageing in the classic French style. In Austria, too (where Pinot Noir is called Blauburgunder), very successful, increasingly burgundian examples are being produced and these, like the best wines of Baden, are worth partnering with game or duck. Switzerland's Pinot Noirs (often blended with Gamay) are mostly lighter and simpler and suited to lighter foods such as *charcuterie* or guinea fowl.

Syrah

Syrah can produce the most exotic and full-bodied of red wines, full of spice and leather, tar, game, blackberries and raspberries. It can also, in cooler climates, give quite simple, fruity wines tasting largely of pepper, raspberry and sometimes herbs. It is also used for red sparkling wine in Australia and in the hottest places for impressive, heavyweight fortified wines in the mould of port. With such versatility it is surprising that Syrah is not more widely planted. In France its home is the Rhône Valley, where steep, inhospitable slopes produce tannic wines of immense concentration and complexity that need years to mature – though, usefully, not as many years as red Bordeaux of equivalent quality. In the Southern Rhône it is blended with other grapes to make a warmer, softer, broader style. Under its alias Shiraz in Australia (its other main home) it gives everything from simple ultra-soft, berry flavoured wines, to firm, peppery wines and headily rich, ripe, minty, long-lived wines. Even the biggest, though, are approachable younger than those of the Northern Rhône.

Although not yet very widespread, in recent years Rhône varieties as a group (white as well as red grapes) have been catching on and in California some excellent wines are being made by a group of winemakers unofficially dubbed the Rhône Rangers. South Africa also has a little, and also calls it Shiraz, but it tends to suffer from the country's tell-tale burnt tar flavours. Early examples from Chile and New Zealand suggest that these are countries to keep tabs on – not least because Syrah is a useful wine at the table. The full bodied styles (which make up the bulk) come to the rescue with all sorts of strongly flavoured meat and game dishes which might overpower many Pinot Noirs or seem too sweet or heavy for many Cabernet Sauvignons. They also go with fatty meats like goose and duck, pork and various types of sausage, and also with hard cheeses.

Syrah and Food

The following are the different styles of Syrah seen around the world – whether as the principal grape variety in a blend or the sole variety in a wine. Some are so similar that, blindfolded, you would be hard-pressed to distinguish between them, but others are poles apart and need to be partnered by quite different flavours and types of food.

HERMITAGE & COTE ROTIE

Syrah has more concentration and tannin, more complexity and tarry, spicy flavour, in the Northern Rhône than anywhere else. The finest wines come from Hermitage and Côte Rôtie where, in the latter, a little white Viognier is sometimes added to give a fascinating and elusive note of musk to the Syrah's berry fruit. Relatively lighter, more approachable wines come from St-Joseph and Crozes-Hermitage – the former nicely supple and the latter a lesser, but very reliable version of Hermitage. Cornas, typically, is big and tarry. These wines deserve to be served with rich beef casseroles, game (which may be well hung) and are also a match for good rare steak.

CHATEAUNEUF -DU-PAPE

Châteauneuf-du-Pape is the flagship of the southern Rhône where Syrah is blended with up to a dozen other grapes, notably Grenache, to make rich, spicy, plummy wines that can mostly be drunk quite young; Gigondas, Vacqueyras and Lirac, all nearby communes, produce similar styles at lower prices. These reds all support substantial food – casseroles, cassoulets and baked dishes incorporating lamb, beef, pork, goose, duck, sausages, beans and lentils.

COTES DU RHONE

The blend of grapes here is similar to that in Châteauneuf-du-Pape, with the best examples having a good proportion of Syrah for finesse and flavour. The vast majority are soft enough to drink young and fresh, although Côtes du Rhône-Villages will be slightly fuller and weightier. These are everyday reds for matching to everyday meat and main course vegetarian dishes, from sausages and moussaka upwards.

PROVENCE AND LANGUEDOC

Syrah is seldom the main grape in the AC wines of the south, but it is judiciously blended to add flavour and finesse to what can otherwise be coarse wines. Corbières, Minervois and Fitou are herby and earthy, with raspberry fruit. They range from slightly rustic everyday wines to those of more serious intention deserving more serious food – lamb with flageolets perhaps. Further east the wines of Provence, in particular Coteaux des Baux-en-Provence, are more blackcurranty, often reflecting an injection of Cabernet Sauvignon. Try them with herb -roasted meat and game birds. There are also some good, inexpensive, early-drinking, spicy, fruity *vin de pays* Syrahs to try with shepherd's pie, cous cous or fassoulia, for example.

AUSTRALIA

Shiraz is altogether softer and suppler in texture with more ebullient fruit than it has (as Syrah) in the Rhône. The richest, most voluptuous, long-lived examples are those made from old vines in the Barossa; leaner, more peppery, herbaceous examples come from cooler vineyards; then there are the masses of simple, cheap wines – mint and bramble-jelly flavoured – which are soft enough to be drunk on their own, but, equally, can be drunk, like the more expensive wines, with barbecued meats (beef, venison, kangaroo). The biggest wines also have the stamina to accompany intensely flavoured stews. Sparkling red Shiraz – full bodied, dark, spicy and vibrantly fruity – should be served lightly chilled at a barbecue, or with Christmas turkey, or, astonishing as it may sound, with foie gras.

Grenache

This is a Mediterranean vine par excellence, growing in hot climates in the south of France, in Spain (as Garnacha) and in North Africa. It gives plenty of peppery, jammy fruit flavour and alcohol, but, lacking structure unless yields are kept very low, it is usually blended with varieties which provide some backbone – Syrah, Mourvèdre, Tempranillo (in Rioja) or Cabernet Sauvignon. It is the main ingredient in Châteauneuf-du-Pape and Côtes du Rhône and is one reason why these wines are seldom long-lived. In Australia it gives cheap bag-in-box and fortified wines, but it is also undergoing a revival in the Barossa where growers have been rediscovering the potential for producing very full-bodied, fruity, peppery wines from parcels of old Grenache vines; Grenache is now appearing on labels in its own right. Outside the Mediterranean only a few California growers treat it sufficiently seriously to make good Rhône styles from it. With the exception of Châteauneuf-du-Pape (*qv*), the average Grenache-based wine is not subtle or sophisticated: choose food accordingly – peperoni, pizza, spare ribs with barbecue sauce, chorizo, etc.

Other Red Grapes

BARBERA

Overshadowed in Piedmont by its majestic sibling Nebbiolo, Barbera produces wine which is broadly similar, but much lighter: a sour cherries flavour replaces Nebbiolo's tar and liquorice and acidity stands in for Nebbiolo's tannin. But Barbera takes well to new oak and in the right hands yields a smoky intensity to balance its high acidity.

Although the most concentrated Barbera comes from Piedmont, it appears in various guises all over Italy, where its ability to retain acidity under the sun is much prized. Grown for the same reason in California, Mexico and Argentina, it is used principally for blending.

Young Barberas go well charcuterie and with anchovy and broccoli sauce (for pasta or soufflé). They are quite good with lambs kidneys and liver and their acidity also ensures that they are the only tolerable red wine partner for smoked salmon. The bigger, oak-aged wines are very good with flavoursome game birds such as widgeon.

CABERNET FRANC

In Bordeaux, and wherever the claret blend is imitated, the lighter, less tannic Cabernet Franc is added to Cabernet Sauvignon to bring notes of green peppers, blackcurrant leaves and raspberries. In the Loire – Chinon, Bourgeuil, Saumur-Champigny and most Anjou-Villages – Cabernet Franc escapes its chaperone and shows what it can do alone, but it needs a hot year to achieve the depth of chocolatey, capsicum and raspberry flavours and the potential to age for five to eight years. Wines from the best years go well with rabbit, pork and beef braised in beer (a tricky dish for wine). The lighter, low tannin wines from the average to cool years are best drunk cool and are a useful partner for fish such as red mullet, sewin and John Dory and for asparagus. They can also be drunk with cheese fondue and the rather more traditional Loire *rillettes*.

DOLCETTO

Dolcetto is the juicy, young, morello cherry-flavoured red that is drunk in Piedmont with all sorts of antipasti and pasta dishes, including some of the dishes with the luxurious white truffle shaved over them. It is lower in acidity than Barbera, much less tannic than Nebbiolo (the name means 'little sweet one') and yet it usually has sufficient bite and concentration for it to partner richer meat dishes including a variety of sausages, than are its traditional Piemontese partners. (The Piedmontese of course have other big red wines to choose from.) Like Nebbiolo, it is a grape of distinctively Italian style that has not moved far from its home. Pockets of it in North and South America and Australia do not achieve the same character.

GAMAY

Gamay is the grape responsible for Beaujolais – light, uncomplicated, and bursting with sappy strawberry fruit and fresh acidity. Nowhere else has succeeded in producing Gamay

Ripe black grapes can look very similar, but when it comes to wine these all make their own statements. Previous page, top to bottom: high acid Barbera, Cabernet Franc (Cabernet Sauvignon's sidekick), Dolcetto (Italy's answer to Beaujolais) and Gamay (the grape of Beaujolais). Below: supple Merlot (left) and majestic Nebbiolo (right).

that has quite the same exuberance, although good vintages produce results in Touraine on the Loire and there is a little in California. Most Beaujolais, including Nouveau with its distinct bubblegum flavour, is particularly good served cool with salamis and hams (smoked, unsmoked, cured and dried) and it partners well fish such as salmon (even farmed salmon), but the deeper-flavoured, fuller-bodied *crus* can take bigger flavours. Morgon (second only to Moulin-a-Vent in weight) is a winner with the tricky-to-partner close-textured sweetness of calf's liver, and is equally, successful when providing a contrast to the rich heaviness of cassoulet. With maturity, Moulin-à-Vent may develop a burgundian character, putting it in the game partners category.

MERLOT

The grape most often used to fatten-out Cabernet Sauvignon used to be less commonly bottled on its own, but California Merlot has become all the rage in the US over the last few years. Merlot has always made up a large proportion of Pomerol and Saint-Emilion, where it is less tannic and generally shorter-lived than Cabernet Sauvignon, although no one would deny the staying power of Château Pétrus. Some of the full-bodied, fleshy California Merlots are also of extremely high quality and go very well with the vibrant Mediterranean flavours of California cooking and even with the spices that are married to them in so-called fusion cooking. New Zealand is making some good examples, too, but in a style which owes more to the French and is suited to slightly simpler, herb-grilled meat dishes.

Down the scale, Merlot from northern Italy is light-bodied and for drinking young (with charcuterie or pasta or on its own); Bulgarian Merlot is fuller and plummier, often with spicy oak and blackberry overtones and a little tannin; and Chile is just beginning to reveal itself as a producer of serious, yet seductively styled Merlot. In general the food for Merlot is similar to that for Cabernet, although its 'sweeter' rounder character suits pork and turkey better and, provided it is not tannic, New World Merlot can partner tuna.

NEBBIOLO

In northwest Italy Nebbiolo makes wines of extraordinary intensity and complexity, but it has hardly travelled from its own base, no doubt because when it is good it is very very good, but when it is bad it is best avoided. It is a demanding and assertive grape which, at lesser levels, can lack suppleness and fruit: it seems incapable of making approachable fruity wines like inexpensive Cabernet Sauvignon, for example.

In the Barolo region it stands most firmly on its dignity, taking its name from the fog ('*nebbia*') that swirls around the Piedmontese hills around harvest time and producing some of the world's most muscular, tannic reds. There has been a move in recent years to make wines of greater fruit and accessibility, but Barolo is still a wine that requires a minimum of five years in bottle for its marvellous flavours of tar and violets, prunes, bitter chocolate and roses to emerge. With time the distinctive tough tannins and marked acidity become coated in velvety richness.

Neighbouring Barbaresco is a slightly lighter, more perfumed version of Barolo. It is delicious with rare roast beef steak, liver and kidneys, where the biggest of Barolos really demand rich beef and game stews.

Apart from these two wines, Nebbiolo appears in various incarnations all over northwest Italy, often under its own name, sometimes under local pseudoynms (such as Spanna and Chiavennasca) and sometimes under the influence of new oak. Most of these versions are lighter, but that still means they are full-bodied and still with the determined Nebbiolo character. Outside Italy a few California producers are experimenting with it, but so far the results show little of the excitement of northwest Italy.

PINOTAGE

Pinotage is a South African speciality likely to be seen increasingly abroad – in bottle, at least. So far no other countries, except Zimbabwe, have been tempted to grow it. It is a cross between Pinot Noir and the Cinsaut grape of southern France and produces a spectrum of wines from fresh and juicy to dense, chunky, tannic reds with flavours of sweet, dusty damsons and – often – new oak. Even the latter, which are good with the sort of robust meat and/or bean stews that also suit Southern Rhône wines (*see* page 69), are best drunk relatively young. Flavours of acetone and tar, and insufficient fruit, still mar some of the wines, but improvements are showing, year by year.

SANGIOVESE

It is hard to imagine Italian food without Sangiovese, the grape which, for many wine drinkers, epitomizes the taste of Italy. Its wine has a tobaccoey, cherry-skins flavour with a twist of tea leaves that in its young and fruity forms washes down pasta, sausages and almost any other food that relishes its acidity. It is the main constituent of Chianti, but is found all over central Italy and often it is blended, because on its own it can be too astringent, too lean, too tannic – even Tuscany doesn't always get enough sun.

As well as being an everyday wine, in Tuscany Sangiovese reaches greatness – and not only in the Chianti Riservas, but also in Brunello di Montalcino, in Vino Nobile di Montepulciano (where it forms the backbone of the blend), in Carmignano and in the so-called Super-Tuscans (*vini da tavola* of exceptional quality made by top estates to avoid the constrictions of Italian wine law, although a new law means these may now qualify for appellations). Brunello, the Super-Tuscans and to a slightly lesser extent Vino Nobile are big wines – intense, spicy and plummy. Rosso di Montalcino and di Montepulciano are lighter versions of the great wines. Some Super-Tuscans are blends with Cabernet Sauvignon (as is the elegant, long lived Carmignano) and this is a remarkably successful combination, or they are 100 percent Sangiovese aged in new oak barrels. These top Tuscan wines, and those of neighbouring Umbria, are particularly good with grilled and roasted meats bathed in herbs – steak, pork, wild boar, hare and game birds. Sangiovese di Romagna never remotely scales the same heights, but its full, rounded fruit goes well with a wide range of meat and pasta dishes.

California's early results look promising, although the wines haven't quite the characteristic Tuscan bitter-sharp twist.

TEMPRANILLO

Rioja is one of the most familiar of all red wines, yet trying to pin down its flavour – and the flavour of its main grape, Tempranillo – is surprisingly difficult. It is somewhere between red Bordeaux and red burgundy in style, though without the assertive blackcurrant of the former or the silky perfume and farmyard gaminess of the latter. Part of the reason is that Tempranillo, which on its own has rounded strawberry, toffee and spice flavours, is blended with the coarser Garnacha (alias Grenache) and often other grapes as well for Rioja. It is then aged in American oak, which has a strong vanilla character – far stronger than the oak used in Bordeaux or burgundy – so that a lot of the taste of Rioja isn't Tempranillo, but oak. Unoaked

Tempranillo bottled on its own (and it is grown all over Spain under various pseudonyms) can be attractively ripe and fruity, but it is not particularly distinctive; it certainly doesn't have the 'look at me' character of Nebbiolo or Syrah. The advantage of Tempranillo, oaked or unoaked, is that it marries well with a variety of medium to quite flavoursome foods, although it is worth saving a leg of lamb or some roast pork for Rioja's fine, mature *reservas* and *gran reservas*. It is also worth bearing in mind that oak-matured Rioja (ie all but the very youngest) has a useful affinity with mushrooms (which are hard on many wines) and lightly-oaked Rioja (*crianza*) can partner some curries (see India, page 134).

As well as Rioja, Tempranillo is the mainstay of the richer, fuller-bodied reds of Ribera del Duero (which, when mature, are good with game and goose) and plays an important role in Penedès, Valdepeñas, La Mancha, Navarra and others. In Portugal it features (though not very importantly) in the port blend as Tinta Roriz and also appears in the increasingly good Douro table wines.

ZINFANDEL

DNA 'fingerprinting' has recently confirmed that this hitherto mysterious Californian vine is the same as the southern Italy's little known Primitivo – which means that it is one of many Italians to have made good in the New World. Not only is it a Californian speciality, it is also a very versatile grape. At its best it makes powerful but supple, black pepper, ripe cherry and blackberry flavoured reds of considerable character that will match lots of well-flavoured, moderately spicy meat dishes, from sausages and barbecues to casseroles and pies. It can also be moulded into much lighter, juicier, berryish reds and even 'blush' wines, although the latter (sweetish rosés often labelled 'White Zinfandel') are not really suited to drinking with food.

Proof that not all the great and distinctive red wine grapes come from France. From top to bottom: Pinotage, *South Africa's very own crossing;* Sangiovese, *a provider of Italian wine at all quality levels from everyday up to superlative;* Tempranillo, *Spain's finest grape (under various synonyms) and best-known for its staring role in red Rioja and Ribera de Duero; and the famous California* Zinfandel *which is now firmly linked with the Primitivo grape of Apulia in southern Italy.*

73

WORLD *Classic* COMBINATIONS

FOR ALL THE NEW FOOD AND WINE STYLES

THAT HAVE DEVELOPED IN A FLURRY OF

CROSS-FERTILIZATION IN THE LAST TWO

DECADES, THERE IS STILL A LOT TO BE SAID

FOR, AND LEARNED FROM, THE TRADITIONAL

PARTNERSHIPS THAT HAVE EVOLVED

TOGETHER ON THE SAME SOIL AND HAVE

STOOD THE TEST OF TIME. THIS DOES NOT

MEAN THAT WE CANNOT ALSO PARTNER

THESE TRADITIONAL DISHES WITH DIFFERENT

WINES — WE CAN AND WE SHOULD.

europe

the new world

india AND THE *far east*

Europe

When in Rome, do as the Romans do, as the famous English saying goes. Curiously, when it comes to gastronomy, Rome is the focal point of one of the few wine producing and wine drinking regions of Europe where the local food and wine are often somewhat at odds – at least they are today. Many of the traditional dishes and specialities, which are still very much part of contemporary home and restaurant cooking, are robustly constituted and powerfully flavoured. The wines that Latium provides to go with them are largely white, very simple and very ordinary – not to say bland. They don't even have the saving grace of tangy acidity (like Vinho Verde, for example) to cut through the sturdy food and complement its pungent flavours. Food and the wine seldom fight, but there is no rapport. Frankly, Rome deserves more – and in the past it had it. The region has never produced serious, big-scale reds, but the whites used to be fuller and more flavoursome. They were also notoriously unstable. Modern winemaking has rendered them stable, but less characterful – and thus a less perfect match for the food.

But Rome is the exception that proves the rule. Elsewhere in Europe's wine regions, wine and food have evolved together, as anyone who has ever eaten meals in Provence, Portugal, the Spanish Basque country and Tuscany will know. It is tempting to speculate which has exerted the greater influence: local ingredients over the style of wines produced, or the type of wine produced over the type of cooking. In many regions it was doubtless the former, but in others, particularly in France where wine and food have for centuries been given equal billing, it is fair to assume that their long and widely celebrated wines have influenced the development of the cuisine. In Bordeaux, for example, the cooking is typically polished, but often fairly simple; in Burgundy dishes tends to be bigger and richer. Perhaps a conveniently neat generalization is to say that locally available ingredients and particular delicacies often exerted the initial influence, but the style of wine that could actually be made in any given region then influenced the type of preparation and cooking of these ingredients.

All this is not to say, of course, that the classic match of local wine and food is the only worthwhile combination (and hence the alternatives recommended for each classic dish on the pages that follow). There may be wines made in similar climates on similar soils from the same grape varieties which are just as successful. More importantly, there are usually other types of wine, sometimes very different ones, that make good partners. It is rare that a dish can be matched happily by only one type of wine. Even where there is a perfect marriage there are usually other very acceptable matches. The fact that foods and dishes which crop up in broadly similar guises in several regions and countries are partnered by quite different local wines – roast spring lamb or *abbacchio*, oysters, fish stews and *bacalhau*, steamed asparagus, sweet egg yolk puddings – only reinforces the point that most food can be accompanied by a variety of wines.

Then there are the countries that do not make wine, or at least not on a major scale. It is stretching the point, I know, to talk of classic combinations in this context, but wine is imported (increasingly so) into northern Europe and Scandinavia and there are plenty of classic dishes from their various and distinctive cuisines which deserve the accompaniment of wine.

France

French cooking is probably the most influential (and the most synonymous with luxury) of any in the world. But trying to pin down what French cooking actually is is another matter: there is *haute cuisine* and *cuisine grandmère*; *nouvelle cuisine* and *cuisine minceur*. As a country that takes both food and fashion seriously, France is apt to impose fashions on its food – and these tend to hasten abroad with all the speed of the latest television series or chef's cookbook.

Yet at the same time there is a strong regionality to French food. Some of this is enshrined in law: many cheeses, plus a few other items like *poulets de bresse*, are *appellation contrôlée* (like the wines) and may only be produced in the areas in which they originated (though of course they are sold, and eaten, all over the country). Some of it is simply traditional, the result of centuries of poor communications and the necessity of self-sufficiency in food and wine: there is little wine from Burgundy drunk in Bordeaux, for example, or vice versa; and while the classic accompaniment to foie gras in the southwest of France is Sauternes, in the other great foie gras region, Alsace, you will be offered a glass of Tokay-Pinot Gris or Gewurztraminer *vendange tardive* or *sélection des grains nobles*.

Whether regional French food is as luxurious as the image of French food *per se* is a matter of historical and geographical chance – whether the local climate produces hardship or plenty, and whether the people have generally been rich or poor. What is invariably true is that even the poorest region of France has the ability to turn simple ingredients into something delicious – which is why peasant dishes like *cassoulet* are today so highly prized abroad.

France can be divided into three parts (though for reasons different from those which Caesar had in mind). In the dairy country of the north, abundant butter and cream are the hallmark of the cooking. In the south, their place is taken by olive oil, while in the southwest the cooking medium is goose or duck fat. Everywhere there is *charcuterie*, because French cooks are frugal, and hardly a trotter, neck or piece of intestine goes to waste. In those parts of the country where wine is produced, it is almost as automatic an ingredient in the cooking as salt or pepper; and in the north, where no wine is made, its place in the kitchen is taken by locally-produced beers or ciders.

Most of the great wine regions of France make a sufficient variety of styles to drink throughout the meal. Notable omissions are sweet whites in Burgundy and good still wines of any colour in Champagne – but then Champagne is unusual among French wine regions in that its wine and its traditional cuisine appear to be at odds with each other. Its wine is the epitome of refinement, while the food is the sturdy, rustic, cold weather fodder of the north, based on root vegetables, game, pâtés and *andouillettes*.

Although there is much determined pairing of meat, and more especially game, with champagne by producers and by chefs, the region's expensive restaurants (of which there is no shortage) have also developed a repertoire of lighter dishes to complement the various styles of champagne, and these are often cooked in champagne sauces. So perhaps what we are seeing is a latter-day adaptation of food to wine of the sort that happened elsewhere a long time ago.

Some pink champagnes, and even some whites, can in fact be surprisingly weighty, but the still red Coteaux Champenois wines are often disappointingly light and acidic, the inevitable outcome of the cold northerly climate. In tacit acceptance of this, you will often be offered a good red from elsewhere – often a classed growth Bordeaux – during the course of a meal in Reims or Epernay.

BORDEAUX AND THE SOUTHWEST

*T*he food and wine of Bordeaux are intricately connected in that it was the wine that brought the wealth which fostered the often elevated food. And Bordeaux is a trading city *par excellence*, so the one food that it lacks to complete a menu, namely a decent cheese, it has brought in from outside and adopted so thoroughly that the original parentage is often forgotten. Mimolette, the hard orange cheese that partners mature red Bordeaux so well, is simply aged Gouda; and Roquefort, which makes a perfect match for sweet Sauternes, comes from the Languedoc.

In other respects, however, Bordeaux can produce a food for every one of its wines, and vice versa. It can draw on oysters from Arcachon (often eaten with little spicy sausages) and superb Atlantic and river fish: sole, lobsters, shad (often stuffed with sorrel) and lampreys, the large eel-like fish cooked in red wine and their own blood to make *lamproies à la Bordelaise*. (Any dish 'à la Bordelaise' involves wine, usually red, with shallots, garlic, parsley and often bone marrow; in *entrecôte à la Bordelaise* the relationship with the grape is further emphasized when the steak is grilled over vine cuttings.)

From the low-lying pastures along the banks of the River Gironde comes what is possibly the finest of all partners for red Bordeaux: *pré-salé* or salt marsh lamb. The tender, milk-fed lambs, available only from Easter until late May or early June, even have their own AC, Agneau de lait de Pauillac. And from the dense, monotonous pine forests of the Landes, bordering the Atlantic coast, there are game birds – *palombes*, or wild pigeons, *ortolans* and *becs fins*, or pipits. There are wild mushrooms, too, particularly ceps which are sold from roadside stands every autumn; and there is a lot of foie gras produced, and where there is foie gras there is *confit* (meat – in this region goose or duck – cooked and preserved in its own fat).

The goose is a notably efficient food producer. The liver (as foie gras), swollen to an ideal weight of one and a half pounds by force-feeding, is the most expensive part, but, like the pig, nothing of the goose is wasted. The rest of the bird can be roasted, or the meat can be preserved in its own fat and used for cassoulet, for flavouring soups and stews, in salads, or, most deliciously, served with garlicky potatoes fried until crisp in the same fat. Surplus fat is used for general cooking purposes; stuffed goose neck is a homely dish, but one which can be made luxurious if the stuffing is of foie gras; the feathers fill pillows and the feet can go for making glue. In armagnac country the liver may be served hot, with a local, late-harvest sweet white Jurançon, Gaillac or Pacherenc du Vic Bihl; in Bordeaux you are more likely to have it cold, with a fine Sauternes, or perhaps a more budget-conscious Sainte-Croix du Mont or Monbazillac.

The wines of Sauternes can make an appearance again with the pudding, though the French often favour drinking champagne at this point. Puddings are often fruit-based, and kind to Sauternes: there are prunes from Agen (which are good cooked with rabbit as well as in desserts) and apples to make into tarts; *clafoutis* with cherries, and a multitude of other pastries. The region of Saint-Emilion has macaroons as its speciality and these appear in *Saint-Emilion au chocolat*, a rich chocolate charlotte, and pine nuts from the Landes forests are another local delicacy, used for example in *pignola*, another rich cake.

CASSOULET TOULOUSAIN

Strictly speaking, cassoulet belongs to Languedoc, partnered by wines like Corbières, but it is also a favourite in the Southwest accompanied by robust reds such as Cahors and Madiran. Personally, I prefer the greater suppleness of a Côtes du Frontonnais, or, even better, the richness-cutting fruit and freshness of a *cru* Beaujolais. Young red Navarra works in a similar way; Australian Shiraz, Grenache and Mourvèdre are heavier alternatives.

COQUILLES SAINT-JACQUES A LA BORDELAISE

A crisp Sauvignon-dominated white Bordeaux or Bergerac is ideal for the delicacy of scallops with butter, shallots and parsley, but a mature, superior white Graves doesn't go amiss; and dry Jurançon is also successful. Sauvignons from Chile, Rueda from Spain and Pinot Blancs (Weissburgunders) from Alsace, Germany and Austria are alternatives from further afield.

TTORO

Like other fish stews, ttoro originated as a way of using up difficult boney fish and, like others, it has become more refined, but the inclusion of hot peppers maintains its distinctive Basque identity. The local Irouléguy rosé suits it well, but rosés from nearby Béarn, from Provence and Navarra can also cope and Loire and New Zealand Sauvignon are useful standbys.

LAMPREYS A LA BORDELAISE

This archetypal dish of eels stewed with their blood in a red wine sauce is only ever drunk with red wine – Bordeaux. The wine shouldn't be too young, grassy or brightly fruity: Merlot-rich St-Emilion and Pomerol, or Graves, often work better than more austere Médocs. Other Bordeaux-type reds and Rhône reds such as Crozes-Hermitage and Vacqueyras work well.

CONFIT DE CANARD WITH CEPS

Occasionally, local white is offered with *confit de canard* – duck preserved in its own fat – but reds are invariably served when ceps are added (and go better, anyway, with confit). This means Cahors, Madiran, Tursan, Béarn *et al*, when you are in the region, but when released from these constraints it is well worth choosing mature, classed-growth Médoc, especially St-Estèphe. Fine California Cabernet and Merlot are also successful, as is the deep, dark, pruney fruit of Catalonia's off-beat Priorato. Avoid young, juicily fruity wines.

BORDEAUX AND THE SOUTHWEST *continued*...

The two main grapes of Sauternes and its lesser, lighter followers (Monbazillac, Loupiac, Sainte-Croix du Mont, Premières Côtes, etc) are Sémillon and Sauvignon Blanc. The same grapes, blended together and aged in oak in the Graves, make the ageworthy dry whites which match local dishes like trout with Bayonne ham. Simpler young Sauvignon and Sauvignon-based blends, often with the simple Bordeaux or Entre-Deux-Mers AC, are ideal for shellfish and plainer fish.

The reds, made from any permutation of Cabernet Sauvignon, Cabernet Franc and Merlot, sometimes with some Petit Verdot and Malbec, can be everyday or aristocratic – tannic and blackcurranty where the Cabernet predominates (basically in the Médoc and Graves) or softer and fleshier where the Merlot takes centre stage (especially in Pomerol and Saint-Emilion). The most expensive wines are intended for long ageing, and are usually then served with relatively simple food intended to show off the wine (salt marsh lamb is perfect). The best come from the Médoc communes of Pauillac, Saint-Estèphe, Saint-Julien and Margaux, plus the top estates of Graves, Saint-Emilion and Pomerol. Simpler wines (look for regional ACs like Haut-Médoc, Côtes de Bourg, Premières Côtes de Blaye or Bordeaux Supérieur) can be drunk within a few years of the harvest. But beware: if your taste is for really well-aged red Bordeaux, then do not seek it in the region itself – the French taste is for drinking wine much younger than it would be drunk in Britain, or even the USA.

While Bordeaux is the capital of the Southwest, it is far from being the whole story, either in food or wine. In the neighbouring regions, like Bergerac, Côtes de Duras and Buzet, the grapes are the same and the wines are similar, although of lesser quality than the best of the heartland. But as one goes further away the influence of Bordeaux fades. Cabernet still pops up, but, in Cahors, Malbec is the main grape and in Madiran the robust Tannat takes over. Go southwest and the wines, red and white, become still more rustic – even idiosyncratic – and the food, likewise, takes on the red pepper flavours of the Basque country.

Red peppers here can go into almost anything, from *ttoro* (fish soup), to *pipérade* (peppers, tomatoes, eggs and Bayonne ham) to the local version of salt cod, or *morue*. Even the fresh fish is of the strongly flavoured kind: sardines, anchovies, tuna and swordfish. Cornmeal is a staple, often made into a polenta lookalike, and *poule au pot* comes from Béarn – which is more than can be said of that Parisian invention, *sauce béarnaise*. More typical of Béarn are thick soups like *tourrin*, with onions, garlic and egg yolks, or *garbure* (vegetables simmered in broth and served with bread *croûtes*). Hearty dishes all; and well matched by the spicy, dark red wines, the rosés and herby whites of the region.

ROAST SPRING LAMB

The perfect accompaniment for a *gigot* (leg) of Bordeaux's sweet and tender salt marsh lamb, roasted with herbs and garlic, is fine red Bordeaux – Médoc especially and Pauillac above all. But it doesn't have to be Bordeaux or even a Cabernet-based wine, although there is a very high strike rate (Coonawarra Cabernet, New Zealand Cabernet-Merlot, Tuscan Cabernet, to name three). Rioja *reserva* or *gran reserva* is another stellar match.

SALMIS OF WOODPIGEON

Game bird *salmis*, especially of pigeon, are popular throughout the Southwest and are drunk with the local red, whether little-travelled Irouléguy, Cahors (fabled but sometimes lacklustre), or globally-esteemed Médoc. This, though, is a good dish for many medium- to full-bodied reds – Northern Rhônes, Ribera del Duero, Portuguese reds (Bairrada, Dão, Alentejo and Douro).

SWEETBREADS WITH TRUFFLES

Were it not for the Perigord black truffles, this might be a white wine dish. Cahors wine is much favoured with truffles, but this refined dish is Bordeaux oriented. The softer and fuller, Merlot-dominated wines (Pomerol, St-Emilion and St-Emilion satellites) and Pecharmant (in Bergerac) are well matched, but more important is a wine that has some earthy, gamey maturity – an echo of the taste of the truffle. For that reason fine, mature burgundy works, too.

ENTRECOTE A LA BORDELAISE

This is an excuse to drink a fine red Bordeaux – one with enough depth to cope with the shallots and wine sauce. Graves is a good choice, but the key is quality and concentration rather than sub-region. Tuscan reds, including Brunello and Bolgheri, top New World Cabernets and Merlots, Rhône reds and burgundy are among the other matches.

RABBIT WITH PRUNES

The traditional partner for this dish (a restaurant staple in much of the Southwest) is Cahors, but it is perhaps not as keen a match for the sweetness of prunes as St-Emilion and Bergerac, Côte du Frontonnais and the better Gaillacs. Rioja, Navarra Crianzas, Australian Shiraz and New World Pinot Noirs also make good partners.

BURGUNDY

Better a good meal than fine clothes, say the Burgundians, though given the high prices for their wines, Charollais beef and Bresse chickens there is no reason why they should not these days have both. Even the name of the vinous heartland, the Côte d'Or or golden slope, gives the game away: this narrow strip of hillside is some of the most valuable agricultural land in all France.

There is a corresponding richness to Burgundian cooking. It is a lavish cuisine, unstinting in its use of cream, wine, freshwater fish, beef and local Morvan ham, and it is food for hearty appetites, worked up during long days in the fields and vineyards. It is also inconceivable without the wine around which it developed. Any dish cooked 'à la Bourguignonne' will have a red wine sauce of mushrooms, bacon and baby onions; red wine sauces also go with eggs or brains (*oeufs* or *cervelles en meurette*). The mustard of Dijon is made not with vinegar but with *verjus*, or the juice of sour grapes; quail may be wrapped in vine leaves and cooked with grapes; and *pochouse* is a popular fish stew, mixing salmon and eel with pike, perch, trout, catfish, carp, white wine and garlic – and, interestingly, drunk with red burgundy in some households and white in others.

Overseas the name of *coq au vin* may be bestowed on any flavourless battery chicken, casseroled with a bottle of equally anonymous red; but properly it is a cockerel, too tough to roast, that needs long simmering in good red burgundy. (Scrawny old hens, past egg-laying age, are likewise the proper starting point for *poule au pot*: the distinctions of the hen-coop are every bit as severe as those of the vineyard. A roasting chicken is a *poularde*; a *poulet* is younger, and a *poussin* younger still.)

As with chicken, so with beef. The point of *boeuf bourguignonne* is that the local Charollais beef is distinctly chewy and less flavoursome than some: not ideal for simple grilling, but perfect for long, slow cooking with red wine. And this is the sort of dish that partners red burgundy. It is a wine that likes earthy, gamey flavours and rich sauces. Except in Chablis to the north, where white wine is more plentiful, most Burgundian cooking relies on red. Pinot Noir is one of the few red wines that, in its lighter manifestations, can partner fish successfully, although many of the local fish dishes – pike in white wine and cream sauce, for example, or chicken with crayfish cooked in cream, garlic and white wine – need a fairly weighty white from the Côte d'Or or a cheaper one from the more southerly Côte Chalonnaise or Mâconnais.

Further south again, in Beaujolais, there is white wine from Chardonnay grapes, but the role of Pinot Noir is taken over by Gamay, which makes wines with vivid, juicy flavours that are perfect with *charcuterie*. Here the place of the bigger red burgundies is taken by the best of the ten *cru* wines from individual villages. A mature Morgon or Moulin-à-Vent can even take on distinctly burgundian characteristics.

The only wine that Burgundy lacks is a sweet white to match the local plums, cherries, currants, raspberries, quinces and wild peaches that are turned into puddings. Burgundians will often have sparkling Crémant de Bourgogne, or a Marc de Bourgogne afterwards.

Classic Combinations

ESCARGOTS A LA BOURGUIGNONNE

Although Burgundians have been eating snails with garlic and herbs since Roman times, there is no single definitive accompaniment to the best known dish, snails stuffed with garlic and parsley butter – no doubt because the flavour of snails is mild and undemanding and garlic-herb butter is similarly accommodating. Bourgogne Aligoté is a typical and very successful partner. Other fairly simple white burgundies and Chablis go well, as do basic red burgundies. Alternatives include Rhône and Provence whites, dry rosés and Spanish *rosados*, Chinon, Bourgueil, Chianti and middle-ranking red Bordeaux.

JAMBON PERSILLE

Bourgogne Aligoté is the classic partner for this – ham set in white wine jelly with parsley and shallots – but Chablis, if anything, goes better. In other whites, look for a crisp, dry, moderately assertive character, avoiding heavily fruity or buttery flavours: try Pouilly-Fumé, unoaked Chardonnays and Chilean Sauvignons Blancs; among reds, try New World Pinot Noirs, Beaujolais-Villages and Italian Barbera.

POCHOUSE

Burgundians make river fish stews with both red and white wine and drink wine of the appropriate colour. Pochouse, the white wine version, is a fairly substantial dish finished with cream and well suited to a Côte d'Or white or polished New World Chardonnay.

COQ AU VIN

Fine red burgundy, preferably Gevrey-Chambertin, is supposed to be the wine for both cooking pot and glass. Use something humbler for the pot and drink the best red you can, whether burgundy, New World Pinot Noir, Douro, Barbaresco or Ribera del Duero.

VEAL KIDNEYS A LA MOUTARDE

The mustard is local Dijon and the accompaniment is red burgundy, preferably Côte de Beaune (eg Santenay, Volnay or Pommard), but many other savoury, not too aggressive red wines work well, including New World Pinot Noir, Rioja, Médoc, St-Emilion and Vino Nobile de Montepulciano.

SABODET LYONNAIS

This hearty boiling sausage is traditionally eaten with a hot, vinaigrette-dressed potato salad and a glass of Beaujolais, preferably a *cru* such as Brouilly or Chiroubles. Alternatives are Valpolicella Classico, reds from Apulia, young Tempranillo and red Zinfandel.

LANGUEDOC, PROVENCE & RHONE

Classic Combinations

he Mediterranean coast is, logically enough, the home of France's contribution to the Mediterranean diet, that fashionable combination of olive oil and vegetables, fish, grains and pulses. Add wild herbs in abundance – thyme, rosemary, savory, marjoram – and lots of garlic, and you have the basic flavours that pervade the region from the Spanish to Italian borders. But to get the full feel of this part of France, you must then add the influences of these same countries – Catalonia extended well into Roussillon from 1160 until 1659, and until the last century Nice and Menton were part of the Italian kingdom of Savoy – and, less romantically, a large dose of grinding poverty.

The south of France may seem to epitomize the good life to modern tourists. But imagine trying to scratch a living from the inhospitable, infertile hills of the interior, where nothing will thrive except sheep, the olive and the vine – and the herbs that flavour everything. The coastal areas can reap a daily harvest of sardines, anchovies, red mullet, octopus, rascasse, lemon sole, mussels and clams, but go inland and until recently you would have been restricted to salt cod, chick peas, dried beans, lentils, and whatever meat you could muster, all washed down with alcoholic red wine.

The strong, vibrant flavours of the region seem to defy poverty. In the more fertile Roussillon, peppers and green olives add a note reminiscent of Spain and the fish stew, *bourride*, is seasoned with garlic, olive oil, onions and herbs. Further east in Provence it acquires tomato, saffron and hot *rouille* and becomes *bouillabaisse*. In both cases it is a way of using the fast-growing, boney Mediterranean fish that have more flavour than texture. Better red mullet and monkfish are served on their own with fennel, or grilled over herbs.

Either way, these technicolour flavours can overwhelm delicate white wines. Young, robust reds, turned out here by the hectolitre, will deal with dried bean stews and, if they are fruity enough, with garlicky fish stew as well. Corbières, Minervois and Fitou are the best-known – and vastly improved – traditional names in Languedoc; Coteaux du Languedoc-Faugères and Saint-Chinian are others to note. Côtes de Provence, Coteaux d'Aix-en-Provence, Coteaux des Baux-en-Provence and, best of all, Bandol all make some impressive, herby, berry-flavoured reds – at a price – in Provence. Of course, there is also a great deal of dry, herby rosé: ideal for washing down *anchoïade* and *tapenade* (anchovy and olive spreads); but until recently there was little white. The climate didn't suit it and the food didn't call for it.

Curiously, though this area has the most interesting food, the finest wine comes from the Rhône Valley. The Syrah grape in the north gives some of France's biggest, most muscular red wines, like Hermitage and Côte-Rôtie, that need five or ten years or even more to mature. The whites – herby, perfumed white Hermitage and voluptuous, dry Condrieu – are rarer but equally expensive. The Southern Rhône is home to warm, spicy, red Châteauneuf-du-Pape and Gigondas, peppery, plummy Côtes du Rhône and some strong dry rosés. But the food is less distinctive. In the north it echoes the rich, sauce-laden cooking of Burgundy, while other dishes, like Valence's *grillade marinière*, beef flavoured with anchovies, point to Provence.

BOUILLABAISSE

There are many Mediterranean fish soups and stews, but *bouillabaisse* is by far the most famous. Served with garlicky, hot-pepper *rouille* and croutons, it is also one of the most flavoursome. Provence rosé suits it perfectly, but so do other dry rosés – Languedoc, Rhône and Spanish. The full, savoury, herby flavours of whites from the Rhône and Provence are the next choice.

SALADE NICOISE

Amid the countless versions of Salade Niçoise all claiming to be the one true version, what is certain is that it depends on the freshest of ingredients – salad leaves, green beans, tomatoes, artichokes, olives, anchovies, lemon juice – and superb olive oil. Made like this (with or without tuna and egg), it merits Provence's best white wines (Bellet, Palette, Cassis, Bandol), but there are plenty of cheaper, crisp, dry, white alternatives – from Lubéron (in Provence) to New Zealand Sauvignons, to Pinot Blancs, bone dry Vinho Verde and many North Italian whites.

RATATOUILLE

Eaten cold, ratatouille is traditionally partnered by a

Provence white or rosé; eaten hot, the wine is red – eg Costières de Nîmes. The formula works, but you don't need to stay with Provence. Many Languedoc-Roussillon reds (Côtes du Roussillon, Minervois, Coteaux du Languedoc, etc) and some of the whites work well. Whites need to be lively and herby more than exotically fruity: Sauvignons are generally good; Chardonnays are not. Red Zinfandel is surprisingly successful, as is, with cold ratatouille, red sparkling Shiraz.

BOEUF EN DAUBE

Daubes are made of all sorts of meat, and even octopus, but beef, slowly cooked with salt pork, calf's foot, red wine, tomatoes, orange peel and olives, is a classic. Coteaux d'Aix-en-Provence and Coteaux des Baux-en-Provence can field ideal partners, but so can the Rhône: Hermitage is not out of place. Nor is Australian Shiraz.

CRYSTALLIZED FRUITS

In France the very sweet *vin doux naturels* of Roussillon (Rivesaltes, Frontignan, Lunel, etc) are often served as an aperitif, but they also accompany the crystallized fruits which are a speciality of Provence. The Rhône's Muscat de Beaumes-de-Venise is equally appropriate and Moscatel de Valencia is a Spanish alternative.

LOIRE & ALSACE

Gourmet and gourmand, the two extremes (though not opposites) of good food, can both find contentment in these regions. The Loire is the more refined, a gourmet heaven: fish is cooked simply *au beurre blanc*, prime pork is baked and shredded into *rillettes*, and the wines have elegance and lightness as their hallmark. Whites, from Sauvignon, Chenin Blanc and Melon de Bourgogne, can be intense but are never heavy. The reds, from Cabernet Franc (Chinon, Bourgueil, etc) and Pinot Noir (Sancerre) are more often light and grassy than deep, dark and age-worthy. Alsace, in contrast, is the land where pig and cabbage flourish, where chicken and game are accompanied by noodles or *spaetzli* and you can feast on foie gras. The wines, similarly, although nearly all are white, are full-bodied, flavoursome, aromatic: even the usually neutral Sylvaner takes on a spicy character.

But look again. The food of the Loire inspired the adjectives Rabelasian and Gargantuan. Think of venison with prunes and red wine, or *andouilles* and *andouillettes*, or *matelote de la Loire* (eel stew with white wine) or fish stewed in red wine – and then for pudding a wedge of *tarte tatin* and a bottle of sweet Vouvray or Coteaux du Layon. In Alsace, conversely, think of the delicacy of *truite au bleu* or *coq au Riesling* – and of the lightness of the local red wine, from Pinot Noir grapes that only just reach ripeness.

The truth is that both regions are lavish in their approach to food and wine. In the Loire a mild climate gives abundant fruit, all turned into tarts and cakes; and prunes are cooked with pork, rabbit, chicken and fish, or poached in wine as a pudding. Yet the food, generally, is simply cooked, and tastes of itself. Flavours are subtle and fresh, rather than heavy and rich: the delicacy of calf's kidneys is emphasized by cooking them in Muscadet; and, instead of the opulence of foie gras or the piquancy of Roquefort, there is nothing better with well-aged Chenin Blanc than a simple pudding of fresh fruit with *cremet*, a little dish of fresh cheese, whipped *crème fraiche* and egg white.

'Little' is not a word often applied to Alsace cuisine. Helpings are copious: there are liver dumplings and dumpling soup, and in Lorraine the local quiche was traditionally served on May Day, after the sucking pig in aspic was cleared away. But if the food and the wines are reminiscent of Germany (after all, only a few kilometres away), both have a French finesse. The *choucroute* is prepared with Riesling (the best partner for Alsace food), and as well as sausages from every conceivable part of the pig, there are pâtés and *mousselines*. There is meltingly creamy onion tart, and the meat for *baeckenoffe*, a slowly baked dish of pork, lamb and beef with potatoes, is first marinated in Sylvaner or Riesling.

The wines have a French fruity-spicy savouriness to them that is totally different to German floweriness. They blend happily with sweet, sour, spicy flavours – even *sauerkraut*, red cabbage and caraway – and Tokay-Pinot Gris is, when late-picked (*vendange tardive*) or nobly rotten (*sélection des grains nobles*), the local match for foie gras.

And of the many fruits here, those that escape the *patissier*, are distilled – for after a large Alsacien lunch, a dry, aromatic *eau de vie* is the perfect preparation for dinner.

FRUIT TARTS

Fruit tarts are a favourite in both Alsace and the Loire and both regions have sweet wines, but in a fine vintage the botrytised Chenin Blancs of the Loire – Coteaux du Layon, Bonnezeaux, Quarts de Chaume, Vouvray – have an intensity of flavour and acidity that is particularly suited to baked fruit. Sweet Austrian wines are a good alternative.

ONION TART

The classic match for *tarte à l'oignon* is Alsace Pinot Blanc, but it is also happy with Sylvaner, Riesling and even Gewurztraminer – and a great many whites from outside Alsace, including New World Sauvignon, Chardonnay and Colombard. Aromatic and fruity flavours work with the sweetness of the onions, and gently buttery flavours go with the rich, savoury custard. Avoid heavy oak.

CHOUCROUTE GARNI

For Alsace *choucroute* (much less sharp than Germany's *sauerkraut*), Alsace Riesling is the undisputed partner. It has the weight to stand up to the pork, bacon and sausages (and goose when included) and the acidity to cut the richness. With the exception of Austrian Riesling, Riesling from elsewhere is seldom as successful (usually it is a touch too fruity), but unoaked Chardonnay often works, as do Pinot Blanc/Weissburgunder and Hungarian whites.

PHEASANT A LA VOSGIENNE

Game dishes such as this filling pheasant, mushroom and noodle pie give Alsace a chance to drink its Pinot Noir, but Pinot Noirs from Burgundy and the New World are just as suitable.

PLATEAU DE FRUITS DE MER

The yeasty freshness of Muscadet *sur lie* is hard to beat with a plate of shellfish, but other brisk, dry whites do go down well – including Sauvignons (especially Sancerre, Pouilly-Fumé and neighbours), *blanc de blancs* champagne, Gros Plant, proper dry Vinho Verde, Rueda and the best dry English wines.

SANDER WITH SORREL SAUCE

River fish – perch, shad, trout, salmon, eel – are often eaten with (and cooked in) red wine in the Loire, but when sorrel (*oseille*) is used, the wine has to have corresponding bite. Savennières (made from Chenin) is perfect, Sancerre and Pouilly-Fumé scarcely less so. Other Sauvignons, especially New Zealand, also go well.

Italy

Italian cuisine is a new concept. Rather, there are kinds of cooking local to each of Italy's sprawling regions, from foggy, mountainous Piedmont in the northwest to the scorchingly hot Salento Peninsula in the southeast. The wine, in a country where vines are grown almost everywhere, is equally regional. To drink Chianti with *fegato alla veneziana* – the wines of Tuscany with the food of the Veneto – is considered a great solecism by the natives of those regions. United Italy is, after all, less than 150 years old.

But modern communications have made their impact, and the old distinctions are not always clear cut. Not so long ago, while pasta was more common in the south, rice and polenta were normal in the north, where potatoes are also valued (best of all, in the form of *gnocchi*). Today, pasta is found all over Italy, although regional distinctions and the matching of shapes with specific sauces still apply. Broad, flat ribbons such as *pappardelle* are used with rich gamey sauces such as hare (*alla lepre*) in central and northern Italy; while thinner spaghetti is chosen for clams and garlic (*alle vongole*). And then there are hundreds of shaped and stuffed pastas – *tortellini, tortelloni, cappelletti, cappellacci, ravioli, cannelloni* to name but half a dozen – which can be filled with anything from spiced meats or pumpkin to spinach and ricotta.

Pizza, the once-lowly food of the poorer south, is perhaps the ultimate example – or victim – of modern communications. It has not only colonized the whole of Italy but much of the world, too (as, of course, has so-called Bolognese sauce). Even *polenta* has become fashionable in the English-speaking world over the last decade; and risotto is perhaps better known by travesties of the real thing, bearing little relation to the refined dish – sometimes delicate, sometimes intensely flavoured – of northern Italy.

Perhaps it is not surprising to find parallels in wine: huge bottles of bland, semi-sweet Lambrusco and vapid versions of Frascati and Valpolicella, churned out for export markets to be the sorry accompaniments to this supposedly Italian cooking.

But the overall picture is far from gloomy. There is nowadays a much more accurate world-wide appreciation of the virtues of true Italian cooking – the emphasis on excellent, fresh, local ingredients relatively simply prepared (very different from the elaborateness of French *haute cuisine*).

In wine, the last ten years have seen a growing understanding and love of the tantalizingly unusual flavours from many of Italy's indigenous vines. The establishment of Cabernet Sauvignon and the international acclaim it has won (alone and in blends) in the seventies and eighties have given Italy the confidence to nurture, and in some cases save from extinction, its own treasure trove of grape varieties.

Thus, both despite and because of the march of modern progress, the specialities of each region remain remarkably clear. While the style of cooking varies from region to region, eating itself conforms to patterns: including the traditional practice of drinking wine as part of a meal. Indeed, many Italian wines positively need to be drunk with food, rather than on their own – and not just the familiar, powerfully tannic reds such as Brunello di Montalcino and Barolo or the more astringent Barbera and Chianti. Less renowned, but admirable reds, such as Salice Salentino and Aglianico del Vulture from the poorer south and rich spicy Sicilian reds made from the Nero d'Avola grape deserve food; so, too, do many of Italy's simple, crisp, but rather neutral whites. They can set off, rather than compete with, the freshest of seafood; or act as a foil for creamy pasta dishes and risotto; or be a simple accompaniment to salad and vegetable dishes.

The order of a full Italian meal is: *antipasto*; *minestra*; pasta; main course of poultry, meat, game or fish; vegetables/ salads; cheese; fresh fruit or, depending on the region, cake, dessert or ice-cream-type pudding. The meat, poultry, game or fish are often treated quite plainly wherever you are – grilled, roasted or baked (if you are lucky, over an open fire) with fresh herbs and garlic, perhaps with some olive oil and usually a lemon for squeezing over the food at the last moment. Playing the same richness-cutting role as the squeeze of lemon, but in a more sophisticated form, is *gremolata* (lemon zest, garlic and parsley) sprinkled over Lombardy's rich veal stew, *osso buco*.

PIEDMONT & TUSCANY

Generalizations are always dangerous in Italy, but it is true to say – and it helps put the wine and food in context – that, broadly, the north has the richest dishes: meat and dairy-based (cooking with butter rather than olive oil), together with rice and *polenta*. A love of *polenta* and of game is found right across the north of Italy from Padua to Piedmont, but in the harsh climate of Piedmont Italian cooking reaches its most robust heights, with wines to match. Chief among these are the many Nebbiolos (Barolo and Barbaresco being the most famous), but Piedmont also has the high acid red Barbera, the more gentle, perfumed, fruity Dolcetto, the white grapes Cortese, Arneis and Moscato and a gamut of other idiosyncratic varieties (Freisa, Brachetto, Grignolino), all of which have a place with food.

Piedmont is also home to the prized white truffle which, if you can afford it in the September to December season, is eaten raw, shaved over almost everything – risotto, *polenta*, pasta, *fonduta* (a type of fondue served with both pasta and *gnocchi*). According to the stage at which the truffle is served, it is usually partnered either by a Dolcetto, or a weightier Barbera or Barolo. (The black truffle, incidentally, which the Piedmontese do not rate, is the pride of Umbria and the Marches where, in addition to being grated over pasta, it is often used with eggs (and stored with them to give them its flavour.)

The Piedmontese love of strong flavours is typified in dishes such as *bagna cauda*, a pungent mixture of olive oil, garlic and anchovy, served hot (hence its name, 'hot bath'), into which you dip crunchy raw vegetables (including, traditionally, the bitter cardoon). *Bollito misto*, another potent dish, is a formidable array of boiled meats cooked together, and served with distinctly sharp sauces, notably 'bagnet verd', the local version of *salsa verde*.

Piedmont shares with Tuscany, another home of big red wines, a liking for roast kid as well as game, including wild boar and hare and, more especially in Piedmont, venison. But Tuscan cooking is generally a touch gentler in its flavours, as are most of its red wines – even the dark and chunky Brunello di Montalcino from south of the Chianti region, made from a particularly dark and thick-skinned clone of the Sangiovese grape which dominates the entire region, occasionally ably assisted by the international superstar Cabernet Sauvignon.

Tuscany has its stews, but the emphasis is on the plain roasting or grilling of its magnificent meat: famously 'bistecca alla fiorentina' legendary beef from the Val di Chiana to the south of Florence. The nearest familiar cut to this would be a T-bone, but the *bistecca* is especially tender and so big that it is served to two or three people, grilled as simply as possible, with olive oil and salt. A Chianti Classico *riserva* is a perfect partner, but not the only one, and not even the only Tuscan one. The equally simple spit roasting of small birds is another firm favourite (of neighbouring Umbria, too), if not a very politically correct one.

Tuscany is also the region best known for its olive oil, which is so admired in the area that the very best is usually eaten on its own with the distinctive salt-free Tuscan bread. A variation is the *bruschetta*, olive oil poured on bread that has been lightly grilled and rubbed with garlic – and now found in corrupt forms in fashionable restaurants across the globe.

PAPPARDELLE ALLA LEPRE

Tuscany's Sangiovese wines go extremely well with the rich hare (*lepre*) sauce but, as pasta (in this case *pappardelle*) is a preamble to the main course, it is not the very best wines which are served – Chianti, but not of *riserva* age and quality, or Rosso di Montalcino rather than Brunello. As a main course (very unItalian), with proportionately more sauce, it can take a bigger wine, even a Brunello. It also suits many other medium- to full-bodied, flavoursome reds, from Teroldego Rotaliano to Aglianico del Vulture, burgundy to Chilean Syrah.

BRASATO AL BAROLO

The best known of Piedmont's robust stews makes it plain from its name which wine should be drunk with it and this is a beef dish for showing off distinguished, old Barolos. Barbaresco isn't considered quite muscular enough, but for those who don't drink Piedmontese reds everyday it is very satisfactory. Other reds with the character to cope include Brunello di Montalcino, Hermitage and other Rhônes, Barossa Shirazes, Australian and California Cabernets, Provence reds and Spain's Toro.

BAGNA CAUDA

Either of two red wines is traditionally served with *bagna cauda*: Freisa, a fresh, slightly astringent and gently fizzy wine; or Barbera, a medium-bodied, still one. Though quite different in style, they share two features: acidity, which cuts through the richness of the garlicky oil; and low tannin, so that there is no clash with the anchovy or the bitterness of the cardoons. A red Vinho Verde might do the same job, but, that aside, it is easier to find alternatives among whites and rosés. German Riesling *Halbtrocken* is one; herby Provence rosé another.

RIBOLLITA

This is a substantial, rustic, bread-thickened, bean and black cabbage soup that is well suited to simple, young Chianti, but also suits Valpolicella, young Spanish Tempranillo and reds from both Languedoc and Roussillon.

CANTUCCI

Cantucci are hard, sweet macaroons designed for eating with (and dipping into) Tuscany's sweet Vin Santo, a strong, barrel-aged wine made from semi-dried grapes. Setúbal Moscatel, sweet sherry, Madeira or Tokay would make reasonable substitutes, but that would be to miss the point – which is the Vin Santo.

EMILIA-ROMAGNA & ROME

Tuscan cooking is far removed from that of northern neighbour Emilia-Romagna. Centred on Bologna, this is traditionally the home of the most opulent cooking in Italy. Cream is used lavishly, as is meat (*pace* Bolognese sauce) and every part of the pig is pressed – often literally – into service. The innumerable salamis and sausages range from the bland pink *mortadella* to specimens like the heavyweight *cotecchino* and *zampone di Modena* (a stuffed pig's trotter), both of which have a richness of texture that sets them worlds apart from even the grandest 'sausage'. Meaty main courses are often cooked with Modena's famous balsamic vinegar. There is air-dried Parma ham – the real thing, from the Langhirano Valley – and there is parmesan cheese – again, the real thing from Parma, properly called Parmigiano Reggiano, as opposed to closely related Grana Padana from the Po Valley.

Just as the cuisine differs, so do the wines. In many ways the food takes centre stage and the wines are the support cast. Emilia Romagna doesn't make serious, muscular reds which might compete indigestibly with the food. It makes smooth, easy-going Sangiovese di Romagna, and none too complex whites like Albana di Romagna (not a very distinguished wine, despite its official classification), and above all it makes Lambrusco. True Lambrusco is a million miles from the commercial export version. It is a lively, fizzing, high-acid red, usually dry, which cuts through and washes down the rich food. A perfect symbiotic relationship.

One place in Italy where the symbiotic food and wine relationship does not seem to exist today is Latium. Romans, as many Italians will tell you, are a law unto themselves, and it is as true of their food and wine. An astonishing number of dishes are distinguished, simply and arrogantly, by the phrase '*alla romana*'. A number of Roman specialities cry out for big red wines, but most of Latium's wine is white and there are hardly any reds of distinction (Torre Ercolana is a rare exception). In the past, Latium's white wines were at least more characterful, but today, certainly, not very interesting whites (Frascati, Est! Est!! Est!!!, etc) predominate.

The dishes for which these wines seem such a curious mismatch include the 'noblest Roman of all', *coda alla vaccinara*, a hearty oxtail casserole with wine, celery, onions, carrots and tomatoes, and *manzo garofolato*, beef braised with cloves. As if not already sturdy enough, both these specialities can be, and are, eaten with tripe rather than pasta.

Another great Roman passion is artichoke, which presents problems of its own to the wine drinker (*see* Tricky Ingredients, page 16). In *carciofi alla romana*, mint (which also flavours tripe in a typical Roman recipe, '*trippa alla romana*', naturally), makes its presence felt in artichokes stuffed with chopped mint, parsley and garlic. But many Romans will make a special visit to the site of the old Jewish ghetto, in the shade of the Theatre of Marcellus, to eat *carciofi all giudea* – flattened and deep-fried artichokes.

Yet Romans do resemble other Italians in their simple treatment of meat: *abbacchio*, for example, at Easter (milk-fed lamb of which one appears to eat half the tiny carcass), or *capretto*, kid – both roasted with rosemary. Lucky diners get to drink one of the few good reds, but for the rest it is white – or a brave excursion into the wines of another region.

Classic Combinations

PARMA HAM WITH FIGS

The traditional partner for Parma ham with figs (or melon) is Malvasia dei Colli di Parma, a soft, gently fizzy white – dry or medium-sweet. On home ground the combination works, but further afield it can be improved upon. Fine German Mosel is perfect. Australian Riesling is a shade obtrusive, but Australian Colombard works well; so do Vin de Pays des Cotes de Gascogne and Pinot Grigio dei Colli Orientali. Try Parma ham alone with lesser white burgundies (St-Veran, Montagny), Beaujolais-Villages, Gamay de Touraine and light Barbera.

COTECCHINO WITH LENTILS

Authentic sharp, dry red Lambrusco is a perfect contrast to this rich, fatty sausage, served with lentils and *salsa verde*, but a Beaujolais *cru* (Fleurie, Brouilly, or Morgon) is just as successful and sparkling red Shiraz is good. Matching weight with weight, California and Barossa Rhône blends work well and just have the edge over Zinfandel which is a touch fruity. Other alternatives are southern Italian reds and full-bodied, savoury whites such as Châteauneuf-du-Pape.

PARMESAN

The speciality that really deserves a deeper, more complex red than Emilia-Romagna provides is cheese. Fortunately, neighbouring Veneto (home of Grana Padana) has the answer in Recioto della Valpolicella – both dry (Amarone) and sweet (Amabile) – and the Bolognese people have no compunction about raiding the Veneto cellar. As for alternatives, young parmesan is very wine-friendly (*see* page 23) – happy with Bulgarian Cabernet, Hermitage, Chianti, Chablis Grand Cru...

ARTICHOKES ALLA ROMANA

Artichokes are notoriously difficult to match (*see* page 16) and, though the mint and parsley in this dish are more help than hindrance, none of Latium's whites is sharp enough. When in Rome, go for the youngest, freshest white; elsewhere, the crispest Sauvignon, Hungarian or modern Greek white.

SPAGHETTI ALLA CARBONARA

One of Roman gastronomy's few secure partnerships is this spaghetti and egg dish with Frascati Superiore Secco. Other local whites will do, as will many, young, unoaked Italian whites. White Mâcon is a useful French option. Reds need to be simple and low tannin – Bardolino or light Barbera.

THE SOUTH, COASTS & ISLANDS

*I*n the south, below Naples, the large quantities of meat eaten further north give way to a diet containing far more vegetables (aubergines, broccoli, courgettes, peppers, tomatoes and so on) and fresh cheeses made variously from buffalo, sheep, goat and cow's milk (*mozzarella*, *provolone*, *pecorino* and ricotta). Cooking in the south is with olive oil, enhanced by the piquant flavours of capers, olives and abundant fresh herbs. Central Italy combines elements of both – a little less rich and hearty than the north, but more sumptuous than the south.

The islands are different again. Sicilian cooking, with its many influences – Greek, Roman, Arab and Spanish among them – is fascinatingly varied and ingenious. The ingredients are largely those of the southern Italian mainland, but with more nuts and dried fruit (used in savoury dishes as well as sweet), together with the candied peels and honey lavished on the legendary pastries and ice-creams. Quite apart from Marsala in its sweet versions, Sicily has some luscious sweet wines with which to enjoy these – Moscato di Pantelleria above all.

A particular quirk of Sicilian cooking, and a product of the traditional poverty of the majority living in feudal conditions under an aristocratic elite, is a love of creating dishes made of fish (cheap and abundant) that are made to resemble meat (expensive and scarce). As well as producing intriguing looking dishes, this practice leads to some acute combinations of flavour: *beccaficcu*, for example, is made of sardines split and shaped to look like the small birds of the same name – fig-eaters, a delicacy of the very rich since Roman times – and they are stuffed, as the birds might be, with raisins and pine nuts. And Sicily has the wines for such food. Despite the southerly latitude, more white is produced than red (as is also the case in Sardinia) and from some unusual indigenous grape varieties such as Cataratto (but these are seldom named on labels). They are essentially modern wines – the islands of Sicily and Sardinia traditionally made strong, often fortified, wines – but they suit the food. The whites are zesty and aromatic; the reds are warmly fruity and spicy with a characteristic bitter twist.

Sardinia's traditional cooking is less distinctive, more rustic and more meat-based (lamb, pork, kid) than Sicilian. It, too, has some interesting, serious reds – notably Carignano del Sulcis *riserva* – but overall it has moved even further down the light white road and these crisp whites do suit the seafood, especially the better Vermentinos.

Both islands inevitably share with all Italy's coastal regions a natural affinity with the sea, exploiting the abundant fish and seafood of the Mediterranean. Every coastal area has its own particular seafood soup or stew – and wine to go with it. Liguria has its Vermentino; the Veneto has any number of crisp dry whites – Soave, Bianco di Custoza, Pinot Grigio, Pinot Bianco – as well as light red Bardolino which can be drunk with fish; the Marches have Verdicchio; and even red wine strongholds such as Tuscany have their selection of *bianchi*.

CAPONATA

In this, the Italian answer to *ratatouille*, aubergines, onions, capers, celery, tomatoes and olives are stewed in olive oil, and vinegar is added to give typically Sicilian piquancy. Almost any young, fresh Sicilian white wine makes an acceptable match (most of the best are sold under brand rather than regional names), but a glass of cool Cerasuolo di Vittoria, a light-coloured, cherry-scented red, makes a more interesting combination. Outside Sicily, the intensity of New Zealand Sauvignon provides an ideal complement.

BECCAFICCU

The oiliness of sardines in this classic Sicilian dish is partly counteracted by the raisin, anchovy and pinenut stuffing, but it nonetheless needs a white wine with crisp acidity. Again, almost any of the island's whites will do – so long as they are lively. Good non-Sicilian partners include Timorasso (a rare Piedmont grape), Muscadet *sur lie*, dry Vinho Verde, Sauvignon (Loire, New Zealand and Chilean).

CASSATA

The original *cassata* is not an ice-cream but a sponge cake filled with ricotta, candied-fruit and chocolate. Sweet Marsala

Superiore is too heavy to be a real success, but Moscato di Pantelleria Passito (from the island of Pantelleria, off Sicily), though powerful, has an apricot character that tunes in naturally with *cassata*. Other Muscats also go well, including *vins doux naturels* such as Muscat de Frontignan, Asti and California and Australian Orange Muscats.

PASTA CON BOTTARGA

Bottarga, the dried eggs of grey mullet, is a Sardinian speciality of pungent, salty intensity. Whether served with pasta or in salad, the traditional accompaniment is Vernaccia di Oristano, an idiosyncratic sherry-like wine. Manzanilla sherry is the obvious substitute overseas, but dry Vinho Verde and Pouilly-Fumé and Sancerre are equally successful.

PORCEDDU

In Sardinia suckling pig is spit-roasted with herbs and aromatic myrtle leaves and goes very well with the ripe, velvety Carignano del Sulcis. A great many other red wines (including Pinot Noirs, Rioja and Bairrada) go with *porceddu*, as they do generally with roast pork, although care needs to be taken here not to overwhelm the flavour. Opulent white burgundy, such as Meursault, is another alternative.

Spain

Throughout her history, Spain has been the gateway to Europe for all sorts of curious and unknown foodstuffs. The Moorish conquest brought with it almond and citrus groves, rice fields and figs. (Who can now imagine Spain without oranges? Or without *paella*?) Then, after the discovery of the New World, the first chocolate, tomatoes, and peppers – both hot and sweet – that Europe had ever seen were unloaded here. To this day chocolate in Catalonia is used more as a savoury than as a sweet ingredient: it flavours meat dishes in a manner reminiscent of Mexican cooking. (Fruit, both fresh and dried, is another distinctive feature of Catalan savoury dishes.)

All round the coast, Spain boasts superb seafood. In the interior, where the land rises to the hot, dry central plateau, meat is the order of the day – often lamb, pork or game, combined in stews bulked out with beans and other vegetables and requiring long and careful simmering. Nowhere are rich sauces used: Spanish cooking is essentially peasant food, lavish where supplies are plentiful but wasting nothing. *Migas*, or crumbs, a classic dish from the centre of the country, consists of fried breadcrumbs with garlic and green peppers – but served with sausages, bacon, olives and vegetables.

Flavoursome rice dishes – of which *paella* is merely the best-known – are popular more or less throughout the country and they are particularly well suited to oaky white wines of the kind that Spain, especially Rioja, has traditionally excelled at. Adding saffron to a rice dish will, however, tip the scales in favour of a dry rosé (*rosado*); fortunately this is another style of wine which Spain does well, particularly in Navarra.

Sausages are another of Spain's most typical products.

There are sausages in every province, and *chorizo*, flavoured with hot red pimento, is everywhere, too. There are about 50 recognized types, excluding family recipes, and while parts of Andalucia may favour wild boar, and Pamplona beef, the long-legged, black Iberian pig is the usual source. The traditional three-day *matanza*, or pig-killing, by which every farmhouse sought to provide itself with sufficient preserved meat to last the winter, still goes on in rural areas. The animal's hind legs are much prized: they are hung up to cure and after nine months have become *jamon serrano*, the delicious and expensive raw ham, at its best from mountain regions, that is in demand all over the country and abroad.

The wines, like the food, can be very roughly divided into those that come from the coastal regions and those from the interior. Most of the best whites are from areas within range of the sea and its harvest of hake, clams, mussels and the rest; further inland, where fish is often limited to salt cod, or *bacalao*, the often rustic reds come into their own. Bear in mind, though, that in most of Spain there is still relatively little emphasis on matching the right wine to the right food. You drink the local wine, whatever that happens to be: if that means red wine with fish, so be it – it is certainly not thought odd, any more than it is thought odd to drink sherry all through a meal in and around the coastal town of Jerez (from which sherry comes and from which the name sherry derives). Here, you start with a *fino* or *manzanilla*, the pale dry sherry styles, and then, if the meal includes a meat course, probably progress to a full-bodied, mature, dry *amontillado* or *oloroso*. The latter might then accompany some Manchego, or similar ewe's milk cheese, before sweet sherries are brought on to go with the puddings.

ANDALUCIA & CATALONIA

Spain's ad hoc approach to food and wine has nevertheless produced some perfect marriages. The lightest, most refined sherries of Andalucia, *fino* and *manzanilla*, take the place of red or white wine with the tapas for which the region is famous, and can continue into the meal proper. Tapas can indeed be the highlight of the meal, but if you have the good fortune to be in a seaside restaurant in Cádiz or Sanlúcar, the speciality will be fried fish, often tiny soles caught that morning.

You can certainly eat meat in Andalucia, but fish is more plentiful. Meat was traditionally expensive and kept for special occasions, with slices of *chorizo* being used to flavour more everyday dishes. Recipes tend to be simple, but ingredients are of good quality – as is the ubiquitous *gazpacho*. Vegetables are taken very seriously indeed. There is wild asparagus, several sorts of pepper, tiny local peas and broad beans, and lots of artichokes: look for *alcauciles con chicharros* (artichoke and fresh pea stew) at Easter.

Almonds are another Andalucian feature. They appear in white *gazpacho* (with bread, garlic, vinegar and olive oil) and in puddings and pastries – especially in the company of egg yolks. *Tocinos de cielo*, custard tarts, are the most famous way of using up yolks after the whites have been used for fining wine – and are a good excuse for a glass of *oloroso dolce*, long-matured sweet sherry, or even an ultra-sweet, raisiny PX, from Pedro Ximénez grapes.

Not only is Catalonia the homeland of sparkling Cava, but it has an altogether greater variety of wines than anywhere else in Spain: Penedès, Alella and Conca de Barberá have dry dry whites that range from light to full-bodied, together with some fine reds; Priorato and Tarragona are noted for their particularly powerful reds and there is even a small amount of good late-harvest sweet white. The grape varieties in this most European part of Spain range from the indigenous, like Parellada and Xarel-lo for whites and Tempranillo, Cariñena and Garnacha for reds, to international names like Cabernet Sauvignon, Merlot, Chardonnay, Sauvignon, Pinot Noir and Gewürztraminer – all perfectly appropriate to a cuisine which spans the seafood of the coast to game, chicken, pork and goat of the mountainous interior.

All Catalan cooking has a Mediterranean air. Olives and olive oil, onions and tomatoes, garlic, rosemary, oregano, bay and thyme are vital ingredients, often joined by dried fruits like prunes or raisins and pine nuts ('*a la Catalana*'). In Tarragona almonds are a favourite and are often made into a thick sauce with garlic, tomatoes, red peppers and bread – *romesco* sauce – which appears with many fish dishes. *Allioli*, a seasoning of crushed garlic and olive oil, in Catalonia may be spiked with a few drops of orange juice. *Sofrito* – tomato and onion cooked gently and slowly in olive oil – is another basic of numerous recipes.

The most elaborate manifestation of Catalan cooking sums up the contradictions of the land. Ampurdán's *mar y montana* (sea and mountain; surf 'n' turf seems an inadequate translation) can combine chicken, cockerel's feet, pig's ears and feet, snails, cuttlefish, lobster, sausage, fruit, vegetables and all sorts of other flavours. *Langosta con pollo* (lobster with chicken) is a more refined version in which the lobster's final role is simply as sauce.

TAPAS

Tapas can be the highlight of the meal in Andalucia. They come in an astonishing variety, from thin slices of peppery *chorizo*, the freshest of prawns, giant green olives and slivers of manchego to scrambled eggs with shrimps or mushrooms (*huevos revueltos*), tortilla, slices of dried tuna (*mojama*) and whole baby red mullet (*salmonetes*). Nothing handles the varied, salty, savoury flavours of tapas so well as *fino* and *manzanilla*, but a crisp, dry rosé from Navarra or Provence is a convenient compromise. Suitable whites must be similarly constituted, tangy but not aggressive or too ripely fruity – eg Sancerre, Penedès and South African Sauvignons, Chablis and Muscadet *sur lie*.

GAZPACHO

Andalucia's most famous culinary gift to the world is *gazpacho*, but the name is given to two quite different cold soups: the tomato-based one, and the more traditional white *gazpacho*. The classic partner for both is *fino* or *manzanilla*, but fresh Sauvignon (Rueda, Penedès, Chile, New Zealand) goes well with tomato *gazpacho*. Unoaked white Rioja, Soave and Bourgogne Aligoté go with white.

KIDNEYS IN SHERRY SAUCE

Riñones al Jerez may come as tapas, or be eaten as an independent course, in which case the accompanying sherry might be dry *amontillado*. For those tiring of sherry, Rioja *crianza* is a good match, as are Dolcetto and Barbera from Piedmont or a *cru* Beaujolais.

RABBIT COOKED WITH WINE AND HERBS

In this typical Catalan dish, rabbit is marinated and cooked in red wine and herbs and flavoured and enriched with cinnamon, tomatoes, chocolate and almonds. The Tempranillo grape, especially good in Penedès and Costers del Segre, is a very good partner, as is Cabernet Sauvignon grown in the same areas. Cabernet Sauvignons from elsewhere (Australia, Languedoc, Romania) also work well, as do Rioja Reserva, Ribera del Duero and Valpolicella Classico.

BACALAO LA CATALANA

Salt cod is eaten throughout Spain with local white or red. Here it is added to *sofrito*, with pine nuts and raisins. Many fresh, young Catalan whites are acceptable partners, but ideally it merits white with more flavour – a traditional white Rioja or oaked Australian Semillon – or young Tempranillo, Chinon or red Sancerre.

THE NORTH

This covers a vast area, from the lush green hills of Galicia, to the raw, exposed land around Madrid, and up again to the Basque country and the fertile foothills of the Pyrenees. In the centre of Spain, where the weather either bakes or freezes, the most famous representative of a dish designed to make meat and game go a long way is *cocido madrileño*, a three-course meal all cooked in one pot: the broth served first, then the vegetables, then the meats.

Further north the soil is more fertile: butter and lard are used more widely and vegetables, combined in an array of inventive dishes, can form the basis of a meal, particularly along the Ebro Valley in Navarra. Asparagus or artichokes may be served with a simple vinaigrette and a white wine wine from Rueda or Rioja; but there are rustic stews as well, like *caldereta ribereña*, combining game or river fish with whatever vegetables are available, according to season.

When it comes to meat, this is sheep country. Lamb is a natural partner for red Rioja and for Ribera del Duero from further west. The latter is the more powerful, a deep, intense wine that needs some years to mature. Rioja – for years Spain's most famous quality table wine – can, at its best (*reserva* and *gran reserva* categories), age to the sort of complexity and delicacy that needs only the most simply-cooked lamb to flatter it, but is more often to be found in less exalted, more everyday forms. Tempranillo is the principal red grape (as it is in Ribera del Duero, although there called Tinto Fino); Viura, Malvasia and Garnacha Blanco are blended for the whites, the traditional oak-influenced style of which is sturdy enough for most local vegetable dishes.

Just as the wines of Rioja influence the style of winemaking in the neighbouring region of Navarra, so too does the cooking style of Navarra spill over into Rioja. The red peppers for which Navarra is well known will be found (often in conjunction with *chorizo*) in anything made 'a la riojana' and the gently oaky, sweetly fruity red wines of Rioja, especially the *crianzas*, are tailor-made for such dishes (as are Navarra's Rioja-like Tempranillo *crianzas*).

The Basque country likes strong, hot flavours. There is *pipperada* (eggs and peppers); *bacalao*, dried and salted cod; baby eels cooked in hot (in both senses of the word) olive oil and chillies; and the blackest squid in its own ink to be found anywhere. Basque wine, predominantly white, manages to cope with such flavours by being light, often fizzy and very sharp. Further west, where fish abounds along the coast, the best wines are the aromatic, zesty whites of Galicia, of which Albariño is the most highly aromatic, famous, fashionable and inevitably expensive. The visitor can either pay the high prices asked for Albariño, or choose one of the cheaper, more modestly aromatic wines from the Ribeiro region. The reds of the area are highly acidic and somewhat earthy – so they suit the fish, as well as the distinctive Basque flavours, but they can come as a bit of a shock to the uninitiated.

PIPPERADA

Scrambled eggs, peppers and *Jambon de Bayonne* is not an easy combination for wine. Most Chacolí, the local Basque wine, is white, slightly fizzy and rather thin and sharp: it may go with *pipperada*, but it is something of an acquired taste. A more appealing marriage is with a *rosado* from neighbouring Navarra. Rosés from France's Southwest (eg Béarn) work in the same way, and dry Australian Rieslings make an attractive contrast.

STUFFED CRAB

Crab is a favourite all along the north coasts. In this Galician dish the crab meat is mixed with onions, garlic, tomatoes and parsley, covered with breadcrumbs and cheese and baked. Albariño is the Galician accompaniment (as it is with all shellfish), but many dry whites work, including Sauvignons, Viogniers and unoaked Chardonnays.

SNAILS WITH, TOMATOES, PEPPERS AND CHILLIS

This is a typically piquant Navarran dish for which the very good local *rosados* are ideal. Southern French rosés (Gascon and Mediterranean) can be substituted, but pink wine is not *de rigueur*. Red Navarra *crianza* and young Spanish Tempranillo, Roussillon and reds from individual Côtes du Rhône villages can all handle the chilli without overwhelming the snails.

COCIDO MADRILENO

Cocido Madrileno is one of many Spanish variations on the traditional substantial stew theme – combining vegetables, chickpeas, cured ham, sausage, marrow, meat, game or poultry. It cries out for one of the many robust local reds. The muscular and aptly named Toro is ideal, while Ribera del Duero is the choice for slightly more refined versions of the dish. California Zinfandel, Australian Shiraz, Châteauneuf-du-Pape, Corbières, Madiran and Alentejo are some of the many full-bodied alternatives.

ESCABECHE

Escabeche originated on the coast as a way of preserving fish in lemon or vinegar. Having moved inland, it began to be applied to poultry and rabbit too. Because of the acidity of the marinade-come-cooking liquid, white wine is essential: young, unoaked Rioja usually copes adequately, Galician whites rather better. Fine German Riesling *Kabinett* and pungent Sauvignons – New Zealand, Chilean, Loire – are a good alternative.

Portugal

To visit this westernmost part of Europe is to go back in time. Food is strictly seasonal; chosen, weighed and wrapped in small shops, pungent with the smell of dried cod and hung with dried beans, almost untouched by modern outside influences. It is earthy peasant food, short on sauces and born of the need to make sparse ingredients go a long way: stews may be thickened with pig's blood and stretched with *chouriço.* Yet the Moorish conquest and Portugal's colonization of places like Goa and Brazil have left their mark and, though the food is often spicier than Spain's, there is a similar taste for almonds and sticky egg puddings.

The wines are often as rustic as the food and are made to be drunk with it, not separately. The traditional taste is for reds well aged in old oak barrels and for oily, rather oxidized whites. These are as uncompromising as the local food and match its hearty flavours, but, unlike the food, they are increasingly being modernized and spruced up for export.

To see how vivid can be the matches of Portuguese food and wine, then, you really need to go there. Vinho Verde is a familiar name abroad, yet the native version – acidic, bone dry and usually red into the bargain – has little in common with the bland, slightly sweetened exported versions. But these cheek-pinchingly astringent, slightly fizzy reds do go with local specialities – with *bacalhau*, the salt cod that is a daily staple in the north and popular everywhere (there are said to be 365 ways of cooking *bacalhau*, though that is probably an underestimate), with *caldo verde* and with the copious amounts of olive oil.

All around the coast there are squid, hake, tuna and sardines, sardines and more sardines. All need wines with flavour and acidity and in much of the country these attributes are to be found in the reds as well as in the whites. There is little importance attached here to matching food and wine: local wine with local food is the rule, and it works.

This of course begs the question of port – the sweet fortified wine largely designed by and for the British. But the Portuguese have made some styles their own. They favour nutty wood-matured tawnies and *colheitas* (tawnies from a single vintage), rather than strapping, plummy, bottle-matured vintage styles beloved by the British. And the Portuguese drink their wood-aged ports after meals or with creamy cheese served with quince jam (*marmelada*).

In the south the food is more aromatic and spicy. Coriander is added with a generous hand, often seasoning the bread-based dishes found in the wheat-growing country of Alentejo. *Açordas* – bread-thickened soups – are made all over the province. Cold *gaspatcho* (sic) is also a speciality, as is a whole range of dishes employing *migas*, or breadcrumbs.

In the Algarve the food becomes lighter. Fish and shellfish are everywhere, sometimes simply grilled or stewed, or mixed with various meats in a cooking vessel called a *cataplana*, with a hinged lid to seal in all the flavours. Clams and pork are a favourite combination.

The south of Portugal has less of a tradition of quality wine than the north. With a few honorable exceptions it is everyday and unpretentious, but the reds at least can be appealing in a vividly fruity way, and all of it can be excellent value. If in doubt about colour, stick to the reds: quality is more consistent and they match the spices and garlic of the stews well.

GRILLED SARDINES

Sardines, eaten the length of Portugal, are still much appreciated at their simplest: grilled and served with lemon and a glass of local wine. Vinho Verde is the best known of these, although traditionally it was more likely to be the red version (even more astringent than the white). Dry white Vinho Verde stands the test of time. Other satisfactory partners for this oily fish include white Gaillac, Mauzac *vins de pays* and the rare Piedmontese Timorasso.

CALDO VERDE

Potato and cabbage soup, generally pepped up with *chouriço*, Portugal's answer to *chorizo*, is eaten all over the north. Again, red Vinho Verde would be a typical accompaniment, but warmly fruity, spicy reds from Alentejo in the south are likely to find more friends. White wines also go well with this soup, such as herby white Bairradas and, in a quite different vein, oaked Chardonnays.

BACALHAU

Though infinitely varied, all Portuguese *bacalhau* (salt cod) dishes tend to be rich in olive oil – and the wine, red or white, must be able to cope. The traditional Portuguese choice was between young and astringent (Vinho Verde) or old and rather oxidized (everything else). Among modern wines, oaked white Bairrada *reserva* works well, but the best all-rounder is Chablis, preferably lightly oaked *premier cru*. Red Sancerre is also good and red Rioja *crianza* and oaked Australian Semillon often work.

SUCKLING PIG

Leitão assado, roast suckling pig, is a speciality of central Portugal where red Bairrada, with its full, peppery, blackberry flavours, makes an excellent accompaniment. Red table wines from the Douro (port country) and Alentejo also go well, as do many other reds – including Rioja *reserva*, burgundy and Beaujolais *crus*. Rich white burgundy and top California Chardonnay are complementary whites.

PUDIM FLAM

Pudim flam, a *crème caramel*, is the most famous of Portugal's rich, egg-yolk puddings. Moscatel de Setúbal, an aged fortified wine from near Lisbon with a flavour of orange marmalade, is a classic match. French *vins doux naturels* (Muscat de Beaumes-de-Venise, etc) make a good substitute, as do botrytised Australian Semillons and, for the very sweet-toothed, Spain's raisiny PX sherry.

Germany

If German food had a symbol, it would be the pig. The porker occupies pride of place in the cooking of almost every region, and there can be nowhere in Germany where *wurst*, or sausages, are not found in a dozen different forms. Behind it (quite a long way behind) would be its country cousin, the wild boar, still hunted in Germany's forests, venison, game of all sorts, and beef cattle. And while Germany is above all a meat-eating country, there are pike, carp, trout and other fish; and from the Baltic and North seas there are herrings, shellfish, sole, turbot and others.

Vegetables? The cabbage reigns supreme, more often than not shredded and pickled into *sauerkraut*. Add caraway seeds to this palette of ingredients, and plenty of fresh herbs, plus a liking for fruit with meat, and the basic sweet-and-sour flavours of German cuisine begin to emerge. If food can be smoked, so much the better; Germans like their dishes to taste strong and piquant. And quantities are generous: in a German restaurant, a platter of venison with pears and cranberries that looks as if it is intended for the whole table really is just for you. What is more, the meat will be of such high quality, and cooked to such perfection, that you will probably eat more of it than you intended. Then you will see the point of another Germany speciality: a shot of fruit brandy, Kirschwasser (from cherries), Himbeergeist (from raspberries) or, in the north, aquavit, to wash it all down.

Few wines can handle these vigorous sweet-and-savoury combinations. But German wine has a style found nowhere else – a particular knife-edge balance of honeyed sweetness and acidity – that relishes this sort of food. It is hard to think of a national food and wine combination that is so perfect on its native soil, and so widely misunderstood outside it. German wines go admirably with food, but the wines in question are not the cheap bottles of sugar-water which have ruined Germany's reputation abroad, and the food is not the roast lamb beloved of so many countries further west. Instead it is the sweetness of pork, the creaminess of trout in a Riesling sauce with herbs, the tartness of red cabbage cooked with apples. Wines aged in new oak cannot handle these flavours. Instead Riesling – light and appley, or rich and minerally – demonstrates why it is the finest of German wine grapes, and grown in every wine region.

Riesling is not, however, the most planted grape: the export of large quantities of cheap blended wine has seen to that. As a general rule, the cheap blends contain no Riesling at all; so look for it on the label. The best of the other grapes are Silvaner (especially from Franken), Scheurebe, Pinot Gris (alias Grauburgunder or Ruländer – particularly Baden's), Pinot Blanc (or Weissburgunder) and, for reds, Pinot Noir (or Spätburgunder).

The complexities of German wine law can be daunting to the novice, but they do make it easier to find a wine to match a particular dish. There are 13 wine regions, but in a nutshell Rhine wines are bigger, especially those from the Rheingau, Pfalz and Nahe, Mosels lighter. Those from Baden and Franken in the south tend to be drier and (relatively speaking) slightly fatter. Baden is also the source of the most international-style reds. (Elsewhere reds can be sweetish and slightly jammy in flavour, which does at least help them to go with the local food.) Anything labelled *Trocken* will be dry, even searingly so; *Halbtrocken* means half-dry, or medium-dry. *Qualitätswein* is basic quality wine. Above that, in ascending order of sweetness, are *Kabinett* – often remarkably low in alcohol, wonderfully light and with a touch of sweetness; then *Spätlese* – generally good with savoury food, including rich goose and duck dishes; *Auslese* – sweet, and perfect with light, slightly tart apple desserts, but also a possibility with venison, goose or wild boar; then come the rich, very sweet *Beerenauslese*, *Trockenbeerenauslese* and *Eiswein* – which can be drunk with puddings, but are also delicious sipped alone after dinner.

However, for such a major wine producer, Germany has remarkably little of its land given over to the vine. Beer, on the other hand, is made everywhere. Beer-drinking regions (the north and the southeast) tend to have more strongly-flavoured food than the wine regions of the southwest. In the latter, the cuisine is more restrained, and wine is widely used in the cooking, just as beer features in recipes elsewhere. But while there is a difference between wine and beer country the real distinction is between north and south.

THE NORTH AND SOUTH

D umplings mark the north-south divide: in the north they are *klösse*, in the south, *knödel*. They may be made from potatoes, bread or flour and flavoured with *wurst*, bacon, cheese, cabbage, plums or just about anything else. *Spätzle* are the smallest, and come from Swabia, but every region has its own, just as it has its own sausages. There are *bratwurst*, *blutwurst* (blood sausages), *rindwurst* (from beef), *liverwurst* and many others, not least Frankfurters. Below the 'Weisswurst line' – a boundary plotted with sausages – there are white Bavarian ones made from veal, brains and sweetbreads, a taste for which has yet to cross the River Main.

Generally, in the north the food is at its most solid. There is excellent sea fish: mostly consumed locally, with the exception of herrings, which are often marinated, salted or smoked before finding their way inland. (There is no wine that can be drunk very pleasurably with a marinated herring. It is probably better to stick to beer or aquavit.) Ham and sausages are smoked, and there is excellent beef and poultry, too. Some of the most notable dishes come from the rich Hanseatic cities of Hamburg, Bremen and Lübeck: Hamburg's *stubenküken* (spring chicken), for example, is simply served on fried bread, or stuffed with the livers, breadcrumbs and herbs.

There is an urban polish to this food that makes it stand out from the more basic dishes of the surroundings, and that makes the cities meccas for lovers of wine. For one thing, the strong seasonings (including lots of sugar) used in much north German food are applied with a lighter hand; for another, the cellars of Bremen and Lübeck were long used for ageing red Bordeaux before it was sent on to Russia, giving rise to a tradition of connoisseurship that still persists. No wine is made locally, but, in common with other places with a history of wine trading, there is good wine to be had.

In the wine country of the south the food is at its lightest. There are delicate soups and sauces made from the first green herbs of spring, river fish cooked in the local Riesling and *zweibelkuchen*, tarts packed with onion and egg-and-bacon custard. In Bavaria food is much more beer-based, although a good, rich Pfalz, Rheingau, or Baden white should have no trouble with a dish like *leberknödel* (beef liver dumplings), usually served with broth. (There may also be chopped spleen mixed in: they are fond of offal in the south, and Bavarians fonder than most.)

But it is in Baden that Germany's 'haute cuisine' is based. Switzerland is a neighbour, as is France's Alsace, and snails, frogs legs, salads of fresh, young dandelion leaves, excellent white asparagus and refined fish dishes all abound. Cream and butter are used, rather than the lard and bacon fat of elsewhere, and, while the wines here lose none of their German character, they add to it a touch of French gloss. The grapes of the Pinot family found in Alsace also excel here and may even be given French-style new oak barrel-ageing. For the biggest surprise of all, though, try real Black Forest gateau. It is to the versions found abroad as Rheingau Riesling is to Liebfraumilch.

Classic Combinations

RED CABBAGE WITH SAUSAGES

This is a solid, flavoursome and comforting dish of red cabbage slowly cooked with red wine, apples, smoked bacon, frankfurters and a mixture of other smoked, fresh and garlic sausages. The best Baden Spätburgunder is easily generously flavoured enough to partner this dish, but it is also one that white wines from the Pfalz can often cope with. New World Pinot Noirs are a good alternative, as is red Zinfandel, Beaujolais *cru* and Australian Shiraz.

EELS WITH GREEN SAUCE

A Mosel Riesling *Kabinett* cuts through the oiliness of eels and complements the creamy fresh herb sauce. No other wine is quite so winning, although Riesling *Kabinett* from other regions is very acceptable. Looking outside Germany, the choice is more difficult: Muscadet *sur lie*, Sancerre and Pouilly-Fumé (and their neighbours) and Austrian Riesling are probably the best answers.

HIMMEL ON AHD

Heaven and earth (*himmel on ahd*) is the name given to this dish of blood sausage with apple sauce and mashed potatoes (mixed together) and fried onions. It is popular in several regions, including the Rhinelands, and is exactly the kind of dish that the fuller, spicy Rieslings of the Pfalz handle well. Chardonnays from the New World are also very successful – more so than Australian Rieslings; red Sancerre is another good partner.

SAUERBRATEN

You can drink white wine with beef, but once it has been marinaded and pot roasted in red wine, as in *sauerbraten*, red is its best ally in the glass (provided vinegar in the recipe hasn't be added with a heavy hand). Baden Spätburgunder or Pfalz Dornfelder are the German choices, but there are any number of other reds to choose from – Beaujolais *crus*, Cabernet Sauvignons and Merlots, Barbaresco and other Nebbiolo wines, or Chianti Classico.

APPLE FRITTERS

Most puddings are too sweet for Riesling *Auslese*, but apple and cinnamon have an affinity with Riesling and these cinnamon-flavoured Rhineland fritters, which may include sweet wine in the batter, should be light and not too sweet. If they are very sweet, try a *Beerenauslese*. Austrian sweet wines, though fuller, make a good alternative, as do sweet Loires and Sauternes.

Switzerland

Switzerland poses several paradoxes to the lover of food and wine. First, it is a wealthy country with a much less wealthy past, so, while it produces the highest of *haute cuisine* and is home to some of the world's finest chefs and restaurants, its native food relies on simple, rustic ingredients like cheese, milk, pork, bread, potatoes and fruit. Second, it has not one culture but three: most Swiss speak German, but in the west French is spoken, and in part of the south, Italian. This in turn gives three cuisines and three styles of wine.

Swiss wine is roughly half white and half red, but Swiss taste is more emphatically for red, so much red is imported (Switzerland is a major importer of burgundy). The local wine is rarely great, but very agreeable with local food, even if the marriages are seldom celestial. Most of the white is Chasselas – light, dry, gently fruity or spicy, depending on the locality; most of the red is soft, fruity Pinot Noir. Acidity is apt to be low in both.

Cheese, as no one needs reminding, is very important in Switzerland. When used in soups, tarts, puddings, fritters or melted over the grated fried potatoes known as *rösti*, a light white or soft red is best. The richness of these foods is usually cut by the salads and fruit of which the Swiss are so fond: not just in *strudels* and tarts, but cherries with roast duck for example, or *schnitz und drunder* (pears and/or apples simmered with smoked pork and bacon), pickled plums with game and apple sauce with sausages.

Sausages are found everywhere, with the German-speaking cantons well in the lead in their love of them. The Swiss are far fonder of pork than beef, so that, while there is air-dried beef like *bundnerfleisch*, pork finds its way into *saucisson vaudois*, the Italianate *luganiga* (served with risotto), *schweinsbratwurst*, *salsiccia* and *saucisses au chou* or *au foie*.

The German-speaking part of Switzerland places less emphasis on wine than any other. Far from regarding Riesling-Silvaner (or Müller-Thurgau), the light, flowery wine most commonly grown here, as an automatic part of a meal, the German-speaking Swiss often drink beer, or even coffee, with everyday meals: wine is for special occasions.

If you want variety in Swiss wines, French-speaking Switzerland is the part of the country to head for – although variety is a relative term when 90 percent of the white wine is Chasselas and 99 percent of the red is Pinot Noir and Gamay. All the same, the Chasselas grape, found under a variety of names including Fendant, Perlan and Dorin, and place names like Chablais, Sion or Dézelay, does exhibit regional differences. Typically, it has a slightly spicy or nutty fruitiness and is a great match for the lake fish, like perch, that are so popular. More interesting, though difficult to find, are whites from Ermitage, herby Petite Arvine and, for very good sweet late-harvest wines, Malvoisie and Amigne. Commonly found red blends are Dôle (in the Valais) and Salvagnin (Vaud), which are good with *charcuterie*.

In the Italian-speaking part, Ticino, Lombardy and Piedmont are the parents of the food. Accordingly there is *polenta* and *gnocchi*, ravioli and risotto – and, to drink, Merlot, Merlot and more Merlot. Most of it is soft and fruity and accompanies the food with ease, although there are a few serious wines with more character. Find them if you can.

Classic Combinations

FRIED FILLETS OF PERCH

In French-speaking Switzerland, this is even more popular than the ubiquitous cheese fondue. Chasselas is the usual partner, but perch is worthy of more distinguished wine – Alsace or top Mosel Riesling, Puligny- or Chassagne-Montrachet, fine Pouilly-Fumé. Bourgogne Aligoté also goes very well.

CHEESE FONDUE

Cheese fondue is a truly national dish, though cheeses (Gruyère, Vacherin, Emmental, Fribourgeois, Apenzeller) vary with region. Unlike Raclette – usually served with red wine in the Valais – Chasselas (under various local names) is traditional with cheese fondue. It is certainly a satisfactory match, but there are good alternatives from beyond the Swiss borders – New World Chardonnay especially so. New World Sauvignons (not Fumés) and *premier cru* Chablis are close seconds and, though reds are less successful, Chinon goes quite well.

SAUSAGE FEASTS

The Swiss indulge their fondness for sausages in autumn sausage feasts which are accompanied by *sauerkraut*, *rösti*, potato salad, beetroot salad or *polenta*, depending on the region. The average, undemanding, fruity Swiss red deals with these quite well, although when *sauerkraut* is on the menu a white is more appropriate. Beaujolais-Villages or *cru*, Côtes du Rhône, Dolcetto, Barbera and Dornfelder are appropriate alternatives, or German Riesling *Halbtrocken* where *sauerkraut* features.

VENISON CASSEROLE WITH WILD MUSHROOMS

Furred game – red and roe deer, ibex, chamois and wild boar, often accompanied by *spätzli* – is much appreciated, but only the finest Swiss Blauburgunder (Pinot Noir), rare Syrah and Humagne Rouge have the structure and complexity to do it justice. Fortunately red burgundy and Northern Rhône do not have to travel far to Switzerland. Alternatives are New World Syrah, Mourvèdre or Cabernet.

BUNDNERFLEISCH

Served wafer-thin with a grinding of black pepper, air-dried beef is an appetizer from eastern Switzerland. A light-bodied Blauburgunder would be the local partner, but one of the lighter Beaujolais *crus* is even better. Light, north Italian red made from the almondy Schiava grape (eg Lago di Caldaro Classico, aka Kalteresee) and Hungarian Kékfrankos are alternatives.

Austria

ustria is a mere stub of its former self. When it was the hub of the Austro-Hungarian empire, people flooded into Vienna from Hungary, Slovenia, Romania, Poland, Italy, Moravia and Bohemia – and with them brought their tastes in food. After World War I all these territories were shaved off, leaving Austria smaller and land-locked. Its food, though, retains vivid memories of all those influences, grafted on to a cuisine that otherwise speaks solidly of cold European winters and the all-pervasive presence of the pig.

The most refined input came from Hungary: paprika is a favourite spice, particularly in the east, where there is good *gulyas* (goulash), and pancakes, also of Hungarian origin, are found everywhere, stuffed with fruit or meat or sliced into the many soups of which the Austrians are so fond. From even chillier Bohemia came the *knödel*, or dumplings, made from potato flour in the Waldviertel and wheat flour or bread elsewhere, and stuffed with every conceivable filling, from lungs (there is a national taste for offal) to *grammeln* (the crunchy bits obtained in lard-making) to cheese to plums.

Lard is in fact the fat of first choice in Austria. Smoked and spread thickly on a piece of black bread, it is the favoured accompaniment to drinks before dinner; white and neutral in flavour, it is the fat in which everything is fried, including puddings. Every part of the pig is accorded similar respect and a favourite meal at a *buschenschanke* (a country inn, serving homemade food and wine) is a plate of various parts of the pig, smoked, cooked, or turned into sausages of various sorts. There may be horseradish or apple sauce as an accompaniment, and the wine will be served in half-litre jugs to wash it down.

And wash it down it does. The flavours of Austria are less assertively sweet and sour than those of Germany, and they tend to have more refinement. The wines (since the climate is warmer) have more body and alcohol and are drier – unless, that is, they are very sweet. There are some very good reds made from local varieties (Blaufränkisch, Saint-Laurent and Zweigelt) as well as increasingly good Pinot Noir (or Blauburgunder) made in the French style, but the bulk of Austrian wine is white. Though there are some Chardonnays and Sauvignon Blancs, which frequently perform extremely well in the face of international competition, most Austrian wine is made from fairly aromatic varieties and is drunk very young, when its fruity acidity cuts through the fatty, floury richness of the food. There is less emphasis, therefore, than, say, in France or Germany on best vintages in Austria. Many Austrian wines, in particular those from the Grüner Veltliner (the predominant grape), Welschriesling, Traminer and Riesling-Silvaner (Müller-Thurgau) grapes are at their best young anyway, but the best Rieslings of the Wachau can certainly improve with age.

The sweetest wines, *Beerenauslese*, *Ausbruch* (an uniquely Austrian category), *Trockenbeerenauslese* and *Eiswein*, come almost entirely from Burgenland and are easily rich enough to cope with the sweet dumplings, *strudels* and pancakes. But, after a meal of soup, pork and fruit dumplings, the prospect of a digestif can be very welcome – and here, too, Austria excels, distilling greengages, quinces, juniper berries, apples, pears, rowanberries, etc.

Classic Combinations

APFELSTRUDEL

Most of Austria's famous cakes (*tortes*) are best left for coffee, but the *strudels* and sweet pancakes (*palatschinken*) are heaven-sent opportunities for drinking the luscious sweet wines made from grapes such as Bouvier, Traminer, Ruländer (Pinot Gris) and Welschriesling. With the most famous of all, the spicy, nutty *apfelstrudel*, an *Ausbruch* is ideal. *Beerenauslese* and *Trockenbeerenauslese* from Germany, New World botrytised and late-harvest Rieslings and sweet Loires all make good substitutes.

SCHINDLBRATEN

This dish of pork with hot paprika is typical of Burgenland's Hungarian-influenced repertoire. A peppery Grüner Veltliner matches the spice and cuts the richness of the pork, but Ruländer makes a more interesting match; Pinot Gris from Hungary and Alsace, and New World Chardonnays also work well. Among reds, Austria's Blaufränkisch handles paprika confidently and Rioja *crianza* copes quite well.

TAFELSPITZ

Tafelspitz, boiled silverside with root vegetables and herbs, would be easy to match to red wine, but for the fact that it is served with gherkins, rock salt and horseradish (the latter often grated into apple sauce). No wine really likes these flavours, but Austria's red Zweigelt deals with them reasonably well, as does Dolcetto. A Beaujolais *cru* will usually scrape through.

WEINER SCHNITZEL

An import from Italy, breaded veal excalope is Austria's favourite Sunday lunch dish, usually served with potato salad and a few glasses of Grüner Veltliner, or perhaps a more complex Weissburgunder. This, though, is the sort of simple dish that suits a variety of medium-bodied white wines – moderately aromatic or lightly oaked – and light-bodied reds, such as Sancerre, other light Pinot Noirs, Chinon and Bourgueil.

PIKE FRIED WITH GARLIC

With no coast of its own, sea fish are expensive, but freshwater fish are plentiful (as are white wines to go with them) and include trout, perch, carp, eel, char and pike. Garlicky fried pike from the Danube is a typical dish, well partnered by Grüner Veltliner. Austrian Rhine Riesling and Sauvignon are also possible, but a shade too aromatic. Alsace Sylvaner, Muscadet *sur lie* and Bourgogne Aligoté are other alternatives.

Greece

Tourism has not been good for the image of Greek food and wine. Visitors return to their home countries with the unshakeable conviction that it consists of meatballs or moussaka, preceded by *taramasalata* or hummus, accompanied by Retsina or Ouzo – and the menus of Greek restaurants abroad only confirm this view. The image of itself that Greece finds most marketable is one of clichés, in which the most interesting wines of the eastern Mediterranean are reduced to a tired, resinated white, and an ingenious, largely vegetarian cuisine is reduced to the eponymous salad of tomatoes, black olives and Feta cheese.

It is true that Greek food is less varied than Turkish and Lebanese. There is no luxurious court cuisine like that of Istanbul, the capital of the Ottoman Empire which ruled Greece for so long, and there is little mixing of sweet with savoury flavours. But in its basics Greek food is similar to that of other eastern Mediterranean countries: chick peas and other legumes, cheese and fish are the sources of protein, with lamb or goat on high days and holidays; vegetables, given richness by the lavish use of fruity olive oil, are still far more important than meat. Lemons feature everywhere and *avgolemono*, egg and lemon sauce, thickens and flavours many soups and casseroles. Then there are the herbs – oregano and thyme above all, but also parsley, dill and basil – and the wild greens that come under the collective heading of *horta* – anything from rock samphire to dandelion leaves to curly endive. These may be blanched, then dressed with oil and lemon, or packed into the filo pastry *pittes*, or pies, beloved of Greeks.

Whatever the filling for these – indeed, whatever the dish – it is seasonal. Peas and artichokes are available in the spring, courgettes in early summer (only recently have tomatoes been on sale all year). But 'seasonal' in Greece does not just mean the weather: the seasons of the church have their appropriate menus, as does every family celebration. Lent means abstinence from all animal products, even eggs; Easter, weddings and baptisms mean roast lamb or goat.

Having been an almost entirely peasant culture for so long, wine is a part of daily life – an alternative to Ouzo, but not something to ponder over. That said, the current revival of good Greek wine is revealing qualities that seem tailor-made for the direct flavours of Greek food. European grape varieties like Cabernet and Chardonnay are extremely limited; instead there are hundreds of unique indigenous grape varieties, and with modern winemaking some of the whites – Assyrtiko and Robola, for example – retain their acidity even at these southern latitudes. The predominant flavours of Greek food – olive oil, lemon juice, sharp feta cheese – all need acidity in the wine; so do the flavoursome fish – fried anchovies, sardines or *picarel*, or grey mullet baked with olive oil and tomatoes, or cuttlefish with spinach.

Greece is even richer in reds and these, too, often have relatively marked acidity. In the north there are Naoussa and Côtes de Meliton and in the Peloponnese there is Nemea – all big, deep, spicy reds that can handle strong flavours. Even the offal which is so popular (the liver, lungs, heart, sweetbreads and spleen are often sold and eaten all together), which would normally need softer reds, is here so often flavoured with lemon, or sometimes tomatoes, that acidity in the wine is not a problem. And for very garlicky or oily dishes, there is always Retsina.

OCTOPUS IN RED WINE

Squid, cuttlefish and octopus are all stewed in red wine (and sometimes white) in Greece, as they are in Spain. In the classic octopus stew (*htapothi krassato*), onions, tomatoes and oregano lend themselves to a rich, aromatic sauce which is ideally partnered by Greek reds such as Nemea. Perhaps not surprisingly, youngish, lightly oaked Spanish Tempranillos work well, too, as do the full, ripe reds of Apulia in southern Italy, Sardinia's Carignano del Sulcis, Barbera from Piedmont and California Sangiovese.

HARE IN SHARP ONION AND TOMATO SAUCE

Game is highly regarded in Greece and the most common way to cook it, especially hare and rabbit, is in a *stifatho*, a sour-sweet sauce made with vinegar, baby onions, tomatoes, garlic, rosemary and allspice. Sturdy, spicy Naoussa copes well with both the sauce and the strong meat. Or try Chianti Classico or Crozes-Hermitage.

MEZE

Retsina is the traditional accompaniment to *meze*, a collection of bite-sized portions of the likes of *hummus*, *taramasalata*, *tzatziki*, aubergine purée, artichoke salad, Feta, deep fried calamari, stuffed vine leaves, herby meatballs and moussaka – which is all very well if you like Retsina. I don't, but it isn't easy to find other wines that span all these dishes well. Modern Greek whites and New Zealand Sauvignon, with their high acidities, do pretty well until you get to the moussaka – at which point. Bardolino, Navarra, Béarn and Provence rosés are better.

POT ROAST CHICKEN WITH AVGOLEMONO

Greece's white grapes are well suited to lemony chicken dishes such as this, but in their absence try the tangy, yet buttery, intensity of a New Zealand Chardonnay or the tangy-lime character of Hungarian indigenous whites.

BACLAVA

While the Greeks prefer to drink coffee with their sticky, honey-soaked almond and walnut pastries, other people might be forgiven for bending the rules and drinking one of the country's sweet Muscat wines – of which Muscat of Samos is the best. Sweet French Muscats, such as Beaumes-de-Venise and Rivesaltes, together with Moscatel de Valencia, are good alternatives.

Scandinavia

Scandinavia has given the world a famous dish, gravad lax, and a distinctive form of eating, the smorgasbord, the Swedish term for a meal with different guises in Denmark, Norway and Finland. Smorgasbord typifies eating in Scandinavia – both formal and informal, tempting and hunger-satisfying. The dishes are set before you in profusion, but there are customary constraints on how you eat and drink – and drinking can be very formal. As you eat, so you drink and toast each other, usually with a shot of aquavit or schnapps that cuts through the food – herrings, rye breads, beetroot, eggs, ham, cold roast pork, smoked eel, warm vegetables and salads, all accompanied by sauce *remoulade* (a piquant, herby mayonnaise), mayonnaise or mustard – followed by a sip of beer.

Swedish smorgasbords have a set order – that sense of formality again. It starts with herring – pickled, smoked, cured or marinated. Next come other cold fish dishes (the Scandinavians love fish) and the famous gravad lax: salmon boned and split lengthways, the flesh covered with a mixture of fresh dill, sea salt, pepper, sugar and brandy, then sandwiched together, weighted under a board and left for up to a week (originally, they say, buried in the ground). It is served with a sweet dill and mustard sauce. Next come 'small warm dishes' ('*måvarmt*'), scaled-down versions of main meals, such as fried fish fillets, fish balls in sherry sauce, pork medallions, or chicken vol-au-vents, followed by a selection of cold pâtés and meats. Cheese and fruit and perhaps a fruit compote follow. Various breads are always to hand – rye, and others flavoured with typical Scandinavian touches of caraway or poppy seeds.

Even if they did not have aquavit or schnapps, you could hardly blame the Scandinavians for not choosing wine as an accompaniment to a smorgasbord. It is not only hard to find one that suits all the components but some of them – not least the herrings – are hard to match in their own right. The two wines that best meet the challenge are fino sherry and German Riesling, preferably a good *Kabinett*, or *Spätlese*, from the Mosel, or a *Kabinett* from the Pfalz (despite the two very different styles of these regions). It is worth noting here that beetroot has an affinity with Scheurebe, but the flavour of this wine can be slightly dominant for the other dishes. If you are having more than one wine, the meat-based warm dishes are the cue to switch to fruity but structured red, such as Beaujolais-Villages, Saint-Emilion or Barbera d'Asti.

Rye bread, dark, dense and slightly sweet, is the basis of the Danish '*smorrebrød*': every ingredient except shellfish is placed on a piece of rye; shellfish are piled on white bread; *remoulade* is applied generously; and there is plenty of pork and ham. Danish food is generally the richest of the Scandinavian countries: other favourites are eels fried in butter, *frikadeller* and steak tartare, the latter two often served with buttery mashed potatoes.

Other general Scandinavian passions include fresh crayfish (the new season being celebrated with a round of crayfish parties), caviar and game. Waterfowl, woodcock, grouse, hare, elk, venison and reindeer are all popular – and smoked reindeer tongue is a Lapp speciality. Game is frequently cooked and served with cranberries, Arctic raspberries or cloudberries, and juniper-berries are another widely used flavouring.

Classic Combinations

ROAST VENISON WITH CRANBERRIES

Cranberries don't do favours for any wine, but one grape with a particular affinity with roast venison, Mourvèdre, stands up to the tart, sweet berries well. Mourvèdre is found on its own in Bandol, and sometimes in Australia and occasionally in California. More widely seen alternatives are big red burgundies (eg Nuits-St-Georges), Northern Rhône Syrahs, or mature Australian Shiraz.

GRAVAD LAX

Salmon, sugar, salt, dill and mustard might sound testing for wine, but in practice there is one excellent match and some other very acceptable ones. High quality, concentrated yet delicate Mosel Riesling *Kabinett* has the perfect balance of sweetness and acidity to cope with the sweet and sharp notes of the sauce and the Riesling flavours complement both salmon and dill. Australian Rieslings don't work nearly so well, but fine Australian and New Zealand Chardonnays, with ripe fruit, clean acidity and judicious oak, are a success; so, too, is Chardonnay-dominated vintage champagne.

FRIKADELLER

These small delicate meatballs, made from veal, or a cunning proportion or veal, pork and beef, provide an opportunity to drink medium-bodied red wines of some age and finesse – Bordeaux, burgundy, Rioja *gran reserva*. The savoury character of white burgundy also goes quite well, but it shouldn't be too grand or opulent an example.

STEAK TARTARE

Raw beef is not a problem for wine, but raw egg yolk is very uncompromising, and most of all with tannin. A Beaujolais Villages or *cru* is about the best bet, but you don't have to stick with red: a fresh white burgundy, such as a good Mâcon or St-Véran, makes a reasonable partner.

GOOSE STUFFED WITH PRUNES

There is a reverence for traditional feast days throughout Scandinavia and roast goose with prunes is a traditional choice at Christmas and at Martinmas. Pork may be similarly stuffed, sometimes with apples as well, and both are typically served with sweet-and-sour red cabbage and caramelized potatoes – demanding flavours for wine. Traditional Australian Shiraz, full-bodied and ripe, is one option. Another is German Riesling, ideally a Pfalz *Spätlese*, to cut through the richness.

Northern Europe

*A*lthough England and Wales produce some aromatic, light-bodied white wines, none of the countries of Northern Europe are classic wine areas. Britain, Belgium and the Netherlands are basically beer-brewing nations, but ones with a long tradition of importing wine, above all red Bordeaux. The UK even has its own name for it – claret – and a tradition of eating plainly roasted or grilled meat that is ideal for showing it off. The most perfect match would probably be Médoc with sweet spring lamb (Welsh vying with South Downs for supremacy), a marriage much favoured, of course, by the Bordelais who have their own special local lamb (*see* page 80). But it is by no means the only option. In Belgium, you might well be served wild boar, venison or veal kidneys with fine Bordeaux and in Holland a hearty one pot stew. In a neat reciprocal gesture, it is Dutch cheeses that are often served at Bordeaux châteaux with the finest mature wines. Mature Gouda (or Mimolette) has a smooth texture and a mellow nutty character that complements claret as few other cheeses do.

Britain may be very much a meat-eating culture, but as an island race the British have no lack of fish and shellfish – even if many of the most succulent lobsters and crabs find their way to tables in France and Spain. Humble fish and chips, eaten in or out of newspaper, can be transformed by a well-made dry white wine – anything from Grand Cru Chablis to Chilean Sauvignon or Pinot Grigio. (The fish, naturally, must be absolutely fresh.) And small towns still have fresh seafood stalls selling such treats as potted shrimps (made from tiny brown shrimps), for which a medium- to full-bodied Chardonnay with some oak maturation is a perfect partner.

Oysters were once so abundant in Britain that the poor could object to being fed them too often. The tradition of cooking with this once-cheap foodstuff survives in steak and kidney pudding, where a few oysters give a pungent richness to the gravy and accompanying wine needs to be red and fairly full. Jugged hare and oxtail stew, every bit as typical of British cooking, make broadly similar demands of wine, although jugged hare, in particular, is an excellent opportunity to show off fine red burgundy, Saint-Emilion or Ribera del Duero. Hare is just one of a whole menagerie of furred and feathered game that is part of the culinary tradition. Pheasant, grouse, partridge, widgeon, snipe, rabbit, venison are others – all with an affinity with flavoursome reds, not least burgundy and Syrah from the Northern Rhône.

As if this, along with the famous roast beef, were not protein enough, Britain is also strong on cheese (Cheddar, Stilton et al) – and boasts one of those famously few near perfect food and wine marriages: port with Stilton (*see* Cheese, page 22). Then there are the puddings: steamed and baked, tarts and pies, fools, syllabubs, custards and trifles. Mind you, it has taken the revolution in cooking of the last 20 years and a Swiss chef to discover that bread and butter pudding must have originated in heaven (with a glass of botrytised sweet wine).

If beef is symbolic of Britain, in Belgium it is mussels. Served with or without chips and cooked in umpteen ways, wine must be chosen accordingly, but mussels themselves are inherently wine-friendly. Not so herrings in Holland, especially new herrings eaten cold from street stalls in spring. Nothing helps these down so much as drop of 'Genever' ('juniper') gin.

LANCASHIRE HOTPOT

This is a classic, warming English casserole, with lamb chops and root vegetables layered under sliced potatoes. It goes with many red wines, but doesn't want anything too refined. Cabernet Sauvignon based wines are a natural ally – red Bordeaux (from ripe years but less elevated properties), Bulgarian, Romanian, Provence and many New World Cabernets and Merlots. But Cabernet doesn't have a monopoly: wines from the south of France (Minervois, Fitou, Côtes du Roussillon), Nemea (from Greece), Montepulciano di Abruzzo, Teroldego Rotaliano, Rioja *crianza* and Bairrada are all in the frame.

EELS

The Belgians, the Dutch and the British all have an appetite for eels, but different ways of dealing with them. The Belgians, like the Germans, often serve them with a creamy herb sauce (*see* page 108). The Dutch are fond of them smoked, which is difficult for wine, but *fino* and *manzanilla* sherry, New Zealand Sauvignon and mature German Riesling all work well. The British set them in savoury jelly – an

acquired taste which needs
fino, *manzanilla* or something
dry, sharp and cheap.

OYSTERS & SMOKED SALMON

It is hard to beat a glass of
non-vintage brut champagne
(of which Britain, in most
years, is still the leading
importer) with a plate of
Colchester or Whitstable
'native' oysters, although
Chablis, another favourite
with the British, is also spot
on, especially at *premier cru*
level; Pouilly-Fumé, Muscadet
sur lie and Gros Plant are not
far behind. Champagne and
Chablis also seem to have
been made for the finest
Scottish smoked salmon,
although, again, there are
other partners: Alsace's
aromatic whites are preferred
by some people, mature
German Riesling or the very
freshest of *fino* sherries by
others. If you are determined
on red, young, unoaked
Barbera is possible.

ROAST SIRLOIN

So famous has British beef
always been that sirloin has a
history almost as old as the
kingdom itself. Properly hung
and rare, with Yorkshire
pudding cooked beneath the
joint and served first, it flatters
a great many red wines,
including mature Cabernet
Sauvignon and Merlot-based
wines, Barbaresco, Chianti
Classico and Douro.

THE *New World*

Strictly speaking the New World means, or at least it certainly used to mean, the world discovered by Christopher Columbus – North America – but in the last 20 or 30 years or so the term has become rather more inclusive. The wine world (encompassing anyone who makes, drinks or discusses wine) has appropriated the expression New World and applied it to all the countries that were settled by Europeans between the fifteenth and nineteenth centuries and which have begun within the last three decades to make wine in a recognizably modern style.

In most cases the new table wines have risen at the expense of traditional fortified wines, sometimes completely supplanting them. The significance of this is that they heralded the habit of drinking wine with meals. In Australia, New Zealand and South Africa, strong 'sherry' and 'port' type wines were widely consumed – but not with meals (and they were not intended to be). In the United States, until quite recently, it was usual to drink any alcohol beforehand only – and it was almost never wine. European wines were imported to all these countries, but they did not feature in most people's lives except as memorably rare luxuries. Nowadays Chardonnay and Cabernet, Merlot and Sauvignon Blanc, Pinot Noir, Chenin Blanc and all the rest are not only readily available but they are designed as much for drinking with food as without it. And European wines are still imported to a greater or lesser extent, depending on exchange rates, international politics and, of course, on local taste.

The situation in South America is slightly different in that the contemporary wines, made predominantly in Chile and to a lesser extent in Argentina, have been created essentially for export markets. Local South American taste still generally adheres to the rougher, less fruity, more oxidized flavours of traditional styles and grape varieties – and to Pisco (brandy). But the cuisines of these countries are very distinctive and it is perfectly possible to match wines like Chilean Sauvignon and Argentine Malbec to traditional dishes.

Classic combinations of food and wine in the so-called New World are thus different in conception and reality from the classic combinations of wine growing Europe: in short, they are newer. But it is not just that the wine is new. Innovative new cooking has burgeoned during the last two decades, especially in the United States and Australasia.

This is partly the result of immigration and foreign travel, exposing chefs to excitingly different flavours, textures and techniques, especially in the last decade to those of the Far East. In California, a place never known to miss an opportunity to coin a cult phrase, the meeting of the west coast's typically sunny flavours with Far Eastern spices and cooking techniques has inspired the term 'fusion food'. Not that fusion food limits itself narrowly to the food and styles of the western United States and southeast Asia: an early recruit to fusion food were the tapas of Spain.

The other reason for the new dynamism in cooking was wine itself – wine cultures were emerging in previously baron lands. The unquestionable quality of the new wines made an improvement to the old colonial and early settler type of cooking imperative. Having seen what could be done with grapes, it may also have alerted cooks (both home and professional) to the magnificent quality and variety of their native foodstuffs. The famous traditional dishes have certainly not been abandoned, but, alongside the likes of Caesar salad, barbecued spare ribs, colonial goose, pecan pie and pavlova, new and original dishes have emerged and these, at least as much as the old ones, are being matched to the wines.

America

NEW YORK AND THE EASTERN STATES

The East Coast is the region where the early traditions of cooking retain their strongest hold. Fish and shellfish are legendary, including the famous Maine lobsters, intense in flavour from their life in icy waters; littleneck and cherrystone clams from Massachusetts; the blue point oysters of Long Island; and the seasonal softshell crabs of the Chesapeake Bay. These may be very simply prepared, but they also come together in the ancient one-pot cooking method which produces the fish, clam or corn chowder (from the French 'chaudron' or cauldron) of New England. Inland, the 'boiled dinner' is made with chicken, beef or ham in place of fish. Sometimes all kinds of food are thrown together, as in clambake: chicken, sweet potatoes, onions, lobsters, clams and corn, ideally cooked over hot stones covered with seaweed.

Corn – maize or sweetcorn – has been a recurring theme ever since the founding fathers were first introduced to it by friendly Indians in the seventeenth century. The Indians also showed them maple syrup, which explains that distinctive feature of American cooking, the sweet-and-sour sauce, more sweet than sour. Ribs for the barbecue are brushed with marinades sticky with maple syrup; hamburgers, hotdogs and steaks are served with relish and mustard (often hot *and* sweet); even the original baked bean – Boston baked beans, slow-cooked in a pot inside a bread oven – gets its characteristic rich sweetness from the addition of maple syrup. Previous generations would not even have thought of drinking wine with this sort of food. For the current generation the trick is to find a wine that can cope with the distinct sweetness. California wines, with their ripe fruit, are a natural choice – rich red Zinfandels, especially, but also Merlots and, when not too tannic, Cabernet Sauvignons.

New York City is a case on its own, where the dishes of countless nationalities have been adapted to American life. Pastrami was originally Romanian, but try telling that to anyone in a Jewish delicatessen on Seventh Avenue. And that same customer probably varies his diet with lox and bagel, spaghetti and meatballs, and pizza. Unsurprisingly, Italian wines have always been popular and respected with these, but New Yorkers are no slouches in the importing of French wines. New York State also has its own blossoming wine industry. The Finger Lakes area is long-established, but in the last two decades vineyards have also been planted along the Hudson River and – making excitingly elegant Chardonnays – on Long Island.

While traditional American foodstuffs remain prominent in the Eastern States, they are nonetheless being challenged by cooking that uses less familiar flavours, ingredients and methods. Oriental spices are much in evidence and a variety of oils, carefully chosen according to the dish, are being used instead of cream, butter and fat. Cooking in broth is one of the most fashionable methods, and simple grilling is giving way to pan-roasting, for more unified flavours.

To what extent these innovations will take root in the more traditional areas is debatable. Pennsylvania was originally settled by Germans, who brought their sturdy cooking with them. This is a land of *sauerkraut*, filled noodles, *schnitz und gnepp* (ham, apples and dumplings), robust stews and shoo-fly pie, a very sweet pastry made with molasses and raisins. To go with these there are Rieslings – dry and sweet – from adjoining New York State.

Classic Combinations

CAESAR SALAD

There are any number of versions of this American classic claiming to be the true one. What most agree on is that it is a salad of cos lettuce dressed with olive oil, egg, lemon, anchovies and black pepper, to which garlic-fried croutons and grated parmesan are added just before serving. A New York State Chardonnay goes with it very well, but it is happy with many other medium- to full-bodied Chardonnays, both Old World and New World and including sparkling Chardonnays.

BOSTON FISH CHOWDER

The fish chowders of New England are substantial soups which include bacon (or salt pork), potatoes, onions and milk (or cream), as well as the cod or haddock. They are ideal for Chardonnay, and a New York State Chardonnay, particularly one from Long Island, is an apt and successful match. Burgundy also works very well including oak-aged *premier* or even *grand cru* Chablis.

BARBECUED SPARE RIBS

Not many wines come out on top from an encounter with sweet, spicy, sharp barbecue

sauce, but full-bodied
California red Zinfandel
triumphs. California and
Chilean Merlots often manage
quite well, but Australian
Shiraz is better.
Gewurztraminer (especially
Alsace) and ripe, full, but not
oaky Chardonnays are white
wine options; medium-dry
whites, especially German
Kabinett, work well, but they
may not be what you want to
drink with ribs.

THANKSGIVING
TURKEY

With chestnut stuffing,
cranberry sauce, sweet
potatoes, squash and
succotash (*see* page 35), the
Thanksgiving turkey is difficult
for traditional European
wines, but ripe New World
fruit can cope. Red Zinfandel
is especially good, very closely
followed by Australian Shiraz.
Full ripe Merlots and
Cabernets are quite good and
California Chardonnay is the
white wine to consider.

TUNA TARTARE
WITH CORIANDER
AND MUSTARD

Tuna tartare is typical of the
new New York cooking style:
normally a lightish California
or Oregon Pinot Noir is an
option, but here the fresh
coriander makes Chardonnay
a better choice – Carneros,
Long Island, Australian or New
Zealand, but it must be high
quality and moderately subtle.

America

THE SOUTH AND THE WEST COAST

The south varies dramatically in its food resources. The riches of one area contrast with the poverty of others. In the mountains of Tennessee or Arkansas there was always scarcity: Kentucky burgoo is now made with beef or chicken with vegetables, but used to be based on squirrel, or any other mammal straying across the hunter's path. The lush landscape of Virginia is home to the famous Richmond ham; the rich waters of North Carolina supply the materials for She-crab soup with crab roe.

Pigs are the traditional livestock, and pork appears in all its manifestations, but menus further south also boast 'gator steaks, green sea-turtle and terrapin, while catfish – blackened with hot Creole spices or just pan-fried as plain as possible – is the genuine fast-food of the 'boondocks'. The coast teems with fish and shellfish of all kinds, including stone crabs (a Florida speciality), blue crabs, oysters and shrimp. They are immortalized in the Seafood gumbo of New Orleans, home of spicy Creole cooking. This famous cuisine is the offspring of a marriage between the European tradition of this originally French colony and the black slave cooks who for so long had to produce it.

For all the new influences in New York, the west coast, too, has seen an enormous change in its cooking in the last 15 or so years – and all because of the wine. California cuisine, based on a super-abundance and variety of local fresh produce of all kinds, is made to partner the wines – the Chardonnays and Cabernets, the Merlots, Zinfandels and Pinot Noirs, the Sauvignons, the Rhône-style wines and Italian blends. There is even a phrase for it: 'cooking to the wine'; two other phrases, 'CalItal' and 'CalMed', indicate the approach and materials.

California cooking continues to evolve and innovate, but the principle is constant (and remarkably similar to that of the wine producers): to obtain maximum flavour without being heavy-handed. While the rest of America can still treat garlic with reserve, here it is nothing to find six cloves in a recipe, along with chilli peppers, olive oil, and a mountain of sage leaves and 'Italian' parsley. Mashed potatoes might be given zip with mustard; a steak doused with mustard, garlic, ginger and soy. And Californians are now discovering distinctive regional food: lamb in Sonoma; ducks in Petaluma; and hand-made goat's cheeses dotted around.

If California led the way, the latest hot spot to eat is Seattle, way up on the icy-cold waters of Puget Sound – ideal for producing the very finest fish and shell-fish: oysters are cultivated on a massive scale (with more varieties than anywhere in the States); so are Manila clams and – the largest clam of all – the geoduck, which can weigh 7 kilograms. The recent immigration from Hong Kong and Japan means that, if cooked at all, your fish and shellfish are likely to have been marinated in sake or soy, then grilled or poached in broth, probably with some of the area's abundant wild mushrooms. And then there are the wines. Seattle's food is ideally served by the vineyards of Washington State and Oregon. Between them they provide a whole spectrum of wines: in good vintages, world-class Pinot Noir from Oregon and aromatic whites; excellent Merlot in Washington State, and Cabernet Sauvignon, Riesling, Sémillon, Sauvignon and Chardonnay, too.

Classic Combinations

OYSTERS ROCKEFELLER

The richness of the bread-thickened green sauce on these grilled oysters is said to have been the inspiration for the name of this famous New Orleans dish. It is not in fact a rich sauce in the egg or cream sense; rather, it is richly flavoured, with spring onions, fennel and spinach cooked in butter and pepped up with parsley, tabasco, lime and Pernod. A top quality dry sparkling California wine, made with the grape varieties of Champagne and the same method, makes an ideal partner. The best from Australia, New Zealand and South Africa are alternatives – or vintage champagne.

JAMBALAYA

Jambalaya is one of the hot pepper classics of Creole cuisine. A cousin of the Spanish *paella*, it is similarly based on rice, with the addition of those classics of the region – shellfish and ham. Unlike so much American cooking, a sour note predominates in Creole dishes and also in the closely related, but hotter, Cajun food of the neighbouring Mississippi Delta. Hot chillies, a sour note, shellfish and ham are quite a lot for any wine to tackle, but Sauvignon has the potential. California's oaked and off-dry Fumé styles don't work. The food needs the purity and intensity of bone dry, unoaked, piercingly flavoured Sauvignons; California is making a few, as are Texas and Washington State, but it is New Zealand and the Loire which excel. The herby, flinty Loire wines (Sancerre, Pouilly-Fumé, Menetou-Salon, Quincy) tend to be better with Jambalaya and other Creole dishes. The pungent, but fruitier New Zealand style is better with the hotter, more robust Cajun ones. The best of Chile and South Africa can substitute.

PECAN PIE

This very rich, very sweet nut pie needs very sweet wines. California Orange Muscat and Canadian Ice Wines are North American answers. Otherwise, try Australia's botrytised wines, and even its liqueur Muscats.

DUCK WITH GREEN APPLE RELISH

This dish of char-grilled duck breasts with a modern rendition of apple sauce is typical of contemporary wine-oriented California cuisine. The relish is fresh, sweet and sharp, but not aggressive: New World Pinot Noir – especially from California and Oregon – matches very well, better than traditional red burgundy, although velvety Volnay or Pommard is good.

South America

South America is where much modern European cooking has its roots. It is where European beef first met New World beans; where European garlic and onions met New World tomatoes and potatoes. Every meal is a summary of several centuries of history; nowhere is cultural collision more vividly illustrated in the food and wine. This is partly because of the extraordinary variety of ingredients and styles of cuisine that existed long before the Spanish introduced chickens, cattle, pigs, sheep, olives and coriander. With every sort of climate from tropical to cool, drippingly humid to desert-dry, there are bananas, custard apples, coconuts, pumpkins, strawberries, several sorts of maize, river, lake and sea fish and rare, exotic seafood. What there was not, until Europeans arrived, was wine. To look at how South American wine matches its food is to look at the way European immigrants have maintained the cuisines of their homelands. The countries that grow vines and make wine are those with the highest concentrations of people of European stock and the most European-style food. Chilean Cabernet goes well with the local beef, but neither was native to the country.

Pre-Columbian cuisine is largely found these days in Peru, although here too the Spanish influence is strong and there is a small amount of European-style wine. In neighbouring Ecuador, *ceviche*, raw fish marinated in lime juice, is the speciality; it is hard to imagine any wine producing country evolving such a dish. Colombia's flavours are more subtle, showing the Spanish influences in such dishes as rice with coconut and raisins. In Venezuela grilled beef comes into its own, served with avocado, or hot chilli pepper sauces: again, an ingenious interlocking of two traditions. In the Guianas you can eat Indonesian rice dishes, Portuguese-style pork, or curries introduced by Indian workers, as well as cassava (*manioc*) fritters or *agouti*, an animal familiar to European zoo visitors. Bahia in northern Brazil is full of dishes that mix African, Portuguese and native Amerindian flavours and techniques, but this is a region often looked down upon by smart Europhile Brazilians, and in the south grilled beef takes pride of place. Predictably, it is also the cooler south where most Brazilian wine is made and consumed.

European influences are even stronger in Uruguay, Argentina and Chile. Uruguay and Argentina have similar, beef-based cuisines. The quality of the beef makes it perfect for grilling, though it is also stewed, often with pumpkins, peaches and corn to make *carbonada*. And Argentina has the most enthusiastic wine drinkers in South America. The best red grape, Malbec, gives rich, fairly robust wines that partner the beef well, although, perversely, the fashion among smart Argentines is for white wines, even though few are as interesting as the reds. Among Uruguay's more modern French styles, chunky red Tannat is the most convincing.

The most European of wines are from Chile where a late-nineteenth century status symbol among the rich was a wine estate, a French winemaker and a French chef. The chefs introduced classics like sole *à la normande* and foie gras, but they also combined French techniques with native seafood such as sea urchins and *abalone*; and Creole food is still in evidence. Likewise, Chile's vineyards are regarded as the Bordeaux of South America, although the Cabernet, Merlot, Sauvignon and Chardonnay produced are all tailored to export markets.

EMPANADAS

Spicy meat (usually beef) pasties with raisins are made in several South American countries, but the Chileans are particularly attached to their *empanadas* and almost the entire population seems to eat them on Sundays. The soft, seductive style of Chilean Merlot and the rich, slightly spicy character of Argentine Malbec suit them well. Australian Shiraz and Navarra reds are among the alternatives.

CEVICHE

Ceviche may not have originated in a wine growing South America, but it it is now popular throughout the continent. No wine is entirely happy with so much lime and raw onion, but Chilean Sauvignon (of export quality) handles it reasonably well, as do Sauvignons from New Zealand and South Africa's cool areas. High-acid dry Vinho Verde is also successful (unsurprisingly) and Gros Plant is worth trying.

SHELLFISH STEW

Chile's *chupe de mariscos* is a rich, oven-baked dish made with mussels, lobster, crab, prawns and exotic native shellfish, as available, in a sauce made from fish stock, milk, breadcrumbs, cheese and egg yolks. New-wave Chilean and Argentine Chardonnays complement it well, but so do many other medium- to full-bodied oak-aged Chardonnays from New and Old Worlds.

GRILLED STEAK WITH PEPPER SAUCE

Argentine Malbec and Uruguayan Tannat go very well with grilled steak and cope with South America's pepper sauces reasonably well, but the smooth, ripe fruit and penetrating flavour of Mexican Petite Sirah seems even better equipped for the sauce. California Petite Sirah and Zinfandel are equally well matched. Another alternative is to try a vibrant, full-bodied New World Chardonnay.

STUFFED AVOCADOS

Avocados are widely eaten in South America. In this simple Bolivian recipe, *paltas rellenas*, they are stuffed with a mixture of cooked shrimps, fish, turkey and hard-boiled egg and bound with mayonnaise. Chilean Sauvignon Blanc is an ideal and extremely able partner, as are New Zealand and Hungarian Sauvignons. Chablis and champagne both work well, as would a number of other crisp, dry, flavoursome white wines.

Australia

Cooking down under has come a long, long way since the height of sophistication was a perfect 'pav' (pavlova) and most meals reflected the worst aspects of old-fashioned British cuisine: the Adelaide 'floater', a meat pie adrift on a sea of mushy peas and drenched in tomato ketchup, may still exist, but visitors are not encouraged to go in search of it. Today, the key influences are Asian, classic French and American southern states, with more than a smattering of Italian, and the touch is light in handling the magnificent native materials.

It is a cuisine that has grown up to match the wines which have come an equally long way in barely two decades. That is not to deny that some marvellous, long-lived reds were being made in southeast Australia in the fifties (and not only by the legendary Max Schubert of Penfolds), but these were wholly overshadowed by the fortified wines. These so-called ports and sherries have now given way to a table wine industry that is second to none in modernity. Consistent quality, ripe flavours, inter-regional blending and rapid mastery of almost all the major wine types and grape varieties have been the key features of Australia's international success so far. The next stage, or rather the current one, is to develop – and preserve – more distinctive wine types and regional identities: Barossa Shiraz, sparkling Shiraz and Hunter Valley Semillon are three obvious ones, but new, cooler regions are burgeoning and they are making wines in a more elegant, less oaky style, often aimed specifically at food. Sauvignon Blanc is being mastered in the Adelaide Hills; there is impressive Pinot Noir in the Yarra Valley; and increasing numbers of entirely unoaked Chardonnays.

The revolution in Australian eating began with the first wave of Mediterranean immigrants – the discovery of the importance of freshness, and the excitement of garlic, peppers, shallots and aubergines, all of them easy to grow in the abundant sunshine and ideally suited to the ruling 'barbie' culture. Now, though, magnificent steaks of beef and, yes, kangaroo (tender textured meat with a flavour that is somewhere between venison and beef and which goes perfectly with Shiraz), might share their place on the barbecue with a handful of quail, whole fish or fish steaks. And any of them might first have been marinated, then smothered with fresh herbs or with spices from the Far East.

Australia, of course, is an island, albeit a vast one, and the quantity and range of its seafood is as great as any. There is lobster – gigantic in scale compared with its Maine or Scottish cousins, but every bit as good. There are strange and delicious varieties of crab (mud crab, blue swimming crab and others) and there are clams, oysters (the famous Sydney rock oysters among them), yabbies and hefty Pacific prawns. These are the kinds of foodstuff that immigrants from the Far East, who have added another dimension again to Australian cooking, have a particular flair for handling. Where the freshwater crayfish of Australia might once just have been chucked on the barbie, now they are served live at the table, to be swiftly cooked in a bowl of simmering broth, flavoured, perhaps, with lemon grass, ginger and garlic. There is a nod to Scandinavia, too, in the making of gravad lax, ideally with salmon from the colder Tasmanian waters, a fish so good it makes the only smoked salmon to rival Scotland's.

Classic Combinations

PEPPERED STEAK WITH ROAST GARLIC

There are numerous versions of peppered steak, but the key elements are top quality steak, crushed black peppercorns, brandy and cream. With the additional flavour of roast garlic this is a dish that suits youngish, medium- to full-bodied reds, including Australian Cabernets and Cabernet-Shiraz blends, red Zinfandel, St-Emilion and reds from Tuscany and Italy's south.

SCALLOPS IN LEMON GRASS BROTH

With a Thai-influenced broth, these scallops call out for the fresh crispness of a Sauvignon. This has been a tricky grape in Australia, but there are now a few very good, tangy, crisp ones, especially from the hills beyond Adelaide. They are gentler than New Zealand's Marlborough Sauvignons – an advantage with delicate scallop flavours. Chilean, Loire and Hungarian Sauvignons are successful alternatives.

CHAR-GRILLED SQUID SALAD

Char-grilling enhances squid's mild flavour and adds a distinctive smoky-burnt note. The zesty freshness and characteristic lime and toast flavours of an Australian Riesling, preferably from the Eden or Clare valleys, complement both the char-grilled squid and the dressed salad leaves. New Zealand and Austrian Rieslings, and Sauvignons which are not too pungent, such as those from Bergerac, are alternatives.

COLONIAL GOOSE

Traditional dishes such as this are currently unfashionable, but they are surely due for a revival. This is a dish of classic simplicity, a boned, stuffed joint of lamb. It was made by early settlers to stand in for the traditional Christmas goose and is a perfect dish for showing off today's fine Australian Cabernet Sauvignons: a Coonawarra, its characteristic mintiness complementing the herbs, is particularly appropriate, but most Cabernet-based wines are suitable. Rioja *reserva* is good, too.

MACADAMIA NUT AND RUM ICE-CREAM

Australia's rich, sticky, raisiny liqueur Muscats, notably from Rutherglen, are better than any other wine at penetrating the palate-numbing effects of ice-cream. They also cope with the difficult flavour of rum. PX sherry, Malmsey Madeira and French *vins doux naturels* are the best substitutes.

New Zealand

The quality and variety of New Zealand's raw materials is superb – the fish and seafood exhilarating. Fish and chips is a hang-over from the British, but in New Zealand today it can be a gastronomic dream: the fish might well be tarakihi cooked in a beer batter as light as the best Japanese tempura. Other fish – blue cod, blue nose, kingfish, snapper, gurnard – might be cajun-spiced, char-grilled or served up with saffron-braised fennel. A yellow fin tuna steak will be seared, as simply as possible, but then it might be served with chilli potatoes. Ravioli in New Zealand come filled with such mixtures as tiger-fish and mussels. And the greenshells (or green-lipped mussels) that cost a small fortune on the other side of the world, are ten a penny in New Zealand – and every bit as delicious stuffed, steamed, baked or served in coriander- and chilli-infused broth.

New Zealand wines, predominantly white, intensely flavoured and high in acidity, are ideally suited to all this seafood: the Sauvignon Blancs, especially those from Marlborough, have set a new standard and style worldwide; and the Chardonnays, despite much greater competition in the global market, are reaching great heights. The cool climate is also ideal for producing the base wine for champagne-type sparkling wines and for bringing out the essential aromatic qualitites in Riesling and Gewürztraminer.

The climate also means that red wine will always be second to white, but with every recent vintage (in spite of the vagaries of the weather) there has been striking progress. Cabernet Sauvignon, Merlot and Pinot Noir are the principal red varieties: the tricks now are to find the most suitable spots to plant them; and in many – perhaps most – cases to blend Merlot and Cabernet together to subdue the herbaceous character of Cabernet Sauvignon on its own.

If persevering with red wines sometimes looks like masochism on the part of the producers, you have only to look at the food available to see why they do it. The fertile New Zealand country is ideal for livestock. New Zealand lamb, eaten a few miles from its source rather than thousands of deep-frozen miles away in Europe, is sweet flavoured and delicate in texture: North Island Merlot-Cabernet blends are its natural partners. The same wines may partner cervena, a flavoursome and tender venison, but, depending how it is cooked, Pinot Noir (probably from Martinborough or Central Otago) might be better. Pinot Noir also comes into its own with the duck currently so fashionable, cooked in infinite ways, in Auckland restaurants and, very sensibly, New Zealanders have no qualms about Pinot Noir with fish.

What makes the lamb and cervena different today, apart from more sensitive cooking (instead of overcooking), are the accompaniments: these might be mash flavoured with olive oil (produced from Marlborough olives) and local garlic, wild rice pancakes, polenta or tabbouleh, together with roasted peppers or an exotic native vegetable such as kumara. Also known as the 'Maori potato', the infinitely adaptable kumara is made into chips to be eaten as an appetizer, reduced to thick, spicy soups, roasted with olive oil, or just cut up and tossed into stews. It is fine with red wine in meat dishes, but on its own, in soup for example, it is happier with Sauvignon or Riesling – both of which New Zealand has in abundance.

Classic Combinations

SPICED HOKI FISHCAKES WITH GREEN SALSA

Another typical, and typically successful, combination of a native fish (New Zealand's answer to cod) and flavourings drawn from distant cultures – in this case Cajun. The slightly fuller, riper style of Sauvignon from Hawkes Bay just has the edge over Marlborough's. Loire, Chilean and South African Sauvignons all work well, as does New World Chardonnay with good acidity – especially New Zealand, Tasmanian, Yarra Valley and cool climate South African.

GREENSHELL MUSSELS IN CORIANDER BROTH

New Zealand Sauvignon Blanc, which might seem the naturel partner for these succulent sweet mussels, in fact tends to overwhelm them, but an intensely aromatic, herbaceous Marlborough Sauvignon is the perfect answer when green-lips are cooked in a broth infused with fresh coriander and chilli. Or try Pouilly-Fumé, Sancerre or Chilean Sauvignon.

DEEPSEA DORY WITH CREAMY GARLIC SAUCE

This is a fine flavoured fish similar to John Dory. Sautéed

and served with a creamy,
but not too pungent, garlic
sauce, it is an ideal showpiece
for the complex flavours of
one of New Zealand's top
Chardonnays. A top white
Côte d'Or burgundy or
California Chardonnay (eg
from Santa Barbara) would
not go amiss either.

STUFFED SADDLE OF RABBIT

A Martinborough Pinot Noir is
an ideal partner for rabbit,
especially as prepared here,
with a herb stuffing and a
mushroom sauce. Red
burgundy, Oregon and
California Pinot Noir could all
be substituted, as could Rioja
Reserva and, when not too
heavy, Australian Shiraz.

CARAMELIZED LEMON TART

Although they are not seen
much outside New Zealand,
there are some fabulous
late-harvest sweet wines. Made
from Sauternes-like blends of
Sémillon and Sauvignon
(sometimes with Sauvignon
predominating) and from
Riesling, they tend to be so
sweet and concentrated and
have such fresh acidity that
they even stand up to the fruit
ice-creams in vogue in New
Zealand restaurants. With this
caramelized citrus tart, the
zesty intensity of a late-harvest
Riesling is a perfect match –
and one that can't be
equalled, never mind bettered.

India AND THE Far East

Classic combinations with Indian curry? With a Chinese meal? With the fiery fresh flavours of Thai food or Japan's piquant raw fish dishes? Surely not? It is, I admit, a rather elastic use of the phrase – even more so than applying it in non-wine producing northern Europe or the relatively new wine producing countries of the New World. It hardly needs saying that the peoples of India, China and Southeast Asia do not, traditionally, drink much western-style wine.

Grape wine is in fact produced in parts of India and China and, surprisingly, in most provinces of Japan, but, with the exception of that made in Japan, which is often made at least partially from imported grape juice, most of it is the product of joint ventures with partners from the West and its destination is markets in the West or incoming tourists and business travellers. Sake, Chinese rice wine, jasmine tea and green tea are far more commonplace – and cognac is still the most popular western drink.

But there is a validity to the term classic combinations here, for there are some wines that go very much better than others with particular foods of the Far East - and some that go very well indeed. I am talking not so much of specific wines to partner specific dishes, but wines that go with the mood of a range of, say, Thai or Cantonese dishes. In most Far Eastern cultures (Japan excepted), all the savoury dishes are put on the table at the same time to be shared by all those present (rather than being served as a series of courses to each diner separately, as in the West). In such circumstances it is usually impractical to think in terms of choosing a wine to match each dish. You could easily end up with seven different glasses of wine before you.

And there is a very simple and valid reason for seeking partners for the cuisines of the Far East: their sphere of influence has greatly expanded in the last two decades; their cooking methods and ingredients have rippled through the world's professional and domestic kitchens – above all those of the English-speaking world, but even France herself has not been immune.

Sometimes the influence has taken the form of exact and exacting authenticity – a truly Japanese or South Indian restaurant run with every possible attention to detail. But increasingly in the last decade, or two, the influence has been felt in a more diffused way: through foreign cooks who have borrowed more or less deeply from the repertoire of techniques and flavourings to give native foodstuffs in New York, Auckland, Sydney or London a taste of the exotic, complex and infinitely varied food of the Far East. Over the same period, wine drinking has become much more a way of life in these English-speaking countries, as the so-called New World of North American, Australian, New Zealand, South American and South African wine has emerged as a powerful force.

Last but not least, although the drinking of imported wine is still very much a minority sport, it is on the increase, especially among the Chinese in Hong Kong where rich businessmen have developed a taste for the most expensive Pomerols. These they drink not with Western type food but with authentic Chinese food – shark's fin soup, dried *abalone*, roast duck, braised goose (Hong Kong is a melting pot of China's regional cuisines). Although Pomerol is a big wine for Chinese food, there is an appropriateness about its lush, soft, round, almost sweet character.

India

There is no denying that some Indian food, particularly that from the south, is searingly hot. With spices such as asafoetida, tamarind and raw fenugreek, it may have bitter, sour and astringent flavours too, but to imagine that all Indian food, even all south Indian food, is too hot for wine is to miss the point of this intricately flavoured, spicy and varied cuisine – and, equally, it is to miss out on some fascinating wine and food mixed marriages. Wine drinkers might sometimes choose to modify some dishes to make them kinder to wine, and avoid others altogether, but there is no need to stick to *lassi*, lager or water.

To talk of Indian cuisine as if one style of cooking enveloped this vast and ancient civilization, with its many languages and cultures, is rather misleading. But there are common threads. Above all there are the spices. The use of these – the way they are first prepared by heating and then blending together – is at the heart of all Indian cooking, for it is flavour more than heat that the Indian cook seeks. Secondly, there is long, slow cooking. There are fast-foods Indian style – the northern tandoori recipes and stir-fried dishes – but it is slow simmering that unites the country's myriad curries. They are also complex in flavour – not merely hot – and it is this that the wine drinker needs to consider.

With other countries, it is usually useful to look at key ingredients, flavourings and garnishes to see what predominates and what, if anything, needs special attention in terms of wine (a fruit sauce, a piquant garnish). But with Indian food the end result is your starting point: it is not only that there might be 20 spices in a recipe, it is the endless permutations of preparation and blending that produce different dishes, irrespective of the meat, vegetables, pulses, grains or fish which may have been added. What you really want to know is how pungently hot, sour, sweet, bitter, heavy or delicate the sum of the many individual parts is. Scrutinizing ingredient lists also tends to flash all sorts of warning lights at wine drinkers – chilli, ginger, mustard, pepper, coriander, cumin, lime, tamarind, yoghurt, coconut, fenugreek, cinnamon, cardamom, cloves, fennel seeds, jaggery (raw cane sugar), dried fruits, nuts et al. And yet the final dish may be mellow and aromatic, rather than startlingly pungent, as in a chicken korma – creamy with yoghurt and sweet with onions (in fact most curries start with the frying of onions, garlic and fresh ginger). It is also worth remembering that for all the spicy and aromatic dishes, there is accompanying plain steamed rice or soft, chewy bread.

As for those threatening sounding ingredients: chilli, though it can numb or burn the palate, doesn't actually ruin the taste of wine, it just saps it of some of its flavours. Much the same applies to fresh ginger. Coconut is seldom a problem; and, although yoghurt (as in cooling *raitas*) is no great friend of wine, mild to medium spicy, yoghurty dishes can be matched by a good quality, zesty, judiciously oaked New World Chardonnay – from Coonawarra perhaps. The one real offender is chutney: with this you must make use of palate-clearing rice or bread.

Bearing all this in mind, and steering clear of dishes of vindaloo strength, you need a wine that has the flavour to stand up for itself. This rules out most of the lightest and cheapest wines (strip away some of their flavour and there is nothing left). It also rules out fragile old wines, and the subtlest and most expensive. An aromatic character is an asset, as is the sweetness of ripe New World fruit. Where there is oak, it needs to be softly vanilla-flavoured, not very toasted or spicy.

Recommended Wines

On the whole, white wines provide more matches, and with vegetable dishes most matches. And with dishes strong on tamarind and lime, acidity is particularly important. **New World Chardonnays** from the slightly cooler areas are good with the creamy, coconuty dishes; top quality **Sémillon** is good, too, as are less common, but interestingly flavoured grape varieties like **Verdelho** and **Marsanne**. Aromatic, dry **Muscats** and Muscat blends (New and Old World) go well with delicate – spicy but not too rich – dishes. But fall back on **Alsace Gewurztraminer** for particularly highly spiced dishes that are proving difficult to partner; alternatively, try a very well-chilled New World **dry sparkling** wine. Note that Sauvignon and Riesling tend to be rendered somewhat one-dimensional, although the unusual blend of **Chardonnay and Sauvignon** works.

With red wines, one of the keys is to go for low tannin or mellow tannin (your tastebuds already have enough to cope with). The New World scores well here. Faced with curry, Pinot Noirs usually lose their quintessential aromas and fruit, but warm climate **Zinfandels, Shirazes, Merlots** and **Cabernets** can be good – served coolish – with the richer North Indian dishes. You must avoid tannic and peppery wines, however: rather than being complementary, peppery wines find their pepper flavour accentuated at the expense of the wine's fruit by the spices in the food.

For those who would prefer to experiment in the Old World, the fruit of a good **cru Beaujolais** or a **Rioja crianza** will work with a spectrum of dishes, but, with the more powerful, try wines made from the velvety, warmly fruity, bitter-spicy **Negroamaro** grape from Apulia in the far south of Italy (for example Copertino and Salice Salentino). I have also enjoyed a fine ten-year-old **Médoc** with a Balti Chicken Tikka. The wine was mellow and complex, the food highly aromatic and complex, and the two tangoed. That the wine was from a seductively, ripe vintage was, surely, significant; that both wine and food were complex in flavour was also, I think, significant, but I shall never understand the alchemy.

Another school of thought recommends traditional **fortified wines** – characterful liquids like Madeira (especially Verdelho and Bual), sherry (dry or sweet, depending on the dish) and ruby port. Personally, I find them too strong and, in the presence of curries, too spirity – but if you are a devotee they might be worth a try.

China

*I*f the use of spices is at the heart of Indian cooking, the cornerstone of Chinese cookery is the blending of flavours, textures, aromas and colour to produce an overall effect that is harmonious and balanced in every way. For all the regional variations, the twin emphases on freshness of flavour and on contrasting textures run throughout the country, from the delicately flavoured cooking of Canton in the South to the richer, sweeter style of Shanghai in the East to the hot and spicy, chilli-infused style of Sichuan and Hunan in the West. In no other cuisine, save Japanese, is the texture of food so pivotal: there must be variety and contrast not just between dishes but between ingredients in the same dish. Although this does not impinge directly on wine choice, it has a bearing, as it governs the Chinese cook's choice of ingredients.

Spices, flavourings and sauces play an important role, but are generally used in moderation. Even in Sichuan cooking, they are there to enhance, not to overwhelm, let alone obliterate, the main ingredients. Key flavourings are fresh ginger, garlic and spring onions – the 'trinity of stir frying' – together with soy sauce, salt, sugar, pepper and cooking oil (preferably peanut). Others, depending on region, are rice wine (*fino* sherry is the nearest, but not very near, Western approximation); Sichuan peppercorns – not actually pepper and rather more sharp and spicy than hot; chillies, both dried and fresh (but the fresh ones are usually less hot than in southeast Asia); five spice powder; chilli bean sauce or paste (hot and spicy); fermented black beans (slightly salty and pungent); and other sauces, such as oyster (rich and savoury, rather than fishy) and hoisin (sweet), some of which are used in cooking, some for dipping only. Herbs are few and far between: fresh coriander, with its citrus-sour character, is the principal one and it is used in sauces and stuffings as well as as a garnish.

So far as main ingredients are concerned, the Chinese love vegetables, particularly when quickly and lightly cooked (stir-fried or steamed) to preserve their crisp, crunchy texture, or pickled or served raw for the same reason. Cabbages of various kinds, long beans, *mooli*, mangetout, aubergine and mushrooms are just a few of the popular ones. When it comes to meat, pork is by far the most important, although beef and lamb both feature. Duck is widely enjoyed, but chicken is more highly prized and is often the centrepiece of a banquet. All kinds of fish and seafood are enjoyed (and not just the heads, fins and edible jelly-fish which make westerners squirm). All these are eaten against the neutral backgrounds of rice, dumplings, noodles and pancakes, and the highly nutritious tofu which can act as substitute for both dairy products and meat.

First impressions, at least on paper, might suggest that Chinese food is reasonably easy to match to wine, or at least easier than Indian food. Flavours are mostly mild and the key concerns of the cook – retaining freshness of flavour and balancing the textures – do not on the face of it present a problem, but there are some unexpected trip wires. One of them is that several contrasting dishes are served at once in a typical meal: finding a wine to suit them all may have to be something of a compromise (the Chinese, of course, drink their thin soups as a beverage). Secondly, a lot of wines – including many from the New World and most reds – are too assertive for the gentle flavours. Thirdly, there is the sweetness of many of the savoury dishes – not least in the classic sweet-and-sour sauces where the sour element is a further complication.

Difficulties notwithstanding, there are certainly wines to go with Chinese food. The best all-rounders are **German** wines, above all good Rieslings. As a grape variety, **Riesling** has the advantage of going well with ginger, coriander and spring onions, and the delicate but insistent fruit flavours, racy acidity and gentle, balancing sweetness of a *Kabinett* or slightly weightier *Spätlese Halbtrocken* are well suited to many Chinese savoury dishes. The more powerful style of New World Rieslings is worth trying, especially Australia's medium-dry Rieslings, but they lack the quintessential German delicacy and balance.

Sweet-and-sour sauces are difficult, but the ripe sweetness and subtle spiciness of a **Pfalz Kabinett** is good, particularly with pork and duck. Alternatively, wheel out the old standby, **Alsace Gewurztraminer**: it is too powerfully flavoured for most Chinese food, but can, even when technically dry, handle sweet spare ribs and the sweet spicy sauces (hoisin or sweet bean) served with Peking duck. German Gewürztraminer tends to be too light, but look out for those from Hungary,

Chile, New Zealand and South Africa.

Another wine that accommodates many dishes, even spare ribs, is **non-vintage champagne**. *Demi-sec* has the ideal level of sweetness, but *brut* (which is not, after all, absolutely bone dry) is nearly as successful, easier to find, and a great deal more reliable.

Acceptable matches can also be made with modern Italian dry whites, such as **Lugana,** which are neither too neutral nor too highly flavoured; with Swiss wines made from **Chasselas,** such as Fendant; with inexpensive white wines from **Baden**; and with wines simply described as **medium-dry white** from the **New World**.

In general, red wines are not good news with Chinese food, but again, Germany comes to the rescue. Lightly chilled, low tannin, light- to medium-bodied, soft, fruity **Pinot Noirs** often work well, including German Spätburgunders (ie Pinot Noirs) from Baden. Light French Pinot Noirs, eg Sancerre, tend to be too dry, but California and Chile both now produce some quite cheap Pinot Noirs with the right attributes: though weightier than Germany's, they focus on fresh, sweet, rounded fruit and early consumption. And if money is no object, try a top Pomerol.

Thailand

Recommended Wines

The flavours of Thai food are vibrant, expressive and sometimes explosive – at once, hot, sour, salty and sweet. Contrasting textures are important, especially the refreshing crunch of crisp vegetables and salads, but texture is not the lynch pin that it is in Chinese cooking. The Thai cook is much more concerned with seasoning and with the often dramatic confrontations of opposing flavours.

Equally, although Indian influences are apparent, especially in the curries made fiery with chillies, Thai cuisine is quite different. Where India uses cooked or dried spices and herbs, Thai curries – and other dishes – are made with fragrant fresh herbs and spices – chillies, lime leaves (preferably kaffir), lemon grass, citrus juices, green coriander root, coriander leaves, galangal (akin to ginger) and various basils. The result, even cooled, mellowed and enriched with coconut milk, is never bland. Indeed, there is a profundity of flavour to much Thai food.

Among the other key ingredients are the distinctive, salty, slightly pungent fermented fish pastes and fish sauce (*nam pla*), used instead of salt, and the powerfully concentrated, flavours of dried shrimps or prawns. There are hot, spicy relishes and dipping sauces, of which *nam prik num* is both important and archetypal – with its chillies, garlic, shrimp paste, tomatoes (fresh of course), fish sauce and lime. There is pickled fish (*pla raa*) and sour lime pickle. There are the nutty flavours of roasted peanuts (famously used in satay dipping sauce) and, in the northeast of Thailand, the distinctive nuttiness of roasted ground rice. There is palm sugar, used to give sweetness both to savoury dishes and to sweetmeats and desserts.

These, then, are the seasonings and flavourings added to meat, poultry and fish. The most common meats are pork and beef, together with offal (including liver, tripe and udder) and chicken and duck. Any of these may be made into spicy sausages. In the south, with its vast expanses of coastline (and large numbers of Moslems), fish and shellfish are far more significant: prawns, shrimps, oysters, crab, lobster and squid are all highly popular. And, just as the north has its sausages, so the south has its spicy fishcakes.

For the wine drinker, this may all sound murderous, but chilli and ginger (as we have seen) do not ruin the taste of wine; lemon grass, coriander and basil are perfectly happy with wine, especially fresh-tasting whites; coconut (as in India) is not problematic; and the salty fish sauces and pastes and pickled items simply need wines with marked acidity and flavour.

The other key point here is that these dishes are not eaten on their own. There is always rice and often simply cooked noodles, too. The rice may be the sticky, glutinous variety of the north, steamed absolutely plainly, without even salt, or it may be fragrant jasmine rice. Whichever, it softens the impact of the curries, fiery salads (Thais love salads) and the fiercely hot clear soups and soup stews (both of which are called *kaeng* and are put on the table at the same time as all the other dishes, Chinese style, rather than being served before, western style).

The sort of wine that suits a variety of Thai dishes is young, fresh, crisp, dry, not too light-bodied and has good intensity of flavour and acidity. Almost invariably that means white wine, but not the German wines that go so well with Chinese food.

Classic German wines tend to be overwhelmed by Thai food, although **Riesling *Kabinett*** is a match for milder noodle dishes, France has more to offer, but, if there is an all-rounder, it is not a country but a grape, **Sauvignon Blanc**.

Sauvignon works in its classic, dry, pungent, minerally, grassy French form – Sancerre, Pouilly-Fumé, Menetou Salon. It works in the closely related, but slightly fuller Austrian form (especially Styrian). It also works in the more overtly fruity, ripe gooseberry style of New Zealand Sauvignons and also, increasingly, those of Chile and South Africa. Tangy New World Sauvignon blends with either Sémillon or Chardonnay also work, but classic white Bordeaux (Sémillon and Sauvignon) falls flat, as do most other French Sauvignons. Inexpensive, crisp, zesty Vin de Pays des Côtes de Gascogne, though insubstantial, is a better bet.

Chablis is also better, because of its acidity and steely intensity of flavour, but you have to be prepared for the food to strip the wine of some of its flavour and character. The same applies to ***brut*** champagne: Thai food makes it taste a little sweeter and blander (*demi-sec* is a complete mis-match).

Chardonnays, other than in Chablis and champagne, are not generally very successful, but a notable exception is ripe, oak-influenced **New World Chardonnay** with pork, chicken and even beef satay: the oak, fruit and butter in the wine complement the coconutty, peanut sauce.

Although most red loses out with Thai food, there are occasions when it works. Beef curries are the obvious case: the hottest, creamiest, most coconutty need the cut of **Sauvignon,** but a slightly milder, aromatic curry, in which the beef flavour is prominent, is better with red wine. Old World wines are more sympathetic – New World reds tend to be too powerful and fruity – but, that said, there are no easy or failsafe matches. *Cru Beaujolais* doesn't clash but is much diminished by the food; Merlot and Pinot Noir clash; Côtes du Rhône is acceptable but rather too peppery; more successful are **cheap Sicilian red wines,** which are designed for export markets and are typically medium-bodied with a spicy, softly fruity character. But the best partner I found for a red beef curry was a **Portuguese Cabernet Sauvignon**. It had the weight of a *cru bourgeois* Bordeaux, but was spicier and more supple. But I would still urge caution rather than conviction with red wine.

Japan

While one of the difficulties of matching wine to Chinese food is that it is easy to underestimate the delicacy of the flavours, with Japanese food the unexpected snare is more likely to be the reverse – underestimating the force of some of the flavours and their potential for slaying accompanying wine. Japanese food appears gloriously light and healthy, but it can pack a powerful punch, with sharp, vinegary notes, tear-jerkingly pungent ones and, as in Chinese food, some distinct sweetness permeating some of the savoury dishes.

Of all the Far Eastern cuisines Japanese can thus be the most treacherous for the wine drinker, but – if any justification were needed for drinking wine with Japanese food – the Japanese have been keenest to adopt the habit. That doesn't mean that wine is usual at Japanese meals – green tea and sake (rice wine) are still the staple drinks – but the number of wine drinkers and the amount of Western-style wine imported is growing. Happily, it is not doing so too much at the expense of the traditional food. Western food is eaten and Western influences are being absorbed into Japanese dishes, especially in smart restaurants where garlic, considered healthy, is highly fashionable and cognac sometimes replaces sake in recipes, but generally Japanese cuisine remains true to its traditions and consequently highly individual.

The Japanese cook has always required the freshest and highest quality of ingredients and aims to preserve the clarity of both flavour and texture by cooking them as briefly as possible. Poaching, grilling and pickling are key techniques. Fish and vegetables, in great variety, are fundamental – scarcely any red meat or dairy products were eaten until late last century – but rice is still the ultimate staple, even though consumption has dropped markedly. It is short-grained, slightly sticky, slightly sweet and, traditionally, it is served towards the end of the meal to allow time for drinking sake – to consume sake and rice together is viewed as gastronomic tautology. Along with a bowl of rice, and tea to drink, the other basics of a Japanese meal are a soup (most often *miso*) and a dish of pickled vegetables. Typically, three or four other dishes are then added: fresh fish, a fresh vegetable, perhaps chicken or other fowl, beef, or just some noodles (hot in soup, or, in summer, cold).

This may all sound relatively innocuous, especially as the pickles are not of the puckering astringency of traditional English ones, but Japanese seasonings and dipping sauces are not mild. Even when they are similar to Chinese, the Japanese cook uses them for greater impact. There are light and dark soy sauces, rice vinegar (relatively soft, like balsamic), *wasabi* (extremely pungent green horseradish which is made into a paste and used as a relish, especially with raw fish dishes), ginger, white radish, spring onions, sake, *mirin* (sweet sake), *miso* (salty, yeasty, fermented bean paste in many forms), sesame seeds, Japan or *sansho* pepper, sour plum paste (very sharp), lime-like citrus fruits and, increasingly, garlic. Hot red chillies are also used to add fire to some of the tart dipping sauces.

These are flavours which present an assault course for wine – and *wasabi*, above all, needs to be applied with caution if any wine is to survive – but what helps the wine drinker is sheer definition of flavour in Japanese food. Because of the liking for vinegar and citrus, wines nearly always need to be well endowed with acid: this directs you most often to whites; light to medium wines suit the weight of Japanese food; and intense, even assertive, flavours (but not oak) match the seasonings.

Recommended Wines

With the raw fish dishes, above all *sushi* (*canapés* of rice and raw fish, often wrapped in roasted *nori* seaweed) and *sashimi* (thin, diamond-shaped slices of raw fish), served variously with soy sauces, pickled ginger and *wasabi,* fine **German Rieslings** are very successful – *Kabinett* especially, including *Halbtrocken* from good vintages. **Non-vintage brut champagne,** especially *blanc de blancs,* and the best and driest of New World champagne-type sparkling wines also make sound accompaniments. Other alternatives include dry **New World Riesling** (it is less likely to overpower Japanese food than Chinese) and the high acidity of **English whites** such as Seyval Blanc. Sauvignon Blanc tends to be a touch too assertive, but Loire, New Zealand, Austrian, Chilean and cool climate South African **Sauvignons** (eg from Constantia) come into their own when *wasabi* is making its presence felt in a big way. The fresh, yeasty dryness of **manzanilla** and **fino sherry** works quite well and these sherries also go with the ubiquitous *miso* soup, and noodle dishes with *miso* (they are the closest Western style wine in taste to sake).

The same wines can generally be drunk with *tempura* (deep-fried fish and vegetables in the thinnest of batters), with the savoury steamed soup custards (*chawanmushi*), *nabemonos* (fish and/or vegetables cooked in a single pot at the table) and poultry dishes, but they can also be replaced with other dry whites, such as **Chablis, Pouilly-Fuissé, Italian Pinot Bianco, Jurançon, Verdicchio dei Castelli di Jesi,** provided flavourings and dipping sauces are not too strident. Japan's most vinegary marinated and soused fish dishes are, however, a no-go area for wine.

With beef dishes, such as *shabu shabu* (where each diner quickly cooks his own very thin slices of beef in simmering broth at the table) and the famous *teriyaki,* red wines can be drunk, but they must not be heavy, tannic or jammy. Because of the dipping sauces, particularly with *shabu shabu,* acidity is again an asset. **Loire reds** (Chinon, Saumur, Sancerre) work well, as does good **Beaujolais,** especially Fleurie. **Baden's** reds are another option, as are **Pinot Noirs** (even though acidity is not notable) from Oregon, Chile and California (medium price bracket). **Côte de Beaune** red burgundies can also be quite successful and Pomerol is worth considering.

MATCHING

Wine and MATCHING Food

WHETHER OR NOT YOU ARE ARMED WITH

ALL POSSIBLE DETAILS ABOUT A DISH AND

FULLY UNDERSTAND THE PRINCIPLES OF

MATCHING WINE TO FOOD, THERE ARE STILL

TIMES WHEN A FEW QUICK SUGGESTIONS

ARE VERY HANDY. EQUALLY, THERE ARE

OCCASIONS WHEN, APPROACHING THE

MATCHING PROCESS FROM THE OTHER END

WITH A SPECIAL BOTTLE OR AN UNFAMILIAR

ONE, AN INSTANT RECOMMENDATION IS ALL

YOU NEED TO INSPIRE IDEAS OF YOUR OWN.

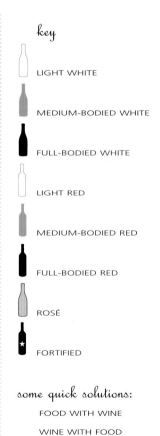

key

LIGHT WHITE

MEDIUM-BODIED WHITE

FULL-BODIED WHITE

LIGHT RED

MEDIUM-BODIED RED

FULL-BODIED RED

ROSÉ

FORTIFIED

some quick solutions:

FOOD WITH WINE

WINE WITH FOOD

FOOD WITH WINE

AGLIANICO DEL VULTURE
Italy (smoky spicy full-bodied red):
rabbit, hard cheese

ALIGOTE
France (tart dry white):
aperitif with dips, tortilla, mussels, snails, cod, trout

ALTO ADIGE
Italy (light crisp dry white):
spaghetti carbonara, simple fish or salads;
(light to medium-bodied red eg Merlot):
beef carpaccio

AMARONE
Italy (rich strong dry red):
powerful game casseroles, parmesan

AMONTILLADO
Spain (dry nutty concentrated sherry):
consommé, olives, tapas, salted nuts

ANJOU ROUGE
France (juicy medium-bodied red):
gammon steaks, lamb chops, nut cutlets

ARNEIS
Italy (dry fragrant quite complex white):
pasta with creamy sauces, simply prepared white fish and seafood, onion tart

ASTI (SPUMANTE)
Italy (light sweet sparkling white):
puddings: jelly, fruit salad, pavlova, lemon soufflé, light chocolate mousse or Christmas pudding

AUSBRUCH
Austria (luscious sweet white):
bread-and-butter pudding, apple strudel, crème brûlée, apricot tart

AUSLESE
Germany/Austria (sweet white):
fruit salad, apple pie; roast goose or duck with fruit sauce

BAIRRADA
Portugal (ripe full-bodied red):
roast pork, beef ragoût, aubergine stew, spicy nut cutlets

BANDOL
France (tannic aromatic vigorous red):
barbecued meats and vegetables, beef en daube, game

BANYULS
France (rich sweet fortified):
Christmas pudding, coffee and chocolate cakes or strong blue cheese

BARBARESCO
Italy (deep full-bodied red):
roast game, beef, offal (not sweetbreads), ceps, truffles

BARBERA D'ASTI
Italy (medium-bodied firm fresh red):
antipasti, spaghetti bolognese, tomatoes, parma ham; the only red that can take (just) smoked salmon

BARDOLINO
Italy (very light crisp red or rosé):
antipasti, cannelloni, seafood soup or stew

BAROLO
Italy (rich full-bodied red):
well-hung game, rich beef and game stews

BARSAC
France (rich sweet white):
peach brulée, raspberry soufflé, tarte tatin

BATARD-MONTRACHET
France (rich full-bodied dry white):
scallops, lobster or salmon with hollandaise or creamy sauces

BEAUJOLAIS
France (vibrant light to medium-bodied red):
charcuterie and cold roast meats, pork chops, fish in red wine sauce, mushrooms on toast

BEAUJOLAIS-VILLAGES
France (fruity medium-bodied red):
kidneys with mustard, charcuterie, sausages, salmon

BEAUMES-DE-VENISE, MUSCAT
France (very sweet fortified white):
caramelized oranges, rhubarb crumble, chocolate puddings

BEAUNE
France (medium- to full-bodied red):
rabbit casserole, roast duck with cherries, wild mushroom fricassée;
(medium- to full-bodied white): *fish pie*

BEERENAUSLESE
German/Austria (concentrated sweet white):
spotted dick, sachertorte, fruit-based puddings, pancakes

BERGERAC
France (medium-bodied red):
roast chicken or lamb steaks; **(dry crisp white):**
fish and chips, courgette soufflé

BERNKASTEL
German (fine penetrating dry to sweet white from the village, not Bereich), for the off-dry *Kabinett* style:
poached trout, sweetbreads in cream, cucumber mousse

BIANCO DI CUSTOZA
Italy (light dry white):
grilled cod, seafood soup, spinach and ricotta ravioli, quiche

BONNES-MARES
France (fine full-bodied red):
roast game, duck or goose, kidneys and morels

BORDEAUX
France (medium-bodied dry red):
lamb, Irish stew, rare roast beef (hot or cold) with old clarets; **(crisp dry white):** *grilled fish, mussels, poultry and seafood*

BOURGOGNE
France (medium-bodied red):
duck breast, oeufs en meurette, game, truffles; **(medium- to full-bodied white):**
fish in creamy sauces, cheese soufflé, roast chicken

BOURGUEIL
France (light- to medium-bodied red):
rabbit, duck pâté, charcuterie, carbonnade, shepherd's pie, asparagus

BROUILLY
France (fruity medium-bodied red):
cold meats, cotechino, stuffed peppers

BRUNELLO DI MONTALCINO
Italy (rich full-bodied red):
oxtail, game casseroles and pies, mushroom stews, hard cheeses

CABERNET SAUVIGNON
France/everywhere (tannic deeply flavoured red):
France: *red meats, especially lamb; poultry; mature hard cheese;*
California: *full-flavoured meaty casseroles;*
Australia: *kidneys or kangaroo or beef;*
New Zealand: *lamb;*
Chile/Argentina: *full-flavoured meat dishes;*
Eastern Europe: *sausages, lasagne, turkey;*
Italy: *char-grilled meat or game*

CAHORS
France (tannic concentrated red):
cassoulet, confit de canard or steak and kidney pie, braised lamb shanks, or try Cantal cheese

CAVA
Spain (sparkling dry white):
drink as an aperitif or with scrambled eggs and smoked salmon

CHABLIS
France (firm dry white):
white fish, eg Dover sole, turbot; shellfish or oysters; trout with almonds, poached salmon; brandade; kedgeree; deep-fried food; Chaource cheese

CHAMBERTIN
France (full-bodied red):
coq au vin, roast guinea-fowl, partridge, grouse; or hare or venison

CHAMBOLLE-MUSIGNY
France (medium- to full-bodied red):
roast poultry or pheasant, game, veal kidneys with ceps, truffle omelette

CHAMPAGNE, BRUT
France (fine dry sparkling):
drink as an aperitif or, oysters, smoked salmon or caviar, or with Chinese food

CHARDONNAY
France/everywhere (from the Old World, medium-bodied fruity dry white):
drink with cheese and egg dishes, asparagus and artichokes, potted shrimps and other seafood, poultry, or dishes with nut sauces;
(from the New World, full-bodied fruity voluptuous white): *richly sauced/flavoured food such as lobster thermidor, guacamole, vegetable terrine, duck à l'orange, or mild creamy coconutty curries*

CHASSAGNE-MONTRACHET
France (rich full-bodied white):
roast veal or richly sauced fish, grilled turbot;
(full-bodied red): *mature cheeses including Brie, game birds*

CHATEAUNEUF-DU-PAPE
France (full-bodied red):
casseroles, eg lamb, beef, venison, game or lentil; cassoulet or roast goose

CHENIN BLANC
France/New World (crisp dry, medium or sweet white):
Loire: *as an aperitif or with delicate creamy fish dishes; if sweet, with fruit-based or almondy puddings;*
New World (dry): *curry, stuffed courgettes*

CHEVALIER-MONTRACHET
France (luxurious full-bodied dry white):
mussels, lobster, prawns, scallops in cream sauce, duck or goose

CHIANTI
Italy (fruity medium-bodied red):
spinach and ricotta cannelloni, cold meats, simple light meat dishes, pizza, barbecues

CHIANTI CLASSICO
Italy (full-bodied red):
roast pork, grilled steak, white truffles with pasta

CHINON
France (juicy medium-bodied red):
asparagus, goat's cheese, fish (eg red mullet in red wine), charcuterie, not too heavy meat dishes, eg stews in beer or stout

CHIROUBLES
France (medium-bodied fruity red):
steak tartare, Brie, rabbit in red wine, boiled or grilled gammon

COLOMBARD
France (light dry white):
light salads and snacks, Thai food

COLLIO
Italy (light dry white), eg Sauvignon:
shellfish, corn on the cob, pork with ginger and garlic

COMMANDARIA
Cyprus (rich sweet concentrated dessert wine):
Christmas pudding or cake, chocolate ice-cream

CONDRIEU
France (full-bodied very aromatic white):
crab, lobster, creamy curries; pork with rosemary

COPERTINTO
Italy (ripe full-bodied red):
hearty stews, barbecued red meat

CORBIERES
France (full-bodied red):
lamb, liver and onions, game pie, potted hare, ratatouille, sausages, mussels Provençal

CORNAS
France (dark sturdy full-bodied red):
beef casseroles, rare steak, wild duck, kidneys

CORTON
France (rich powerful red):
roast or casseroled poultry or game

CORTON-CHARLEGMAGNE
France (rich luxurious full-bodied white):
roast veal, lobster, richly-sauced white fish, fresh salmon and scallops

COTE DE BEAUNE
France (medium-bodied red):
roast pheasant, vegetable rissoles, sweetbreads;
(full-bodied white): *lobster, richly-sauced fish dishes*

COTE CHALONNAISE
France (medium-bodied white):
pasta and poultry, especially in cream sauces, Parma and Bayonne hams

COTEAUX DU LANGUEDOC
France (medium- to full-bodied red):
steak, stews, rabbit with mustard

COTEAUX DU LAYON
France (very sweet yet crisp white):
fruit-based and nut-based puddings and pastries; rich pâtés

COTES DE BOURG
France (medium-bodied red):
lentil stew, spaghetti bolognese, lamb chops

COTES DU RHONE
France (medium-bodied red):
shepherds pie or moussaka, goulash, sausages, vegetarian casseroles, chilli con carne, ratatouille

CROZES-HERMITAGE
France (full-bodied red):
pot-roast pheasant, beef casserole, game and meatballs

DAO
Portugal (solid full-bodied red):
beefburgers, heart (lamb), grilled kidneys, lamb with garlic and rosemary, moussaka

DOLCETTO
Italy (light-bodied red):
Mozzarella or Fontina cheese, cold meat, meaty pasta dishes, stuffed peppers, osso buco, black pudding

ECHEZEAUX
France (fine full-bodied fragrant red):
game birds, venison, mushrooms, truffles

EISWEIN
German (luscious concentrated sweet white):
buttery biscuits, peaches, greengages, fruit puddings

ENTRE-DEUX-MERS
France (light- to medium-bodied dry fresh white):
shellfish, seafood, salads

EST!EST!!EST!!!
Italy (light dry white):
spaghetti carbonara, *mussels*

FITOU
France (full-bodied spicy red):
cassoulet, lamb with flageolets, vegetable bakes, pork sausages

FLEURIE
France (fruity medium-bodied red):
rabbit with mustard, wild mushrooms, nut roast, sausages, charcuterie

FRASCATI
Italy (light-bodied dry white):
light pasta dishes, white fish, chicken chow mein, omelettes

FRONSAC
France (medium-bodied red):
mixed grill, guinea-fowl, roast and grilled lamb

FUME BLANC
California (medium- to full-bodied dry white):
barbecued fish, vegetables and poultry, lightly spiced curries

G

GAILLAC
France (medium-bodied red):
garbure, confit de canard, Bayonne ham; **(dry white):** *pasta and pesto, sardines, mackerel, herrings*

GAMAY
See *Beaujolais*

GATTINARA
Italy (full-bodied red):
pasta with hare sauce (pappardelle alle lepre), porcini mushrooms, Parmesan

GEVREY-CHAMBERTIN
France (fine full-bodied red):
game birds, especially in casseroles (but not when too well hung), coq au vin, duck, mushroom dishes, mature cheeses including soft ripe ones such as Milleens and Camembert

GEWURZTRAMINER
France/New World (spicy medium- to full-bodied white):
pungent cheese dishes, smoked salmon, pork rillettes, pâtés, spicy food, onion tart, cooked red peppers; **(sweet, from late-harvested grapes):** *foie gras and pâtés; puddings*

GIGONDAS
France (full-bodied red):
rich meat and game casseroles; roast goose; moussaka; char-grilled steak

GRAVES
France (medium- to full-bodied dry red):
game terrine, roast lamb; steak, kidney and oyster pie; **(medium- to full-bodied white):** *mussel stew with cream, or any richly-sauced fish dish*

GROS PLANT DU PAYS NANTAIS
France (crisp dry light white):
crudités, oily fish eg mackerel, oysters

HERMITAGE
France (full-bodied red):
beef dishes/casseroles, rare steak, beef wellington, roast and casseroled game, English hard cheeses

JULIENAS
France (fruity medium-bodied red):
steak tartare, coq au vin, escargots

JURANCON
France (medium-bodied tangy dry and sweet white):
dry: *sauced fish, salades composées, cheese fondue;* **sweet:** *foie gras, Brebis cheeses, pastries*

KABINETT
German (light off-dry white):
smoked fish, sushi and sashimi, Chinese food, crab salad

KEKFRANKOS
Hungary (light to medium-bodied red):
toad in the hole, sausage and mash, faggots, beef stroganov

L

LAMBRUSCO SECCO DOC
Italy (sparkling tangy red):
Parma ham and salami, cotecchino

LIEBFRAUMILCH
German (light-bodied semi-sweet white):
drink, if at all, as an apertif or with dim sum

LIQUEUR MUSCAT
Australia (concentrated fortified dessert wine):
Christmas pudding, mince pies, dark chocolate mousse, ice-cream

LIRAC
France (full-bodied red):
rabbit and other game casseroles, smoked ham, barbecued meat

LOUPIAC
France (concentrated sweet white):
strawberry or raspberry mousse, crêpes suzette, bread and butter pudding

LUGANA
Italy (medium-bodied dry white):
braised fennel, pasta and pesto, stuffed courgettes or aubergines, Chinese food

M

MACON
France (medium- to full-bodied dry white):
cream-based dishes, eg pasta, Parma ham, seafood brochettes, roast chicken, blanquette de veau; **(medium-bodied red):** *pork or charcuterie, fish cooked in red wine*

MADEIRA
Madeira (tangy dry to lusciously sweet fortified):
dry: *salted almonds, consommé;* **sweet eg Malmsey:** *Christmas cake or pudding, mince pies and brandy butter, baked apples*

MADIRAN
France (dark full-bodied red):
confit de canard, magret, *substantial stews*

MALAGA
Spain (concentrated fortified dessert wine):
steamed chocolate, date or Christmas pudding; ice-cream and fudge sauce

MANZANILLA
Spain (tangy dry lightly fortified white):
tapas, consommé, olives, salted nuts

MARGAUX

France (complex medium-bodied red):
roast lamb with herbs, fillet steak, roast duck or goose

MARSALA

Italy (fortified tangy dry to concentrated sweet):
dry: *aperitif with nuts or oily antipasti;*
sweet: *chocolate and almond gâteau, sticky toffee pudding*

MARSANNE

France/Austria (full-bodied fruity dry white):
spicy or coconutty dishes, creamy curries

MEDOC

France (medium-bodied red):
simply roast or grilled meat such as lamb (especially with Pauillac or St-Julien), roast pork and garlic, roast chicken, kidneys, cheese soufflé

MERLOT

France/everywhere (soft medium- to full-bodied red):
beef with stout, bean stew; **(New World):** *try calf's liver and grilled food including tuna*

MEURSAULT

France (full-bodied dry white):
chicken with truffles, monkfish or scallops in cream sauce, asparagus with hollandaise

MINERVOIS

France (medium- to full-bodied red):
ratatouille, lamb with flageolets, squid with tomato stuffing, spicy sausages

MONBAZILLAC

France (concentrated sweet white):
pears stuffed with blue cheese, sautéed foie gras and apples, crème caramel

MONTEPULCIANO D'ABRUZZO

Italy (medium- to full-bodied red):
lasagne, rabbit and peppers, chicken with olives, spaghetti bolognese, pizza

MONTEPULCIANO, VINO NOBILE DE

Italy (full-bodied red):
roast boar or pork, roast pigeon, quail

MONTILLA

Spain (tangy dry white):
aperitif with salted nuts or savoury biscuits

MONTLOUIS

France (dry, medium-sweet or sweet white):
dry/medium: *aperitif or delicately-flavoured shellfish or fish in creamy sauces;*
sweet: *fruit tarts*

MONTRACHET, LE

France (finest rich full-bodied dry white):
chicken with crayfish, rich-sauced lobster, turbot

MORELLINO DI SCANSANO

Italy (fruity medium to full-bodied red):
roast marinaded lamb, mixed grill, pork chops

MOREY-SAINT-DENIS

France (fragrant medium- to full-bodied red):
game birds and venison, roast or casseroled

MORGON

France (juicy full-bodied red):
casseroles, braised beef with olives, cassoulet, coq au vin

MOSCATO D'ASTI

Italy (light sweet sparkling white):
baked Alaska, meringue nests, Christmas pudding

MOSEL

German (light aromatic white):
smoked mackerel with black peppercorns, Gravad Lax, duck à l'orange

MOULIN-A-VENT

France (juicy full-bodied red):
baked ham, beef wellington, steak tartare

MUSCADET

France (light crisp dry white):
moules marinières, oysters, plateau des fruits de la mer, herb omelette; light antipasti and salads, mackerel

MUSCAT

France/everywhere (dry to very sweet grapey white):
dry: *chicken with grapes, avocado salad;*
sweet: *puddings – exotic fruit salad, mince pies, chocolate, nut and ginger-based puddings*

NAVARRA

Spain (medium dry white):
fried whitebait, bouillabaisse;
(rosé): *grilled red mullet;*
(red): *chorizo, spicy vegetable couscous, lamb*

NEMEA

Greece (strong full-bodied red):
meatballs, goulash, moussaka, kleftiko

NIERSTEIN

German (light medium-dry to sweet white), best wines only, medium-dry *Kabinett* style:
Chinese dishes, including dim sum, or light salads, or drink as aperitif

NUITS-SAINT-GEORGES

France (full-bodied red):
any game, venison steaks, goose confit, kidneys with wild mushrooms

OLOROSO

Spain (full-flavoured dry to sweet fortified):
dry: *olives, hard cheese;*
sweet: *trifle, crème brûlée, chocolate gâteau*

ORVIETO

Italy (crisp dry to medium-sweet white):
dry: *pasta carbonara, grilled plaice, other light fish dishes;* **sweet:** *fruit salad, almond biscuits*

P

PASSITO

Italy (concentrated sweet white):
Blue cheese, baked peaches, praline ice-cream

PAUILLAC

France (fine medium to full-bodied red):
lamb with rosemary, stewed pigeons, roast guinea fowl

PINOT BLANC/BIANCO

France/Italy (medium-bodied dry white):
good with fish, cheese and egg dishes: quiche lorraine, pike in cream sauce, pasta and pesto; also try with Thai green curry

PINOT GRIS/GRIGIO

France/Italy (light to full-bodied white):
Pinot Gris: *cold dishes and spicy dishes, courgette or onion flan, pork with juniper;*
Pinot Grigio: *mushroom ravioli, linguine with cream and Parmesan;* **sweet:** *foie gras, smooth liver pâtés, puddings*

PINOT NOIR

France/everywhere (Old World: fine light- to full-bodied red): *roast poultry, game, charcuterie, meatier fish eg red mullet;*
(New World: ripe medium- to full-bodied red): *cold meat or game, partridge with spiced damsons, duck with mango, tuna, salmon*

POMEROL

France (medium- to full-bodied red):
pork with prunes, char-grilled or simply roast lamb or steak, wild duck and ceps, Camembert

POMMARD

France (velvety full-bodied red):
wild boar, sautéed ham or kidneys, pheasant and truffles, other game

PORT
Portugal (sweet fortified):
Stilton, blue cheeses and Cheddars, chocolate cake or pudding, nuts

POUILLY-FUISSE
France (full-bodied white):
pasta, poultry, fish in creamy sauces, asparagus quiche, gougères, salmon en croûte

POUILLY-FUME
France (crisp concentrated dry white):
trout meunière, smoked salmon sandwiches, creamy chicken pie, goat's cheese

PULIGNY-MONTRACHET
France (fine full-bodied dry white):
lobster, crab soufflé, monkfish

R

RECIOTO
Italy (concentrated sweet red or white):
red: *blue cheeses;* **white:** *foie gras and puddings that are not too sweet: cakes, biscuits, fruit fools*

RETSINA
Greece (strong medium-bodied white):
taramasalata, olives, spiced chick-pea bake

RHEINGAU
German (dry to sweet intense white):
medium-dry: *sweetbreads, braised celery, pork, duck or goose with fruit sauce;* **sweet:** *fruit pies and tarts,* langues du chat *biscuits*

RIBEIRO
Spain (crisp dry white):
smoked mackerel with black peppercorns, deep fried courgettes or aubergines;
(red): *sardines*

RIBERA DEL DUERO
Spain (full-bodied red):
beef en croûte, spit-roasted boar and other roast meats, mature hard cheeses

RICHEBOURG
France (luxurious full-bodied red):
game birds, venison, magret, calf's liver

RIESLING
Germany/everywhere (Old World: light aromatic dry to sweet white): *stir-fried or poached dishes, eg poached sole; avocado salad, roast hot or cold goose, duck, wild-boar; apple and raspberry puddings;* **(New World: ripe aromatic dry to sweet white):** *southeast Asian curries, sun-dried tomatoes, roast vegetables, puddings*

RIOJA
Spain (medium- to full-bodied red and white):
red: *casseroled or roast lamb, game or poultry, mushrooms, truffles;* **white:** *onion tart, tapas, barbecued chicken*

ROMANEE-CONTI, LA
France (fine complex full-bodied red):
See *Vosne-Romanée*

ROSE D'ANJOU/DE LOIRE
France (dry to medium-dry):
aperitif or gentle salads

ROUSSILLON, COTES DU
France (full-bodied red):
vegetable-based dishes, spiced pork or beef, snails with anchovy butter

RUEDA
Spain (light- to medium-bodied dry or sherry-like white):
simple or garlicky fish, seafood and poultry, green vegetables and salads

RULLY
France (medium-bodied red):
roast pork, coq au vin; **(dry white):** *jambon persillé, artichokes, cheese fondue*

S

SAINT-EMILION
France (medium- to full-bodied red):
roast beef, wild boar with chestnuts, roast turkey, lobster in red wine, chicken casserole, truffles, Camembert

SAINT-ESTEPHE
France (medium- to full-bodied red):
roast lamb, lamb en croûte, lamb with flageolets, lampreys in red wine

SAINT-JOSEPH
France (full-bodied red):
Toulouse sausage, barbecued kebabs, beef casseroles, roasted vegetables, game

SAINT-NICOLAS DE BOURGUEIL
France (light to medium-bodied red):
See *Bourgueil*

SALICE SALENTINO
Italy (ripe full-bodied red):
game stew, stuffed aubergine, some curries

SANCERRE
France (medium-bodied crisp dry white):
poached trout, smoked salmon sandwiches, avocado mousse, goat's cheese, sashimi; **(light red):** *brandade, fish like red mullet or salmon*

SAUMUR-CHAMPIGNY
France (light-bodied red):
lighter meat dishes such as spring lamb, cheese and herb soufflé, salmon-trout

SAUTERNES
France (luscious sweet white):
salty blue cheeses, foie gras, duck with orange and honey, cream-based puddings eg crème caramel and brûlée

SAUVIGNON BLANC
France/everywhere (tangy dry white): Loire: *seafood salad, Thai food, asparagus quiche;* **New World:** *more intense flavours and denser textures such as hollandaise and mayonnaise sauces, asparagus and shellfish, tomatoes and Thai food*

SAVENNIERES
France (intense, crisp dry white):
river fish, sorrel sauce, goat's cheese soufflé

SEMILLON
France/Australia (Old World: medium-bodied dry white – usually blended): *prawns, mussels and many other fish;* **(New World: ripe and full-bodied white):** *fish pie, richly-sauced fish, spicy pork dishes;* **(botrytised):** *Roquefort cheese, cream-based puddings, honey-roast poultry*

SHERRY
Spain (fortified dry to sweet):
dry fino to medium amontillado: *gazpacho, olives, grilled sardines;* **very sweet oloroso:** *mince pies, fudge or chocolate ice-cream, treacle pudding*

SHIRAZ
Australian (ripe full-bodied red):
rich meat stews, barbecued meat or vegetables, chilli con carne, roast goose, duck and turkey with traditional trimmings

SILVANER
German (light dry white):
cheese choux puffs, quiche lorraine, poached fish or poultry

SOAVE
Italy (light dry white):
pasta and pesto, spinach and ricotta tortelloni, chicken salad, light fish dishes

SPARKLING SHIRAZ
Australia (full sparkling red):
roast turkey, mature goat's cheese, rich pâtés

SPATBURGUNDER
German (light- to medium-bodied red):
boiled ham; sausages – smoked, fresh and garlic; stuffed mushrooms

SPATLESE

German (light medium-sweet white):
pork with mustard, cold roast pork and duck, sun-dried tomatoes, crab mousse

SYRAH

France (aromatic usually full-bodied red):
game and cold meats, beef cooked in red wine, liver, wild mushroom dishes, hard cheeses

TACHE, LA

France (fine full-bodied red):
See *Vosne-Romanée*

TAVEL

France (full-bodied dry rosé):
fish soup, stuffed red peppers, ratatouille and couscous

TOKAJI

Hungary (dry to intensely sweet white):
dry: *aperitif with nuts;* **sweet:** *Christmas pudding, treacle tart, crème caramel, mild creamy blue cheese, foie gras*

TOKAY-PINOT GRIS

France (full-bodied dry to sweet white):
See *Pinot Gris*

TREBBIANO

Italy (light dry white):
pasta carbonara, spinach canelloni, sardines, weiner schnitzel

TROCKEN

German/Austria (light dry white):
fairly plain fish dishes, light salads

TROCKENBEERENAUSLESE

German/Austria (intense sweet white):
apple and sultana tart, Black Forest gâteau, pavlova, crêpes suzette

VACQUEYRAS

France (full-bodied red):
cassoulet, rabbit stew, stuffed peppers, snails in garlic butter, pigeon

VALDEPENAS

Spain (medium- to full-bodied red):
stuffed squid, olive and garlic bread, herb-roasted lamb or braised lamb shanks, kebabs, or try with any cooked mushroom dishes

VALPOLICELLA

Italy (fruity light red):
deep fried mushrooms, tuna and bean salad, lentil patties, sausages, bresaola

VENDANGE TARDIVE

France (intense sweet white):
baked custard tart, terrine of foie gras, Munster cheese

VERDELHO

Australia (ripe tangy dry white):
spicy dishes, including Indian, roast vegetables;
Madiera (fortified medium-dry white):
salted nuts and olives, game consommé

VERDICCHIO

Italy (light dry white):
linguine with cream and smoked salmon, fish and chips, seafood salad

VERNACCIA DI SAN GIMIGNANO

Italy (light- to medium-bodied dry white):
pasta and pesto, salmon carpaccio, fish stews

VIN JAUNE

France (concentrated maderized dry white):
duck with olives, ripe hard cheeses

VIN DE PAILLE

France (concentrated sweet white):
apricot soufflé, sweet omelette, apple charlotte, praline gâteau

VIN SANTO

Italy (concentrated sweet white):
cantuccini biscuits, apple fritters, panforte, walnuts, hazelnuts and pecans

VINHO VERDE

Portugal (crisp light dry white):
oily fish such as sardines, light green vegetable meals and salads

VIOGNIER

France (medium- to full-bodied dry white):
lobster or scallops with saffron, crab, carrot and orange soup, spiced parsnips, chicken korma and other mild to medium curries; it also goes well with rosemary

VOLNAY

France (medium- to full-bodied red):
roast veal, duck or beef, mushroom or game dishes

VOSNE-ROMANEE

France (perfumed medium- to full-bodied complex red):
saddle of venison, not too well hung game birds, casseroles, ceps and truffles, mature cheeses

VOUGEOT, CLOS DE

France (fine full-bodied red):
boeuf à la bourguignonne, grand game dishes

VOUVRAY

France (dry to sweet white):
dry to medium: *delicately-flavoured fish like trout in cream, goat's cheese soufflé;* **sweet:** *tarte tatin, baked pears, apricot and peach tarts, nut pastries*

WHITE ZINFANDEL

California (medium-dry medium-bodied rosé):
aperitif or prawn cocktail – nothing serious

ZINFANDEL

California (aromatic powerful red):
well-flavoured, spicy dishes (can have a touch of sweetness eg barbecue sauce with spare ribs), game casserole, Thanksgiving turkey and its traditional accompaniments, steak with mustard and soy sauce, ratatouille, stuffed peppers, anchovy and olive antipasti, and even dark chocolate biscuit cake

WINE WITH FOOD

AIOLI:
crisp dry white or rosé such as Soave Classico or Provence rosé

ALMOND CAKE:
sweet white eg Coteaux du Layon, Muscat de Rivesaltes, Australian botrytised Semillon or Setúbal Moscatel

ALMONDS, SALTED:
tangy dry aperitif, such as fino sherry or Sercial Madeira

ANCHOVIES, SALTED:
difficult, but try fino or manzanilla, white Ribeiro, Spanish rosé or Muscadet sur lie

ANTIPASTI:
easy-drinking Italian red or white such as Dolcetto or Verdicchio, or try a young dry rosé

APPLE PIE OR FRITTERS:
Riesling Beerenauslese or sweet Chenin Blanc such as Côteaux du Layon

ARTICHOKES:
tangy white eg a modern Greek or Hungarian white, New Zealand Sauvignon, young white Rioja, or a crisp Chardonnay

ASPARAGUS:
crisp Sauvignon eg from Chile, Constantia, Bergerac or Bordeaux; Mosel Kabinett or young Chardonnay, including burgundy or Chablis when served with melted butter; or try red Cabernet Franc such as Anjou-Villages

AUBERGINE, STUFFED:
aromatic herby red such as Bandol or Côtes du Roussillon

AVOCADO VINAIGRETTE OR SALAD:
clean crisp white, especially Sauvignon, eg from New Zealand; or non-vintage brut champagne, Chablis or other young Chardonnay

BACON, BOILED:
fruity soft red such as a California Pinot Noir, Beaujolais-Villages, young Tempranillo or inexpensive Shiraz

BANANAS, BAKED, FLAMBEED OR FRITTERS:
well-balanced sweet white such as Loupiac or Muscat de Beaumes-de-Venise

BARBECUED FISH:
Australian Semillon, oaked or unoaked

BASS, GRILLED:
complex dry, not too fruity white eg mature Chablis or Roero Arneis; red Chinon at a pinch

BEAN CASSEROLE:
full and spicy red such as an Australian Shiraz or Fitou

BEEF, BOURGUIGNONNE:
full-bodied Pinot Noir eg Gevrey Chambertin or one from Western Australia

BEEF EN CROUTE:
sophisticated mature red such as claret or Merlot or Argentinian Cabernet Sauvignon or Malbec

BISON STEAK:
top Pomerol or New World Merlot, or Australian Shiraz or Cabernet Sauvignon

BLACK FOREST GATEAU:
intensely sweet white such as Trockenbeerenauslese, or for a contrast, Australian sparkling Shiraz

BLACKBERRY AND APPLE CRUMBLE:
refreshing very sweet white eg New Zealand botrytised Riesling or Austrian Ausbruch

BLINIS:
something refreshing, sparkling and luxurious such as champagne

BLUE CHEESE:
rich sweet red, white or brown – port, Recioto, Sauternes, Bual Madeira

BOUILLABAISSE:
medium to full dry rosé such as Tavel or Rioja rosado, or herby southern French white

BRANDADE:
firm full dry white eg premier cru Chablis or young light red eg Sancerre

BREAD AND BUTTER PUDDING:
rich, sweet wine such as Sauternes, Ste-Croix du Mont, Australian botrytised Semillon or sweet Austrian wine

BRESAOLA:
juicy medium-bodied Italian red such as young Chianti or Valpolicella Classico

BROCCOLI MORNAY:
avoid grassy Sauvignon and Cabernet – try Muscadet sur lie or Mâcon Blanc-Villages

CAESAR SALAD:
well-flavoured white, especially Chardonnay, eg from California or NY State

CALF'S LIVER:
medium- to full-bodied fruity red such as Rioja crianza, Morgon (or other Beaujolais cru), Salice Salentino

CANNELLONI:
medium-bodied red such as Chianti Rufina, Montepulciano d'Abruzzo, Parrina or California Sangiovese

CARPACCIO:
fresh red eg Dolcetto, fine Tuscan red such as Carignano or pink champagne

CASSEROLES, MEATY:
sturdy red such as California Cabernet or Zinfandel, Bairrada, Hermitage or Copertino; chicken in red wine: Côte Chalonnaise Pinot Noir; lamb: Eastern European Cabernet, Nemea, Naoussa or Côtes du Rhône; beef: Gevrey-Chambertin, Vosne-Romanée, Cornas, Barolo

CASSOULET:
intense fruity red eg Morgon, or a more robust one eg Cahors, Corbières, Copertino

CAULIFLOWER CHEESE:
full-bodied white such as Australian Semillon-Chardonnay or clean, fresh Sauvignon

CAVIAR:
champagne, mature vintage or non-vintage

CEVICHE:
piercingly fresh Sauvignon eg from Chile or New Zealand, or dry Vinho Verde

CHARCUTERIE:
easy-drinking young red such as Beaujolais, Chinon, Côtes du Rhône or Chilean Cabernet Sauvignon, or try Swiss Pinot Noir or Dôle

CHATEAUBRIAND:
grand elegant red such as mature claret or New World equivalent

CHEESE: See page 22

CHEESECAKE:
California Muscat, Sauternes or other botrytised Semillon, or Asti

CHERRY TART:
vibrant sweet wine from the Loire Valley such as Coteaux du Layon, or German Riesling Beerenauslese or California Black Muscat

CHICKEN:
(in general): many styles of red or white – the grander the dish, the finer the wine, from red Bergerac to white St-Véran, to mature clarets like Pomerol; (smoked): oaked Chardonnay – New World, vin de pays, Mâcon or Chalonnaise

CHILLI CON CARNE:
full-bodied, spicy red eg Zinfandel, Shiraz

CHINESE FOOD:
crisp aromatic white such as Riesling Kabinett, Gewürztraminer, New Zealand Sauvignon Blanc, or light reds such as the lighter Baden Spätburgunders; or Pomerol

CHOCOLATE:
fortified sweet wine: Malága, liqueur Muscat or 10-year-old tawny port; with chocolate pudding: Muscat de Beaumes-de-Venise, youngish Sauternes

CHORIZO:
fruity-spicy red: Navarra, Pinotage or Grenache

CHOUCROUTE:
crisp aromatic white such as Alsace Riesling, Pinot Blanc or Hungarian Furmint

CHOWDERS:
rich buttery white eg California or southern French Chardonnay

CHRISTMAS CAKE:
rich sweet fortified wine such as Malmsey, liqueur Muscat or very sweet sherry

CHRISTMAS PUDDING:
Asti or rich, sweet fortified wine eg liqueur Muscat, Málaga or Banyuls

COD:
not too fruity medium to full-bodied white such as Mâcon or white Rhône

COFFEE GATEAU OR ICE-CREAM:
sweet Muscat wines, especially fortified ones such as Rutherglen liqueur Muscat

CONSOMME:
dry fortified wine eg fino or amontillado sherry or Sercial Madeira

COQ AU VIN:
red burgundy or top California Pinot Noir

CORN ON THE COB:
full-bodied oak-aged Chardonnay eg California, or Alsace or Hungarian Pinot Gris

CORNISH PASTY:
straightforward medium-bodied red such as Sangiovese di Romagna or Valdepeñas

COUSCOUS:
spicy red Shiraz, Petite Sirah or well-chilled dry rosé or Lebanese or Morrocan red

CRAB:
fine, full-bodied white, eg Côte de Beaune, Viognier, Riesling Spätlese, vintage champagne

CREME BRULEE:
rich sweet wine: Sauternes, botrytised Sémillon, fortified Muscat or Austrian Ausbruch

CREME CARAMEL:
the same sort of rich, sweet, even fortified wines as crème brûlée

CREPES SUZETTE:
refreshing sweet white such as Orange Muscat, Asti or sparkling Vouvray

CROCODILE TAIL:
fresh full savoury white eg premier cru Chablis

CROQUE MONSIEUR:
full-bodied fruity dry white like Australian Chardonnay, or light red: Beaujolais or Dôle

CRUDITES:
fresh dry white such as Pinot Blanc, Pinot Grigio or Alsace Muscat

CURRIES:
aromatic and spicy or fruity whites, eg New World Chardonnay or Marsanne, or dry Muscat or Gewürztraminer; or low tannin reds such as Shiraz and Rioja crianza

CUSTARD TART:
sweet white such as Muscat de Beaumes-de-Venise or Monbazillac

DATE PUDDING:
rich, sweet fortified wine such as liqueur Muscat, Málaga or PX sherry

DIM SUM:
crisp, dry white such as Chilean Sauvignon, Australian Riesling, Mosel Kabinett, champagne

DUCK:
(in general): rich, gamey red such as Nuits-St-Georges, Pomerol, Carneros Pinot Noir, Salice Salentino or Australian Shiraz; (with orange): ripe dry to medium-sweet white eg Australian Chardonnay, Pfalz Auslese, or even Barsac; (smoked): white burgundy or Vin de Pays de l'Ardèche Chardonnay, but not New World Chardonnay

EEL, SMOKED:
tangy dry fino sherry, New Zealand Sauvignon

EGGS:
best served with dry sparkling wine for brunch dishes, or not too oaky Chardonnay, or medium-bodied Pinot Blanc

FAGGOTS:
medium-bodied juicy red: Gaillac or Barbera

FISH PIE:
creamy medium- to full-bodied white: Alsace, Baden or Austrian Pinot Blanc, or Chardonnay

FISHCAKES:
crisp aromatic white such as New Zealand Sauvignon or Chablis or young Chardonnay

FOIE GRAS:
concentrated sweet white such as Alsace Pinot Gris, Sauternes, Jurançon, Tokaji, Recioto di Soave; or sparkling red Shiraz

FONDUE, CHEESE:
well-structured, ripe white eg California Chardonnay or New World Sauvignon

FONDUE, MEAT:
full juicy red such as Morgon or California or Coonawarra Cabernet

FRANKFURTERS:
light fruity red such as German Spätburgunder or Alsace Pinot Noir

FRUIT COMPOTE OR SALAD:
sweet, grapey or sparkling white eg Muscat de Rivesaltes or Asti or Moscato spumante

FRUIT-BASED PUDDINGS:
sweet Loire wines (eg Bonnezeaux or Quarts de Chaume) or sweet (Beerenauslese level) Rieslings from Germany, Austria, Australasia, Canada

GAME:
sophisticated medium- to full-bodied reds, especially Pinot Noir (including burgundy) and Syrah (including Northern Rhônes)

GAME CASSEROLE:
full-bodied red eg Hermitage, Gevrey-Chambertin, Barbaresco or Barossa Shiraz

GAME PIE:
mature medium- to full-bodied red such as fine claret, Rioja riserva, Ribera del Duero, Crozes-Hermitage or red burgundy

GAMMON:
See *Bacon;* see *Ham*

GAZPACHO:
fino or manzanilla sherry or young Sauvignon

GINGER:
in curries and puddings – Muscat-based wine

GNOCCHI:
light Italian wine eg white Pinot Grigio or red Merlot or Valpolicella

GOAT'S CHEESE SALAD OR SOUFFLE:
Loire Sauvignon (Pouilly-Fumé or Sancerre), New World Sauvignon or Loire Cabernet Franc

GOOSE:
mature gamey red such as Pomerol, Morey-St-Denis, Côte Rôtie or Shiraz or Pfalz or Rheingau Riesling Spätlese

GOOSEBERRY FOOL:
sweet Riesling – botrytised Australasian, German Beerenauslese or Austrian Ausbruch

GOUGERE:
smooth fairly full dry white such as mature Graves, Mâcon-Villages or Tokay-Pinot Gris

GOULASH:
fairly robust fruity red eg Costières de Nîmes, Primitivo, young Tempranillo

GRAPEFRUIT:
best avoided, but otherwise Gros Plant, Pouilly-Fumé, bone-dry Vinho Verde

GRAVAD LAX:
Mosel Riesling Kabinett, top New World Chardonnay or blanc de blancs champagne

GROUSE:
mature fine red such as Echezeaux, Hermitage, Barbaresco, super-Tuscan or Amarone

GUACAMOLE:
aromatic crisp dry white eg New Zealand (or similar) Sauvignon or dry Muscat; or non-vintage champagne

GUINEA FOWL:
elegant Pinot Noir such as Volnay or Oregon, or mature white burgundy

HADDOCK, SMOKED:
good quality oak-matured but not oaky white eg Graves or New World Chardonnay; or crisp Sauvignon for contrast; at a pinch dry Languedoc rosé

HAGGIS:
medium- to full-bodied red eg young claret or New World Cabernet

HAM:
medium-bodied red such as Chinon, Givry or California Pinot Noir; or white such as Côte Chalonnaise

HARE:
fine gamey full-bodied red burgundy such as Morey-St-Denis, Vosne-Romanée or Nuits-St-Georges; or Ribera del Duero; or Barbaresco

HAZELNUT SHORTCAKE:
concentrated sweet white eg Loire Chenin Blanc or fortified Muscat

HEART, STUFFED:
Full-bodied red such as Shiraz-Cabernet, Bairrada or St-Joseph

HERRING:
crisp but not too assertive white such as Muscadet sur lie or Aligoté; marinated: German Riesling Kabinett or fino sherry

HUMMUS:
very crisp dry white such as modern Greek or Hungarian

ICE-CREAM:
fortified Muscat eg Australian liqueur Muscats or Muscat de Beaumes-de-Venise

IRISH STEW:
flavoursome young red such as Vin de Pays d'Oc Cabernet or Côtes du Ventoux

JAMBALAYA:
penetrating crisp dry white especially Sauvignon Blanc eg Sancerre or New Zealand

JOHN DORY:
full-bodied classic Chardonnay, especially burgundy and top California wines; with creamy sauce, Alsace Pinot Gris or Ruländer

KANGAROO:
deeply flavoured ripe red eg Shiraz, Australian or California Cabernet or St-Emilion

KEBABS, MEATY:
hearty fruity red eg Tempranillo, Zinfandel, Douro or Alentejo

KEDGEREE:
full-bodied white: Mâcon or South African Chardonnay or Pinot Blanc, or sparkling

KIDNEYS:
medium to full savoury red such as Nuits-St-Georges, Crozes-Hermitage, oaked Barbera or mature Shiraz

KIPPERS:
Islay malt whisky, or tangy manzanilla

LAMB, ROAST:
fine mature red such as claret, its New World equivalents and Rioja; casseroles: heartier reds eg Nemea, Rioja crianza, Corbières

LANGOUSTINES:
classic white burgundy or aromatic dry Albariño

LASAGNE:
fruity medium- to full red such as Rosso di Montalcino, Romanian Cabernet or Primitivo

LEEK GRATIN:
spicy dry white eg Alsace or Hungarian Gewürztraminer or Australian Riesling

LEMON TART AND SOUFFLE:
botrytised and Ice Wine Rieslings from the New World, or youngish Sauternes or similar

LENTIL RISSOLES:
quite hearty red eg Valdepeñas or Teroldego Rotaliano, or white Châteauneuf-du-Pape

LIME AND COCONUT
FLAVOURED CURRY:
*highly aromatic white like Gewürztraminer
or Australian Verdelho or Riesling*

LIVER, CASSEROLES:
*robust red such as Bairrada or Languedoc;
pan-fried: finer, lighter-bodied red such as
Pinot Noir or Rioja. See also Calf's Liver*

LOBSTER:
*fine full-bodied white like top Chardonnay,
especially burgundy; Condrieu, mature white
Graves or rosé champagne when in rich sauce*

LYCHEES:
Late-harvest Alsace Gewurztraminer

MACKEREL:
*refreshingly acidic dry whites: Muscadet,
Gaillac, Vinho Verde or young Italian white*

MARROW, STUFFED:
*fruity dry white such as South African
Chenin, Australian Chardonnay or Verdelho
or Riesling – or match the stuffing*

MAYONNAISE:
Chardonnay with good acidity

MEATBALLS:
*medium-bodied red such as Chianti Classico,
Côtes du Rhône or Minervois*

MELON:
*semi-sweet sparkling Clairette de die,
Moscato spumante or port*

MERINGUES:
Recioto di Soave, Muscat de Rivesaltes or Asti

MERGUEZ SAUSAGES:
*spicy full-bodied red or rosé such as
Grenache, Shiraz or Rioja rosado*

MILLE FEUILLES:
*sweet sparkling white such as Asti
or champagne rich*

MINCE PIES:
liqueur Muscat

MINESTRONE:
*full-bodied dry white eg Côtes du Rhône
Blanc, Corbières or Marsanne or Chianti*

MIXED GRILL:
*red such as young claret, Bulgarian Cabernet
or Beaujolais-Villages*

MONKFISH:
*full-bodied dry white eg California
Chardonnay or Puligny-Montrachet,
or even California Pinot Noir*

MOUSSAKA:
*medium- to full-bodied red eg St-Chinian
and other southern French reds, Tuscan
reds, Rioja crianza, Naoussa*

MUSHROOMS:
*rounded, well-flavoured mature red
eg burgundy, Rioja or claret, or white
Châteauneuf-du-Pape*

MUSSELS:
*crisp dry white such as Muscadet, Chablis
or Verdicchio*

NOODLES, JAPANESE:
*light crisp dry or off-dry Riesling,
or fino sherry*

NUT ROAST:
*fleshy medium-bodied red eg Chilean Merlot
or Cabernet-Shiraz*

NUTS:
*sweet fortified wine such as Madeira,
tawny port or oloroso sherry*

OCTOPUS:
*herby-spicy red or white eg from Provence,
Greece or Rioja*

OLIVES:
*fino or manzanilla sherry or Riesling; cooked
in a dish: herby reds eg from Provence*

OMELETTE:
*crisp but smooth dry white eg Baden
Weissburgunder or Alsace Pinot Blanc*

ONION TART:
*aromatic fruity dry whites from Alsace,
or New World Colombard, Sauvignon
or Chardonnay*

ORANGE,
CARAMEL/PUDDINGS/CAKE:
*rich, concentrated sweet wine – Sauternes
or Barsac or other botrytised white, New
World Muscat, Muscat de Beaumes-de-
Venise, Setúbal Moscatel; in jelly or fruit
salad: Asti*

OSSO BUCO:
*low tannin red: Dolcetto d'Alba or Bourgogne
Rouge, or full savoury white like Hermitage*

OXTAIL:
*powerful red eg Châteauneuf-du-Pape, Ribera
del Duero, Shiraz, Brunello di Montalcino*

OYSTERS:
*crisp or sparkling dry white such as Chablis,
Muscadet or champagne*

PAELLA:
*dry quite full rosé eg Navarra, Provence,
Tavel, Lirac*

PARTRIDGE:
*mature fine red eg Côtes de Nuits, classed
growth claret, Rhône or Brunello*

PASTA, WITH CREAMY
SAUCES:
*light to medium-bodied dry whites: Alto Adige
Chardonnay or Swiss Chasselas; with meat
sauces: medium- to full-bodied fruity red eg
Dolcetto, Salice Salentino or Chianti Classico*

PATE:
*fruity red Beaujolais cru or southern French
red, or semi-sweet white eg German Riesling
or Scheurebe Spätlese*

PAVLOVA:
*sweet sparkling white eg Asti or rich
champagne, or Trockenbeerenauslese*

PEARS IN RED WINE:
*fortified sweet red such as Banyuls or
Rivesaltes, or white such as German Riesling
Beerenauslese*

PECAN PIE:
*concentrated fortified sweet wine eg liqueur
Muscat or Malmsey Madeira*

PEPPERS, ROASTED
OR STUFFED:
*full-bodied spicy fruity red eg Zinfandel or
Rioja crianza, or zesty dry white Australian
Riesling or Semillon*

PESTO AND PASTA:
*crisp aromatic white eg Hungarian Hárslevelu,
Savennières, unoaked Chardonnay, Argentine
Torrontes; or mature fleshy red St-Emilion*

PHEASANT:
*fine mature red, especially Pomerol
and St-Emilion*

PIGEON:
powerful mature red, eg Côte de Nuits, Crozes-Hermitage or Tuscan Sangiovese

PINEAPPLE UPSIDE-DOWN CAKE:
concentrated sweet white with good acidity such as Côteaux du Layon or New Zealand late-harvest Riesling

PIZZA:
fresh fruity red or crisp medium-bodied white eg Chianti Rufina, California Sangiovese, Refosco or Chardonnay

PLAICE:
clean, dry white such as Pinot Blanc, Chablis or Riesling Kabinett Halbtrocken

PLUM TART:
Riesling Beerenauslese or fragrant sweet Black Muscat

PORK, ROAST:
many medium to full reds, especially Rioja, or full-bodied whites like California Chardonnay

POUSSIN:
as chicken, but leaning more to whites

PRAWNS:
fine dry white eg burgundy, its New World equivalents or Graves, or contrast with New World Sauvignon

PROFITEROLES:
concentrated sweet white: Austrian Ausbruch, Muscat de Beaumes-de-Venise, Orange Muscat

PROSCIUTTO:
light to medium fruity red eg Fleurie, Barbera, Valpolicella Classico, Sancerre, or rosé champagne, or light dry white like Pinot Grigio

PRUNES:
concentrated sweet fortified such as Banyuls or tawny port; or even Sauternes

PUMPKIN PIE:
Very sweet white eg botrytised New World Semillon

QUAIL:
fine not too heavy red eg New World Pinot Noir, mature claret or Rioja, or Carmignano

QUAIL'S EGGS:
blanc de blancs or Chardonnay-dominant champagne or light crisp still dry white

QUEEN OF PUDDINGS:
New World botrytised Riesling or Barsac

QUICHE:
Chardonnay including good burgundy, or dry Pinot Gris or Bergerac Blanc

RABBIT:
lively, medium-bodied red such as Chinon or Chiroubles; or more savoury reds such as Aglianico del Vulture or Côtes du Frontonnais

RASPBERRIES:
Rheingau or Pfalz Riesling, or juicy young red Beaujolais-Villages

RATATOUILLE:
aromatic full-bodied southern French red such as Fitou, or Zinfandel; or dry white or rosé with good acidity

RED MULLET:
flavoursome dry white, or light red such as Chinon, Alsace Pinot Noir or Sancerre, or New World Pinot Noir

RHUBARB FOOL OR CRUMBLE:
botrytised or late-harvest Rieslings from Germany, Austria, Canada, Australasia

RISOTTO ALLA MILANESE:
lightly fragrant crisp white such as Pinot Bianco, Soave Classico or Favorita

ROAST MEAT OR GAME:
highest quality reds available

ROQUEFORT:
concentrated sweet wine especially Sauternes and its country cousins

SACHERTORTE:
concentrated rich, or fortified sweet white such as Austrian Beerenauslese, German Trockenbeerenauslese or Muscat de Beaumes-de-Venise

SALADS:
Sauvignon, Riesling, Pinot Grigio or new-wave Portuguese whites such as Fernão Pires; or try dry rosé or light reds such as young Chianti or Gamay

SALAMI:
light fruity red eg Bardolino, Anjou Rouge or Beaujolais, or dry Australian Riesling

SALMON:
fine full dry white: Chablis, champagne, Alsace or New World Chardonnay; or lighter red: Bourgueil or New World Pinot Noir

SARDINES:
very crisp dry white such as Vinho Verde, Soave Classico or Mauzac vin de pays

SATAY:
oak-aged New World Chardonnay, or Gewürz

SAUERKRAUT:
refreshing sharp dry white such as Mosel Riesling Kabinett or Scheurebe Kabinett Halbtrocken

SAUSAGES:
hearty red eg Eastern European Cabernet, Côtes du Rhône, Corbières, Zinfandel, Shiraz

SCALLOPS:
fine medium or dry white such as burgundy, demi-sec Vouvray, or champagne

SCRAMBLED EGGS:
refreshing sparkling white, ideally champagne

SEAFOOD AND SHELLFISH:
crisp dry white, still or sparkling, such as Muscadet sur lie, Chablis, Bergerac, champagne, New World Sauvignon Blanc, or unoaked or lightly-oaked Chardonnay

SHEPHERD'S PIE:
fruity peppery red such as vin de pays Syrah or Côtes du Roussillon

SKATE:
firm dry white such as Alsace Riesling, lightly oaked Chardonnay or Sauvignon Blanc

SMOKED SALMON
blanc de blancs champagne, lightly oaked Chardonnay or dry Alsace white

SNAILS:
crisp savoury dry whites such as Aligoté or Chablis, or dry rosés or young reds like Chianti

SOLE:
fine whites such as burgundy and its New World equivalents, Graves or Arneis

SORBETS:
light sweet sparkling white eg Moscato d'Asti, Asti or Clairette de Die

SOUFFLE:
fine red or white: claret or red burgundy for cheese; Graves or white burgundy for fish; late-harvest white, eg Gewurztraminer séléction de grains nobles, for sweet

SOUPS:
dry sherry or match the wine to the main ingredients

SPAGHETTI:
lively fruity red such as Chianti Classico or Montepulciano d'Abruzzo for meat sauces; fresh crisp white eg Pinot Grigio or Collio for carbonara or creamy sauces

SPINACH SOUFFLE OR QUICHE:
full-bodied fresh dry white such as New World Chardonnay; at a pinch, low tannin red such as Beaujolais

SQUID:
refreshing dry white such as Bianco di Custoza or Pinot Blanc; or medium-bodied savoury red eg Navarra or Carignano del Sulcis

STEAK:
structured red such as top Cabernet Sauvignon, Shiraz, Rhône, Nebbiolo or Sangiovese

STILTON:
fortified sweet red eg vintage or tawny port or Banyuls, or powerful dry red such as Ribera del Duero, or crisp contrasting Sauvignon Blanc

STIR-FRIED VEGETABLES, SEAFOOD, CHICKEN OR PORK:
crisp light-bodied whites

STRAWBERRIES:
with sugar and cream: Sauternes or Mosel Beerenauslese and their New World equivalents, or sweet Loire such as Coteaux du Layon; with wild strawberries (plain): Margaux or other fine red

SUMMER PUDDING:
Mosel Beerenauslese, Austrian Ausbruch or young red Banyuls

SUSHI:
crisp off-dry or dry white eg German Riesling Kabinett, dry Australian Riesling, champagne or Chilean Sauvignon

SWEETBREADS:
fine dry white such as burgundy, vintage champagne or mature off-dry Rheingau Riesling

SWORDFISH:
full-bodied dry white eg California Chardonnay, Barossa or Hunter Semillon or Australian oaked Marsanne

TAPAS:
tangy dry white or rosé, eg fino sherry, or Sancerre or Provence rosé

TARAMASALATA:
Retsina or high-acid dry white such as New World Sauvignon Blanc, or crisp dry rosé

TEMPURA:
crisp, dry white eg Sancerre or Chablis

THAI FOOD:
crisp dry white, especially Loire or New Zealand Sauvignon Blanc

TIRAMISU:
concentrated sweet white eg Muscat de Rivesaltes, Frontignan or Sauternes

TOAD IN THE HOLE:
hearty red Bairrada, Navarra or Cabernet-Shiraz

TOMATOES:
crisp Sauvignon or Vin de Pays des Côtes de Gascogne, or tangy red eg Barbera

TONGUE:
fruity red such as Saumur-Champigny or Beaujolais cru, or full-bodied dry rosé eg Tavel

TREACLE TART:
powerful very sweet or fortified wine eg liqueur Muscat, Malmsey Madeira or Moscatel de Valencia

TRIFLE:
sweet sherry or sweet botrytised wine such as Australian botrytised Semillon

TRIPE:
fruity reds: Anjou Rouge or Côtes du Vivarais; or pungent dry white such as Pouilly-Fumé

TROUT:
medium- to full-bodied dry whites eg Graves or Chablis or light-bodied off-dry German Rieslings or dry Austrian white

TUNA:
soft reds eg New World Pinot Noir or Merlot, or Chinon, or full white California Chardonnay

TURBOT:
fine dry white such as mature Chablis or Côte d'Or burgundy and New World equivalents, or white Hermitage or Condrieu

TURKEY:
many reds and dry whites, from burgundy to sparkling Shiraz: finer wines with grander dishes

VEAL:
fine dry white such as Vouvray, burgundy or Alsace Tokay-Pinot Gris, or mature grand red eg burgundy such as Pommard, or Bordeaux such as Margaux

VEGETABLE TERRINE:
crisp dry aromatic white such as Australian Riesling or Vouvray

VENISON:
rich gamey reds, eg Bandol, California Mourvèdre blends, red burgundies such as Morey-St-Denis, New World Pinot Noirs, Syrahs and Australian Cabernet

VICHYSSOISE:
crisp dry white eg Vin de Pays des Côtes de Gascogne

VITELLO TONNATO:
full-bodied dry white, especially Chardonnay, eg Rully or Carneros

WALNUTS:
fine, mature fortified wine eg tawny port, Madeira or dry or sweet oloroso sherry

WHITEBAIT:
crisp dry white eg Muscadet, Touraine Sauvignon or Orvieto

WILD BOAR:
mature German Riesling, especially Rheingau Auslese or Spätlese; or many reds such as Pommard or California Pinot Noir, Tuscan Sangiovese or Cabernet, Pomerol, Bairrada or Shiraz

YOGHURT (SAVOURY DISHES):
New World Chardonnay

ZABAGLIONE:
Asti or sweet Marsala

INDEX

PICTURE ACKNOWLEDGEMENTS

Cephas Picture Library *Nigel Blythe*: 60 left; *Mick Rock*: 52, 56, 58, 60 right, 60 centre left, 61, 62 top, 62 below, 63 centre left, 63 centre right, 63 left, 63 right, 64, 66, 68, 70 centre top, 70 below, 70 centre below, 70 top, 71 right, 71 left, 73 below, 73 centre below, 73 centre above, 73 top; *Ted Stefan*: 60 centre right
Armin Faber 107
Robert Harding Picture Library: 91; *C Martin*: 79; *Nik Wheeler*: 76
Image Bank *Karl Hentz*: 120; *Jeff Hunter*: 132

Reed International Books Ltd *Anita Corbin/John O'Grady*: back jacket flap, 6; *Jeremy Hopley*: front jacket, 26, 28, 31, 33, 34, 36/7, 81 Bordeaux, 83 Southwest, 85 Burgundy, 87 Languedoc, 89 Loire, 93 South & Islands, 95 Piedmont & Tuscany, 96 Rome, 99, 101 Andalucia, 105 The North, 105 Portugal, 109 Regions, 111 Switzerland, 113 Austria, 115 Greece, 117 Scandinavia, 119 N.Europe, 122, 125, 127 South America, 129 Australia, 131 New Zealand, 135 India, 137 China, 139 Thailand, 141 Japan; *Ray Moller*: back jacket, 9, 10, 11, 12, 13, 14, 15, 18, 22/3, 25, 39, 40/41, 43, 44, 45, 47, 48/9, 50, 51, 52 bottle, 53, 54, 56 bottle, 57, 58 bottle, 59, 60 centre right

bottle, 60 centre left bottle, 60 left bottle, 60 right bottle, 61 bottle, 62 top bottle, 62 bottom bottle, 63 centre left bottle, 63 left bottle, 63 right bottle, 63 centre right bottle, 64 bottle, 65, 66 bottle, 67, 68 bottle, 69, 70 above centre bottle, 70 top bottle, 70 bottom bottle, 70 below centre bottle, 71 left bottle, 71 right bottle, 73 bottom bottle, 73 below centre bottle, 73 above centre bottle, 73 top bottle, 75, 143.

Laytons Wine Merchants and **Nicolas UK Ltd** suppliers of wine bottles for photography.
Michael Johnson (Ceramics) Ltd – suppliers of glasses, all by Riedel. Excluding pages 81, 105,115.